BIRMINGHAM SLAVONIC MONOGRAPHS NO. 30

Kate Sealey Rahman

Ostrovsky: Reality and Illusion

British Library Cataloguing in Publication Data
A catalogue record for this book is available from the British Library

Published by the
     Department of Russian
     The University of Birmingham
     Edgbaston
     Birmingham B15 2TT
     UK

Printed in Great Britain by University of Birmingham Central Printing
Services

ISBN 07044 85273
ISSN 0141-3805

CONTENTS

To Razi

ACKNOWLEDGMENTS

I am much indebted to numerous friends and colleagues for their support and advice in the preparation of this study. I am particularly grateful for the many invaluable articles and references which were passed on to me. I give special thanks to the supervisor of the thesis on which this work is based, Professor A.D.P.Briggs, without whose encouragement I would never have embarked on the project, and whose support and enthusiasm carried me through to its conclusion. I also give special thanks to my family, particularly to my parents, Chris and Angela, my brother, Tim, and my husband, Razi, who listened to me with patience and good humour. Finally, I wish to express my gratitude to Emma Wilson for her help in proof-reading this document.

TRANSLITERATION AND ABBREVIATIONS

Transliteration

Russian words have been transliterated in accordance with the guidelines for Birmingham Slavonic Monographs.

Soft signs which appear at the end of names (for instance, Gogol´, Lyubov´, Pol´) have been omitted when the names appear in the text.

Within the text, surnames ending in -skii have been anglicised, and thus appear as -sky (for instance, Ostrovsky, Dostoevsky). Similarly, Tolstoi is anglicised as Tolstoy. The ending -nyi in a surname appears as -ny (for instance, Bessudny).

Abbreviations

PSS   A.N.Ostrovskii, *Polnoe sobranie sochinenii*, ed. by G.I.Vladykin, I.V.Il´inskii, V.Ya.Lakshin, V.I.Malikov, P.A.Markov, A.D.Salynskii, N.L.Stepanov and E.G.Kholodov, 12 vols, Moscow, Iskusstvo, 1973-1981.

tr.   translated by

Unless otherwise noted, quotations from Ostrovsky's plays have all been taken from *PSS*. The numbers in brackets at the end of each quotation refer to the volume and page number. The translations are all the author's own.

INTRODUCTION

Aleksandr Nikolaevich Ostrovsky (1823-1886) presents us with a curious paradox. Despite being acknowledged as the central figure of nineteenth-century Russian drama—I.Esam refers to Ostrovsky as 'the creator of a Russian National Repertory'[1], G.Noyes describes him as 'the great Russian dramatist of the central decades of the nineteenth century'[2], and E.Kholodov labels him 'the most important and influential figure in Russian theatre of his time'[3]—he is surprisingly little known and studied in the West. In Russia, Ostrovsky is still greatly loved, his plays continue to be performed regularly and there is a wealth of critical analysis. Yet in the West, professional productions of his plays are extremely rare, few of his works have ever been translated, and there is very little critical comment.[4] Only one full-length publication in English is devoted to Ostrovsky's life and works.[5] Yet this man was the sole nineteenth-century Russian writer of note who was purely a dramatist. He wrote nearly fifty original plays—comedies, tragedies, historical plays and a fairy-tale drama in verse—as well as numerous collaborative works and translations. He devoted his entire life to the theatre, working to improve the position of actors and playwrights, and developing new techniques of stage-setting, acting and directing. It was Ostrovsky

---

[1] I.Esam, 'Folkloric Elements as Communication Devices in Ostrovsky's Plays', *New Zealand Slavonic Journal*, 2 (1968), 67-88 (p. 67).

[2] G.R.Noyes, 'Introduction', in *Alexander Ostrovsky: Plays*, tr. and ed. by G.R.Noyes, (New York: Scribners, 1917), 3-8 (p. 1).

[3] E.G.Kholodov, 'A.N.Ostrovskii v 1873-1877 godakh', in *PSS* iv, 460-93 (p. 476).

[4] A list of the principal productions of Ostrovsky's plays in England is given at Appendix B.

[5] The publication referred to is: Marjorie L.Hoover, *Alexander Ostrovsky* (Boston: Twayne, 1981). N.Henley notes the injustice done to Ostrovsky by many contemporary experts on Russian drama. He gives examples of anthologies of Russian plays which fail to mention Ostrovsky. See Norman Henley, 'Ostrovskij's Play-Actors, Puppets and Rebels', *Slavic and East European Journal*, 14 (1970), 317-25 (p. 325).

2

who paved the way for the national 'people's' theatre later developed by Stanislavsky and Nemirovich-Danchenko.

Explanations for such a paradox have been numerous and varied. I.Beasley sees it as a quirk of fate, noting that 'By a curious incident of fate, Englishmen were not introduced to the great national dramatist of Russia, but to another and perhaps less representative writer. Ostrovsky was neglected for Chekhov.'[6] *The McGraw-Hill Encyclopedia of World Drama* also points to fate as the culprit, stating that Ostrovsky 'was fated to be a dramatist at the time when Russian novelists were in vogue and to die just a decade before Chekhov, Gorky and Andreyev introduced the Russian dramatic influence into the mainstream of Western drama.'[7] More commonly, critics have blamed the inaccessibility of Ostrovsky's language, which is full of local speech and idiom, and the difficulty it poses for successful translation. L.Hanson talks of the 'impossibility of translation' of Ostrovsky's plays.[8] R.Lord notes that Ostrovsky's language is 'the most real, vivid and idiomatic ever to appear in the Russian language'[9], whereas I.Zohrab has dedicated an entire article to 'Problems of Translation in Ostrovsky', noting that 'while most of the works of the other Russian literary "greats" of the nineteenth century appeared in successful English translation relatively soon after their publication in Russian, it was only in 1895 that a complete play by Ostrovsky was translated.'[10] In Russia, scholars have even gone to the lengths of producing a dictionary of words in Ostrovsky's plays 'to aid modern actors, directors and translators', and there are numerous studies of Ostrovsky's language—for example, E.Kholo-

---

[6] I.Beasley, 'The Dramatic Art of Ostrovsky', *Slavonic and East European Review*, 6 (1927), 603-17 (p. 603).
[7] *McGraw-Hill Encyclopedia of World Drama*, IV, ed. by S.Hochman (New York: McGraw-Hill, 1984), 54.
[8] L.Hanson, 'Introduction', in *Career Woman: Artistes and Admirers*, tr. by Elisabeth Hanson (New York: Barnes and Noble, 1976), ii-xxxvi (p. xxiii).
[9] Robert Lord, *Russian and Soviet Literature: An Introduction* (London: Kahn & Avril, 1972), 171.
[10] Irene Zohrab, 'Problems of Translation. The Works of A.N.Ostrovsky in English', *Melbourne Slavonic Studies*, 16 (1982), 43-88 (p. 43). The translations in question are those by E.L.Voinich in *The Humour of Russia* (London: Walter Scott, 1895). For the first translations of Ostrovsky's plays into other Western European languages, see the Bibliography at the end of this study (pp. 232-47).

dov's *Yazyk dramy: ekskurs v tvorcheskuyu laboratoriyu A.N.Ostrov-skogo.*[11]

However, this study argues that more important than either fate or language in explaining Ostrovsky's obscurity in the West has been the emphasis on the realism of his drama. Ostrovsky is generally credited with playing a pivotal role in the development of realism in Russian drama. He is frequently described as a 'chronicler of Russian life' (Turgenev referred to him as 'the Shakespeare of the merchant class'[12]). He is seen as the man who first brought the gritty realities of the Moscow merchant world to the Russian stage and who then went on to chart faithfully the social changes wrought by the reforms of the 1860s, describing accurately the rise of the new capitalist class and the decline of the gentry.

All this is undoubtedly true. Ostrovsky did indeed play a crucial role in the development of realism in Russian drama. He did introduce to the stage sections of society (most particularly the merchant class) left all but untouched in previous Russian drama (and, indeed, in the great realist novels of Tolstoy, Turgenev and Dostoevsky). Yet the continual emphasis on this aspect of Ostrovsky's work has served to root it firmly in the narrow sphere of nineteenth-century Russian society. This in turn has given rise to the commonly expressed view that Ostrovsky has little to offer to audiences in the West.

Quotations from literary criticism illustrating this view are almost overwhelming in their number. D.Magarshack (a scholar who has done much to introduce Ostrovsky's work to Western readers) notes that many of Ostrovsky's plays 'deal exclusively with the life of the Russian Merchant class in the middle years of the last century, whose traditions, patriarchal customs and dark superstitions are unintelligible outside Russia.'[13] A.V.Knowles states that Ostrovsky 'established a tradition of realism on the Russian stage', noting that he 'bequeathed a wide and varied repertory which dealt in the main with

---

[11] See *Slovar´ k p'esam A.N.Ostrovskogo*, ed. V.A.Filippov (Moscow: Vesta, 1993); and E.G.Kholodov, *Yazyk dramy: ekskurs v tvorcheskuyu laboratoriyu A.N.Ostrovskogo* (Moscow: Iskusstvo, 1978).

[12] See I.Beasley, 'The Dramatic Art of Ostrovsky' (unpublished doctoral thesis, University of London, 1931), 47.

[13] David Magarshack, 'Introduction', in *Alexander Ostrovsky: Easy Money and Two Other Plays*, tr. by David Magarshack (London: Allen & Unwin, 1944), 6-11 (p. 8).

particularly Russian themes and national problems.'[14] L.Hanson talks of Ostrovsky's 'essential Russianness.'[15] G.Noyes describes Ostrovsky as 'one of the most national of authors ... in him we can study the life of Russia as he knew it...'[16] R.Lord notes that 'it is unlikely that Ostrovsky will ever gain wide appeal outside Russia ... [he] has given expression to that elusive Russian concept 'byt'... add to this the local colour of Zamoskvorechye ... and the English reading public is up against severe odds ... Ostrovsky's milieu is as essentially Russian as Trollope's is English ...'[17] *The McGraw-Hill Encylopedia* notes that 'his work is so closely tied to a specific Russian milieu that it is difficult for foreign audiences to penetrate the wealth of local colour and typically Russian characterization.'[18] And Prince Mirsky is most forceful in his assertion that Ostrovsky's 'plays are always narrowly native and do not have universal significance ... the characters are taken in their social aspect. They are not men and women in general but Moscow merchants and cannot be torn away from the social setting.' Discussing *The Storm*, he notes: 'It is intensely local and Russian, and the saturation of the atmosphere with the very essence of Russian *byt* and Russian poetical feeling make it hardly understandable to a foreigner.'[19]

The quotations listed above are all found in English and American criticism, but they are echoed in works by their Soviet and Russian counterparts. In both Russian and Soviet criticism the words most frequently used to describe Ostrovsky include *realist, bytovik and bytopisatel´*, the last two denoting a portrayer of everyday life. V.Lakshin talks of Ostrovsky's plays providing 'information on the realities of life in the mid nineteenth-century.'[20] (Indeed the belief in the accuracy of Ostrovsky's portrayal of nineteenth-century social mores is so strong that some writers even refer to Ostrovsky for

---

[14] A.V.Knowles, 'Introduction', in *Groza*, by A.N.Ostrovskii (Oxford: Blackwell Russian Texts, 1988), x-xxi (pp. x-xi).

[15] Hanson, xxiii.

[16] Noyes, 8.

[17] Lord, 171-2.

[18] *The McGraw-Hill Encyclopedia of World Drama*, 54.

[19] D.S.Mirsky, *A History of Russian Literature* (London: Routledge & Kegan Paul, 1949), 235-8.

[20] V.Ya. Lakshin, 'Mudrost´ Ostrovskogo', in *P´esy*, by A.N.Ostrovskii (Moscow: Olimp: PPP, 1993), 5-12 (p. 11).

historical details.[21]) V.Setchkarev notes: 'Ostrovsky's plays are so intimately bound up with Russian social conditions that for all their excellent qualities it is unlikely that they will ever attract much of an audience outside Russia ... without an understanding of the patriarchal tyranny, the incredibly limited intellectual horizon and the superstitious attachment to tradition which formed the outlook of this class, it is impossible to make much sense of the characters' behaviour.'[22] Even contemporary writers asserted the peculiar 'Russianness' of Ostrovsky's work. Dostoevsky, writing in 1873, noted that '... at the very least, three-quarters of his comedies remain completely beyond European understanding.'[23]

A typical discussion of Ostrovsky's work in Soviet criticism is found in *Razvitie realizma v russkoi literature*. Initially the comments seem promising. The author, S.Shatalov, quotes V.Lakshin (commenting on *Even Wise Men Err*) as stating that 'the outward simplicity [of the play] conceals its true depth', and complaining that Ostrovsky has not yet broken free of the 'stamp of perceiver of everyday life'. Yet the determination to keep Ostrovsky's work within its social and historical context remains. Lakshin goes on to state that in *Even Wise Men Err* 'Ostrovsky wrote not so much a comedy of everyday life, but more a political comedy, with deep socio-philosophic meaning.' And this, in turn, is denied by Shatalov, who asserts that 'even in "Wise Men", perhaps the most satirical of Ostrovsky's comedies, it is clear that satire is not the main element. Ostrovsky was and remained a brilliant writer of everyday life ...'[24] Again, he uses the word *bytopisatel´*, 'portrayer of the everyday'.

Perhaps the confusion surrounding many Western scholars' understanding of Ostrovsky's works is best illustrated by M.Slonim's comments on Ostrovsky in his *Russian Theater: From the Empire to the Soviets*. He first notes: '[Ostrovsky's] plays in translation do not irradiate any special attraction for a foreign reader and ... are hardly

---

[21] I.Beasley notes that Shashkov's *History of Women in Russia* refers to Ostrovsky for historical detail. See Beasley, unpublished doctoral thesis, 101.

[22] V.Setchkarev, 'From the Golden to the Silver Age (1820-1917)', in *Companion to Russian Studies*, ed. R.Auty and D.Obolensky, 2 vols (Cambridge: Cambridge University Press, 1977) II, 133-85 (pp. 152-3)

[23] F.M.Dostoevskii, 'A.N.Ostrovskii', *Grazhdanin*, 13 (26 March 1873), 423.

[24] S.E.Shatalov, 'A.N.Ostrovskii', in *Razvitie realizma v russkoi literature*, ed. by U.R.Fokht and others, 3 vols (Moscow: Nauka, 1973), II, 314-15.

suitable for the American or European stage. From a purely literary standpoint, they are lacking in psychological depth and seem one-dimensional. The plots are simple, the characterization static, the development of the action seldom holds any major surprise for the spectator and some of the devices employed to enhance suspense appear on the borderline of naivety.' However, in the very next sentence he goes on to state: 'Yet these unsophisticated comedies and dramas are constructed with such consummate craft, they reveal such an infallible sense of stage effects and techniques, they create such an atmosphere of reality and truth, and their protagonists appear so believable and alive, that they never fail to grip audiences from the most primitive to the most refined.'[25] Whatever one takes as 'a purely literary standpoint' (presumably Slonim means to differentiate this from stageworthiness), Slonim's description is full of inconsistencies. How can 'consummate craft and an infallible sense of stage effects and techniques' marry with 'devices to enhance suspense ... on the borderline of naivety'? How can protagonists be both 'believable and alive' yet have 'a lack of psychological depth and static characterization'? How can his plays be 'out of place on the American and European stage' when 'they never fail to grip audiences from the most primitive to the most refined'?

The view of Ostrovsky's work outlined above is not all-pervasive. There are critics who have eschewed the traditional interpretation of Ostrovsky's work as somehow peculiarly 'Russian' and have argued for a more universal reading of his drama. D.Magarshack, for example, has noted elsewhere that 'in later years Ostrovsky turned away from the narrow confines of merchant life to the production of masterpieces of universal appeal.'[26] V.Lakshin also asserts that Ostrovsky's plays 'quickly outgrew the limits of chronicles to take on more universal meaning in terms of character-types, social and psychological scenes.'[27] (Curiously, one critic, C.Manning, who also asserts the universality of Ostrovsky's later plays, finds in this cause for complaint. He notes that 'the picturesque element has gone out of

---

[25] Marc Slonim, *Russian Theater: From the Empire to the Soviets* (London: Methuen, 1963), 74.

[26] Magarshack, 11.

[27] Lakshin, 6.

life. We are coming more and more to the drab type of crooked bourgeois and to face the same problems as the rest of the world.'[28]

However, those voices which proclaim the universality of Ostrovsky's work are few and far between, and despite assertions of 'universal appeal' there is little elaboration as to the nature of such appeal. E.Bristow and I.Esam are rare in their specificity. Bristow argues that 'throughout his plays Ostrovsky raised questions and employed themes which related specifically to the *byt* of each class yet were also universal: How should the family complex be governed? What alienates parents and children? What are the rights of women? Does education eliminate prejudice and vulgarity? What is the role of ethics in business, in government, in the aristocracy?'[29] Esam notes that 'although the dramatist padded and trimmed his plays with details of *byt* or the manners and morals of a specific place and time, these are in fact only accessories. Stripped of all their padding, the plays are about universal and eternal themes, about life and death, about beauty and pain, about the unchanging laws of humanity in history.'[30] Yet even these critics provide little in the way of elaboration or further explanation of their views.

In general, this study aims to redress the balance; to join with Magarshack and Esam and argue that the themes which Ostrovsky discusses in his plays are not limited to a particular time and place, but have far wider appeal, dealing with issues of universal significance. As such it aims to add further weight to those critics who, since William Ralston in 1868, have been arguing that Ostrovsky deserves far greater attention in the West.[31] More specifically, this study examines Ostrovsky's treatment of reality in his plays. It seeks to demonstrate that far from simply depicting the everyday realities of a particular social setting, Ostrovsky's plays explore the theme of

---

[28] Clarence Manning, 'Ostrovsky and The Kingdom of Darkness', *Sewanee Review*, 38 (1930), 30-41 (p. 41).

[29] Eugene K.Bristow, 'Introduction', in *Five Plays of Alexander Ostrovsky*, tr. and ed. by Eugene K.Bristow (New York: Pegasus, 1969), 15-21 (p. 21).

[30] I.Esam, 'An Analysis of Ostrovsky's *Ne ot mira sego* and the Play's Significance in Relation to the Author's Other Works', *New Zealand Slavonic Journal*, 4 (1969), 68-91 (p. 69).

[31] William Ralston was the first Western European critic to discuss Ostrovsky's works. In his review of *Sochineniya A.N.Ostrovskogo v 4 tomakh, 1859-67* in *The Edinburgh Review*, 261 (1868), 158-90, he argues for 'greater reciprocity' in literature between Russia and Western Europe, and states that we should be 'ashamed of our ignorance'.

reality on a number of different levels: social, psychological and philosophical. His plays explore the relationship between real and illusory worlds. They explore the relationship between real and ideal worlds and human psychological mechanisms for dealing with the gulf between our ideals and the reality that surrounds us. They even question the very nature of reality itself, asking whether one perceived reality is any more valid than another. The world depicted in Ostrovsky's drama is a complex web of deception and illusion, peopled, in the main, by characters whose understanding of what is real bears little relation to the actuality of the world around them. Rather than merely presenting us with a fixed, tidy picture of the speech, lifestyle and social mores of a specifically defined group of people in a specifically defined time and place, Ostrovsky's plays present us with a world of uncertain reality. They serve to challenge our perceptions of reality and even to question whether a comfortable notion of reality can ever exist. All these questions resound with universal interest and significance.

This study consists of a detailed analysis of forty-one of Ostrovsky's forty-seven original, completed plays, which seeks to demonstrate how a series of elements relating to reality and illusion occur with almost obsessive repetition throughout his drama.[32] These elements include: the relationship between realism and idealism; deception and conscious role-play; the superficial nature of outward appearance; a blindness to the true nature of characters and events; language relating to blindness and vision; dreams and fantasies; subconscious role-play; a blurring between reality and illusion; the relationship between life and literature; the relationship between life and theatre; and the symbolic use of mirrors and pictures. The study also looks briefly at the depiction of supernatural reality in Ostrovsky's drama. Each of these elements is examined in detail, and selected examples illustrating its presence in the plays are given. Constraints of time and space have prevented examples from all forty-one of the plays appearing in the main body of the study, however a series of appendices describes in greater detail the presence of such elements in each play. Despite the relegation of material to the appendices, extensive quotation has been retained in the body of the work in order to convey a true sense of the

---

[32] A list of Ostrovsky's original, completed plays is at Appendix A.

overwhelming presence of each element. The intention is to build up a convincing picture of the pervasiveness of these elements in Ostrovsky's drama, and thus in turn to demonstrate the centrality of the theme of reality to Ostrovsky's works.

The complexity of the theme of reality in Ostrovsky's plays means that the definition of each element and the examples used to illustrate them necessarily suffer from some degree of arbitrariness or overlap. This is because the elements are frequently interwoven within the plays themselves. The same event may be the result of, say, blindness to reality, deception, and idealism all at one and the same time. Likewise, the same piece of dialogue may be used to demonstrate a series of different elements. The elements discussed in this study appeared to the author to provide the most coherent way of breaking down the complex theme of reality in Ostrovsky's plays into definable facets. Similarly the examples used to illustrate each element are those which seemed to the author to be most significant, although other examples might easily have stood in their place. The two elements 'Blindness to Reality' and 'Superficiality of Appearances' are often particularly interchangeable, though they remain, in the author's opinion, two distinct features, however closely related.

Six of Ostrovsky's original (completed) plays have not been included in the detailed analysis of his works. This was partly due to contraints of time and space, but also because the six discarded plays—five historical dramas and the fairy-tale drama, *The Snow Maiden*—are not generally considered to be among the dramatist's 'realist' works. The particular focus of this study is on Ostrovsky's treatment of the theme of reality in those plays usually considered to be realistic depictions of the social mores of contemporary (or near-contemporary) Russian society. (Plays such as *You Can't Live as you Please* which contain stage directions indicating that 'the action takes place at the end of the eighteenth century' and so forth, are included, as such notes are generally considered to be devices for appeasing the censor. The action itself was intended to be viewed as contemporary.) While not analysed in detail, many of the elements discussed in this study also appear in the six excised plays and for the sake of completeness, they will receive brief consideration collectively in the Conclusion.

10

The study has been divided into two main parts. The first deals with the exploration of the relationship between realism and idealism in Ostrovsky's drama.[33] The second part includes discussion of all the other elements mentioned above, each divided into shorter sections but falling under the generic title 'The Nature of Reality'. The section on realism and idealism has been separated from the main body of the work in this way since it demonstrates, more clearly than any other of the elements discussed in the study, the way in which traditional critical interpretation of Ostrovsky's work has kept his drama locked firmly in the narrow confines of nineteenth-century society.

---

[33] 'Idealism' is defined for the present context on p. 13.

PART ONE

THE REAL AND THE IDEAL

'Noble poverty is good
only in the theatre. Just
try it out in real life.' *A
Lucrative Post* (ii, p. 50)

The portrayal of idealism[1] in Ostrovsky's work has largely been overlooked in critical analysis, yet it forms a key element of his plays. Numerous works depict the struggle of characters to realise their dreams and aspirations, only to have them shattered in the face of the reality that surrounds them. Thus, we see young wards who dream of bettering themselves by making good marriages, only to be forced to marry unpleasant drunkards on the whim of their 'samodur', i.e. wilful and tyrannical, mistresses (*The Ward*); romantic young women who are forced to marry vulgar civil servants or merchants in

---

[1]Although the literary and cultural debates of nineteenth-century Russia were greatly influenced by philosophers such as Schelling and Kant, the words 'ideal' and 'idealism' are intended in their common usage, rather than with any specific philosophical or ideological meaning. Nor are they connected with any specific definition of the 'ideal' advocated at the time: A.Grigor´ev, for example, saw the 'ideal' in specifically Russian traits, such as an 'evangelical love of one's fellow man', and 'an optimistic sense of humour' and frequently noted that this ideal was 'best expressed in Ostrovsky's plays.' [See Victor Terras, *Belinskij and Russian Literary Criticism* (Wisconsin: University of Wisconsin Press, 1974), 220.] It is, however, important to note that debates about the 'real' and the 'ideal' were raging on all kinds of levels at this time—W.Dowler notes: 'In the changed conditions of 1848, the discrepancy between the real and the ideal, the 'is' and the 'ought' became even more pronounced, and the resulting alienation of the concerned even more acute. It was in these conditions that the Russian Intelligentsia was born' [see Wayne Dowler, *An Unnecessary Man: The Life of Apollon Grigor´ev* (Toronto: University of Toronto Press, 1995), 65]—making it perhaps even more surprising that this aspect of Ostrovsky's work has been overlooked.

order to avoid financial ruin (*The Poor Bride, Without a Dowry, Talents and Admirers*); principled young men who find themselves unable to survive without succumbing to the bribery inherent in the society around them (*A Lucrative Post, The Abyss, Truth is Fine, but Luck is Better*); and husbands forced to face the realisation that their beautiful wives are not the paragons of virtue they once thought (*We All Have our Cross to Bear; Rich Brides*).

Ostrovsky even chose to make the conflict between the ideal and the real the overriding theme of his last play, *Not of This World*. Written during his final illness, this play juxtaposes the other-worldly Kseniya (her name means 'alien'), who has been brought up by her mother 'for the next world' and is intensely spiritual, living by a strict moral code, against her very worldly husband, Vitalii (meaning 'vitality'), who lives for worldly pleasures: drink, picnics, women, the operetta. The play charts the couple's struggle as each tries to draw the other into their own world, and finally ends in Kseniya's death. Despite their affirmations of love for one another, the couple cannot survive the duality of their worlds, and again it is the ideal which is destroyed.[2]

The plot development of many of Ostrovsky's plays revolves around this destruction of idealism, with characters moving from a state of idealism, through increasing awareness of the realities of life, to the final realisation that the dreams and ideals they hold are incompatible with this real world. The realities of life may differ, depending on the social milieu, but the conflict between realism and idealism remains the same.

L.Hanson, in his introduction to a translation of *Talents and Admirers*, notes the progression of the plot from the heroine, Negina's, initial state of idealism, to the point where she finally faces up to the choice between ideals and necessity: 'At the opening of the play, she [Negina] appears to be ideally situated: the popular leading lady of a provincial theatre and the fiancée of a good and clever man.

---

[2]I.Esam, discussing *Not of This World*, is one of the few critics to have noted the conflict between the real and the ideal in Ostrovsky's plays, yet even she fails to note the extent to which this theme pervades his work. She talks of such a conflict only in relation to female characters, stating: 'Ostrovsky's heroines, the most active element in his plays, search for perfection in this life, for the Ideal, and come into conflict with a reality which cancels out any possibility of an Ideal.' [See I.Esam, 'An Analysis of Ostrovsky's *Ne ot mira sego*', 83.]

She feels ... that she has the best of both worlds. Reality enters with the Prince's proposition [that she should become his mistress] ... [her] reaction to the proposition ... destroys her ideal world and forces her to grow up. From that moment on, she is driven, step by step and always with reluctance, first to realise that there is an inevitable choice before her, then to face the choice, and finally to make it.'[3]

A close analysis of the play reveals how skilfully the construction of the plot propels Negina towards her final decision, with a constant battle between representatives of both sides of the debate which is closely reflected in the juxtaposition of scenes. Thus in Act One, Scene 1, we are presented with realism in the form of Negina's mother, Domna, bemoaning their poverty, their numerous debts, and the fact that, unlike other actresses, Negina refuses to accept gifts from patrons. Scene 2 sees the entrance of Narokov, a former estate owner, who, we learn, has spent all his money on the theatre he loves and is now reduced to scraping a living as a prompter in the very theatre he once owned. Thus a depiction of idealism follows that of realism and almost immediately we are forewarned about the likely outcome of dedicating our life to ideals at the expense of our material well-being. Domna and Narokov discuss Melusov, Negina's fiancé, a poor, highly principled student, who wishes Negina to leave the theatre, and who is the principal representative of idealism in the play. In Scenes 3 and 4, 'reality' re-enters in the form of Bakin and Prince Dulebov, two characters who demonstrate that their true interest lies not in the theatre itself—Prince Dulebov's conversation with Negina in Scene 5 demonstrates clearly his ignorance of the theatre—but in the actresses, whom they shower with their patronage. Prince Dulebov has come to suggest to Negina that she become his mistress in return for a better apartment and financial security. Negina is still, at this point, rooted firmly in her state of idealism and when she enters in Scene 5 ideals again take the ascendancy, as she responds to his proposal with horror and disgust. From this point on, however, her fate is largely sealed. Reality has entered her ideal world. Symbolically, Scene 6 sees Domna enter and berate Negina for her stupidity in turning down Dulebov's offer, thus making an enemy of him. She blames Melusov for Negina's foolishness—thus reintroducing the notion of idealism; and again, immediately follow-

---

[3] Hanson, xxxiv.

ing discussion of Melusov, the pendulum swings back and realism enters in the form of the actress Smel'skaya (a willing accomplice in the system of patronage) and the mysterious new patron, Velikatov. Melusov himself then enters and idealism again takes the ascendancy with Velikatov admitting that 'the prose of life has overwhelmed me ... my soul has become shallow' (v, p. 229) and praising Melusov's high principles. However he notes, somewhat ominously, that Melusov's conceptions 'have a lot of nobility in them, but very little chance of success' (v, p. 229). In Scene 10, realism is represented as Negina discusses with Smel'skaya her need for a new dress for her benefit performance, and expresses envy at Velikatov's fine horses: 'What horses you have! How I would love to go riding with them sometime!' (v, p. 230). Scene 11 has idealism back in command as Negina and Melusov are left alone to reaffirm their ideals and Melusov praises Negina for refusing the Prince. It is clear, however, that tensions have already entered their relationship. Negina worries about her benefit performance and her need to buy a new dress—realistic concerns—whilst Melusov talks of the need to study and improve themselves, to live honest, hard-working lives— idealistic notions. Consequently, Scene 12 sees Smel'skaya returning with a new dress for Negina paid for by Velikatov and an invitation to dine out at his expense. Negina hesitates, but eventually decides to go. The pull away from the ideal world has begun.

Act Two sees the intensification of reality's intrusion into Negina's world. In revenge for her refusal, Prince Dulebov persuades the theatre manager not to renew Negina's contract for the following season and to postpone her benefit until the end of the fair, when the audiences will be smaller—thus ensuring her financial ruin. Eventually Negina is offered a way out of immediate financial ruin by Velikatov, who offers to buy up all the tickets for her benefit. Negina again struggles with her principles, but has little choice but to accept.

In Act Three, the struggle between the two sides reaches its crisis point, and the plot pattern returns to a continual see-sawing between representatives of the two sides. The Act opens with Domna delighting in the success of the benefit, and Velikatov soon appears with expensive presents and the money Negina has made from her performance (realism—Scenes 1 and 2). This is immediately followed by the entrance of Narokov, bringing flowers and verses he has written extolling Negina's talent as an actress (idealism—Scene 3). Negina is now clearly aware of the realities of her situation. The success of the benefit has shown her the rewards that patronage can bring, yet she remains in poverty and has no job for the coming season. She muses on her future, contemplating whether to leave the stage and marry Melusov (idealism—Scene 4). Yet Domna expresses incredulity that she could contemplate leaving the stage when she has just made so much money; and Bakin enters suggesting that he and Negina should spend the night together (realism—Scene 5). Scene 6 sees Negina wavering between the two sides when she is persuaded to join in with a celebration drink—in contrast with the teetotal Melusov (realism—Scene 6). The situation is finally brought to a head in Scene 7, with the arrival of two letters. One is from Melusov reiterating his love for her and asking her to meet him that night; the other from Velikatov, also stating his love for her and describing his dream of having her at his estate as his mistress, where she would take the leading role in his own theatre. Negina is thus forced to face directly the inevitable choice before her. On this occasion it appears that ideals will win out. She reacts with horror to Velikatov's letter, declares her love for Melusov and her determination to see him that night, and is clearly touched by Narokov's verses (idealism—Scene 7). Yet reality is always around the corner, and Scene 8 sees Bakin planning to harm Negina's reputation by suggesting that he has spent the night with her (realism—Scene 8). Scenes 9 and 10 see the apparent triumph of idealism as Melusov manages to evict Bakin from the house (idealism—Scene 9) and Negina leaves to spend the night with Melusov (idealism—Scene 10). Yet the victory at the end of the Act is somewhat hollow: Negina has announced that she has yet to make a final decision, and the very fact that she agrees to leave with Melusov is a negation of her former ideal of purity.

The final outcome is left in suspense throughout Act Four, which sees all the characters gathered at the station in order to see Negina off. Whether she is leaving for Moscow to try and find a new job, or has decided to take up Velikatov's offer, is left unresolved until the very end, when Velikatov is seen boarding the train. Realism has defeated idealism.[4]

---

[4] It is important to note that the progression from idealism to realism in *Talents and*

Whilst not reflecting the same rigid see-sawing of scenes depicting realism and idealism, a much earlier play, *The Ward*, follows a similar plot progression of an idealist who is forced to face up to the realities of the world in which she lives. Here the idealist is Nadya, the young ward of a rich landowner, Ulanbekova. The play opens with Nadya telling a housemaid, Liza, about the time she spent in Petersburg with Ulanbekova, and of how fine city life is: 'It's all so wonderful, you can't find the words to describe it' (ii, p. 170); she talks of her dreams of improving herself: 'Seeing it all, my dear, I myself decided to try and improve myself' (ii, p. 170), so as to fulfil her one hope (it is significant that Nadya's name itself means 'hope')—that of making a good marriage: 'Now, I have but one hope—to marry a good man' (ii, p. 171).

Again, we have an early warning that Nadya's dreams may not be fulfilled, when Liza notes: 'Life with a husband isn't always joyful! Some have such ones thrust on them, it's a punishment from God!' (ii, p. 171). Nadya dismisses her concerns by stating that she is able to distinguish between good and bad husbands: 'I, thank God, can soon see which are good and which bad' (ii, p. 171). In the next scene, however, it becomes apparent that Nadya's ability to distinguish between good and bad husbands may have no bearing on her fate: the servant Potapych discusses with Ulanbekova's son, Leonid, the mistress's penchant for marrying off her wards at whim: '... we have always got two or three ... wards. She takes a young girl from someone or other, raises her, and as soon as she reaches seventeen or eighteen, then, without any kind of conversation, she marries her off to some clerk or petty official in the town ... whoever takes her fancy ... even a nobleman sometimes ...' (ii, p. 173). He talks of what a 'terrible existence' these young wards have, how the mistress brings them up as young ladies: 'she dresses them as if they were really her own daughters, and sometimes has them sit and eat with her; and she never asks them to do any kind of work' (ii, p. 173), but then sharply reverses their position when she marries them:

Admirers is not universally accepted. I.Beasley suggests that Negina is 'calculating in the manner with which she refuses Dulebov's offer with such a show of injured virtue and later accedes to Velikatov's request as he has more to offer.' There is, however, little in the play to suggest that Negina's horrified refusal of Dulebov is anything but genuine. See Beasley, unpublished doctoral thesis, 268.

'"You, " she says, "have lived with me in wealth and luxury, and have never had to do anything. Now you are married to a poor man, and you will live your whole life in poverty and work. And it is your duty to do this. You must forget, " she says, "about the life you had with me, you must never think about that life, and always remember your true worthlessness and the rank you came from ..."' (ii, p. 174). He notes finally that the wards generally pine away, because 'their husbands, for the most part, turn out to be scoundrels' (ii, p. 174).

Nadya, at this stage, still cherishes her hopes. When Leonid makes a pass at her, despite the warnings of the other servants not to be so modest, she rejects his advances for fear that any scandal might jeopardise her chances of making a good match. Yet once more we are reminded of the gulf between Nadya's dreams and the reality of her position, as Potapych chastises Leonid for using the formal 'vy' when addressing Nadya: 'What are you doing, master, calling her 'vy' as if she were some kind of lady?' (ii, p. 176)

Nadya's fate is sealed in Act Two, when Ulanbekova suddenly announces her decision to marry Nadya to Negligentov, a worthless drunkard, and dismisses Nadya's protests out of hand. Although Nadya does win a reprieve—Negligentov turns up at the house drunk, and Ulanbekova, shocked by his behaviour, reverses her decision—the damage is done, and she realises the futility of her dreams. The Act ends with Nadya preparing to give in to Leonid, and asking Liza to arrange a meeting between them.

In Act Three, Scene 1, Nadya and Liza prepare to meet Leonid. Liza is shocked by Nadya's sudden change of attitude: 'What has happened to you? You never used to talk like this. You always used to hide from him, and now you yourself are going to him' (ii, p. 190). But despite her reprieve, Nadya has realised the reality of her situation, and her powerlessness to decide her own fate. She again talks of her dreams of love and marriage:

> Oh Liza, if life were better, then I wouldn't be coming out here into the garden at night. Do you remember how I used to dream about myself? Yes, and you also, probably, had in your head the thought that you were an honest girl, that you lived like some kind of bird, would suddenly take a fancy to some man and he would begin to court you: come to you often, kiss you ... so that you were both

ashamed and glad at the same time. Even if you weren't rich, you would at least be able to sit with him in company—precisely as if you were a princess, as if every day was a holiday for you. Then you would marry, everyone would congratulate you. Well, yes, and even if life was difficult, even if there was a lot of work, all the same you would live as if you were in paradise, you would be proud. (ii, p. 191)

And of the dashing of those hopes:

While she pampered and caressed me, then I thought that I was a human being, like any other person; ... but when she began to order me about like a doll, then I saw that I have no free will, nothing to protect me ... (ii, p. 192)

Her one thought now is to have something by which to remember her youth: '... that at least my beauty shall not have been in vain ...' (ii, p. 192). Thus, she goes to Leonid and seals her fate. Act Four provides the inevitable conclusion to the play, when Ulanbekova, hearing of Nadya's meeting with Leonid, resolves once more to marry her to Negligentov.

While being grounded in an understanding of reality, Nadya's love scene with Leonid in Act Three has a dream-like quality, as if it were an interlude from real life, a momentary escape from the reality of her situation. Thus Nadya is described as acting 'absent-mindedly and almost mechanically', as if 'in a reverie' (ii, p. 194). She appears to focus on Leonid to the exclusion of everything else around her. At one stage she states: 'I am ready to sit here the whole night and look at you, never lifting my eyes' and is described as 'looking fixedly' at him: '... she stares at Leonid, fixedly and thoughtfully' (ii, p. 194). She fails to heed Liza's warnings to 'Watch out!' (ii, p. 194); and when she returns from her tryst in Scene 6, she again ignores Liza:

Liza. What have you done, what have you done? ...
Nadya (not hearing her, speaks quietly to Leonid). You will come again tomorrow? (ii, p. 198)

and fixes her attention on Leonid: 'slowly, as if involuntarily, they part. Nadya turns back, catches up with Leonid and looks him in the eyes' (ii, p. 198). Thus Nadya appears to be living out her ideal before abandoning it forever.

As stated in the Introduction, the (limited) critical discussion of the theme of idealism in Ostrovsky's drama demonstrates clearly the narrow focus of traditional analysis of his work, interpreting his plays solely in terms of their contemporary context. Critical discussion of Ostrovsky's drama has been greatly coloured by two formative articles by N.Dobrolyubov in 1859 and 1860—entitled respectively 'The Kingdom of Darkness' and 'A Ray of Light in the Kingdom of Darkness'. In these, Dobrolyubov continually emphasises that the essence of Ostrovsky's plays is 'their unadulterated truth', their 'faithfulness to reality'[5], before going on to argue that the underlying motive for Ostrovsky's work was social criticism, the desire to challenge Russian life: '... if our readers, after pondering over our observations, find that . .. the artist has indeed challenged Russian life . .. then we shall be satisfied, no matter what our scholars and literary judges might say.'[6] Ostrovsky's plays, Dobrolyubov asserts, are a protest against the tyranny that is to be found in this 'realm of darkness' (namely Russian society); a protest against its corrupting influence on human relationships, the way it stifles and crushes all that is good in society, leaving potentially good and noble people impotent and apathetic.

For followers of this view, the destruction of idealism in Ostrovsky's work is simply further ammunition in his social critique. For them, Ostrovsky is merely depicting how ideals and principles were stifled and destroyed by the structures and norms of nineteenth-century Russian life. However, while there were undoubtedly elements of social criticism in Ostrovsky's drama, the portrayal of idealism in his work is far more complex. Take, for example, the play *A Lucrative Post*. Here, the play initially appears to follow the usual progression of ideals destroyed by the reality of life. The plot centres on a young university graduate, Zhadov, who is determined to live life according to his principles of honesty and hard work and thus

---

[5]N.A.Dobrolyubov, *Selected Philosophical Essays*, tr. and ed. by J.Finsburg (Moscow: Foreign Languages Publishing House, 1948), 238, 240. Dobrolyubov's hold over the critical interpretation of Ostrovsky's plays is evident from a recently published edition of a selection of Ostrovsky's plays which has, as its only critical comment on the works, a reprint of Dobrolyubov's article 'A Ray of Light in the Kingdom of Darkness'. See A.N.Ostrovskii, *Izbrannye sochineniya* (Samara: Samarskii dom pechati, 1996).
[6]Dobrolyubov, 628.

refuses to participate in the bribery and corruption common in society around him. The play charts his struggles to earn an honest living and support his new wife, until finally he comes to the realisation that he cannot maintain his principled stand against taking bribes and still provide a reasonable standard of living for his family. Again, the ideal falls in the face of reality. Yet, in this play, at the very point at which Zhadov renounces his ideals and goes to ask his uncle to find him a 'lucrative position' in the bribe-taking civil service, he finds that his uncle has been taken to court for corruption and has suffered a stroke. The young hero reaffirms his decision to live according to his ideals, and in a startling reversal, the ideal world appears to have won out over the real one.

Numerous critics have found the sudden reversal of plot progression in *A Lucrative Post* unsatisfactory, and have offered a number of explanations for it. N.Chernyshevsky, writing in 1857, considered that the play would have been 'more solid and complete artistically if it had finished at the point of crisis [at the end of Act Four]', suggesting that 'the fifth act was added by the author in order to save Zhadov from a moral fall'[7]; and A.Grigor´ev also considered the whole of Act Five 'superfluous.'[8] A more modern critic, N.Henley, suggests that Ostrovsky 'wrote Act Five to appease the censor'[9] (although the play was banned from production for six years anyway); while E.Kholodov argues that Zhadov's fall was necessary to show that he was 'not a hero, but an ordinary man', and the sudden reversal of fortune in Act Five was Ostrovsky 'telling his contemporaries that they needed to find in themselves the strength to rise up, even if they are not heroes.'[10] I.Beasley is very rare in her assessment that 'the vindication of [Zhadov's] opinions and his return to them makes a pleasing and appropriate conclusion.'[11]

Critics have also pointed out that the victory of the ideal at the end of Act Five seems rather hollow, as there is no real indication that Zhadov will be any more successful in supporting his wife this

---

[7] N.G.Chernyshevskii, 'Zametki o zhurnalakh', *Sovremennik*, 4 (1857) [see *PSS* ii, 706].

[8] A.A.Grigor´ev, *Yakor´*, 31 (1863) [see *PSS* ii, 708].

[9] Norman Henley, 'Afterword' in *Alexander Ostrovsky: Without A Dowry & other plays*, tr. and ed. by Norman Henley (Dana Point: Ardis, 1997), 72-5 (p. 75).

[10] E.G.Kholodov, 'A.N.Ostrovskii v 1855-1865 godakh' in *PSS* ii, 666.

[11] Beasley, unpublished doctoral thesis, 175.

second time around.[12] Certainly the other characters in the play who attempt to live by their ideals—Dosuzhev and Mykin—are shown to have great difficulty in scraping a living. What this suggests, however, is that the ending of the play seems unsatisfactory not simply because, as adherents of social criticism would have it, the play has failed to present the true 'reality' of grim realism destroying hopes and ideals; but because the ideal itself is somehow flawed. The message of the play is not so clear-cut as to suggest that the bribetakers are simply villains, while the principled idealists are all heroes. Indeed, when one reads the play, Zhadov often appears ridiculous in his ardent protestations as to the 'rightness' of his way of life; while his assessment of his naive, rather silly, wife as 'Perfection!' (ii, p. 46), 'an angel' (ii, p. 68) raises questions about his judgement.[13] In contrast, while his uncle is without doubt an unscrupulous bribetaker, he often appears sound in his judgements about life. When Zhadov asks why the office clerks laugh at his sermons on morality, questioning what is funny about their content, his uncle replies: 'Everything, my friend; beginning with your un-necessary, indecent enthusiasm and ending with your childish, impractical conclusions. Believe it, any clerk knows life better than you. He knows from his own experience that it's better to have a full stomach than to be a hungry philosopher. Of course your words seem stupid to him' (ii, p. 49); and it is he who questions Zhadov's right to marry when he is living in poverty: 'So, what are you preparing for her, what kind of joys in life? Just poverty, and all kinds of deprivation. If you ask me, if you love a woman, then you should try and strew her path, so to speak, with all kinds of delights' (ii, p. 50) ... 'In a word, it's your duty to provide happiness for the woman you love' (ii, p. 51). Indeed the sympathetic depiction of the bribetakers provoked one contemporary critic to complain: 'These persons who are brought on to the stage should rouse in the reader, or spectator, a

---

[12] See Hoover, 53.
[13] The difficulties in assessing Zhadov's role in the play are made clear by the following conflicting critical interpretations: N.Henley notes that 'the play makes it only too clear that the fault is much more society's than [Zhadov's]' [see Henley, 'Ostrovskij's Play-Actors, Puppets, and Rebels', 323], whereas Yu.Aikhenval'd complains that 'in the character of Zhadov, in this talentless, lifeless character, [Ostrovsky] vulgarises honesty.' [See Yu.Aikhenval'd, Siluety russkikh pisatelei (Moscow: Nauchnoe slovo, 1909), 169.]

feeling of repugnance, but in themselves they excite only compassion. Bribery, a social sore, is not brought out in very vivid and disgusting colours in their conduct ... The author should have shown how bribetakers and embezzlers of state funds are tormenting, disgracing and ruining our long-suffering and beloved mother Russia everywhere, at home and abroad', before going on to ask 'why Ostrovsky has brought out a disreputable gentleman like Zhadov as the representative of honest striving?'[14]

This suggestion of flawed idealism is present in many of Ostrovsky's plays which deal with the relationship between real and ideal worlds. The play, *A Hangover from Someone Else's Feast*, for example, contrasts the poor but honest teacher, Ivan, with the wealthy 'samodur' merchant, Tit Titych, who tyrannises his family. Once again, adherents of the social criticism view of Ostrovsky's work would note that the play depicts a society in which a cheating, ignorant merchant can live more successfully than an honest, hard-working teacher. Yet again, the message is ambiguous, as the idealistic Ivan's obsession with learning has led him to disregard the importance of providing adequately for himself and his family. Act One of the play contrasts the idealistic Ivan—who lives for his books and learning, and is continually trying to blot out the 'ignorance' of the world around him—with his more pragmatic landlady, Agrafena, who is far more realistic about the circumstances in which he lives and tries to encourage practical action to improve them, as the opening sequence depicts:

> *Ivan Ksenofontych enters, waving his arms; Agrafena Platonovna follows after him.*
>
> **Ivan.** Ignorance! Ignorance! And I don't want to listen to ignorance! (He sits at the table and opens a book).
> **Agrafena.** Everything is ignorance with you. But what are you yourself? Your only blessing is that you are an educated man! What's the use of it, this learning of yours? You have only one thought—that you are an educated man—but you're worse than us, uneducated ones. You live like a peasant, with neither house nor home!

---

[14] See Dobrolyubov, pp. 225 and 239. The critic was N.A.Nekrasov. His review appeared in *Atenei*, 10 (1858).

Ivan. Ignorance! Ignorance!

Agrafena. It's all one thing with you! Ignorance and ignorance! I'm speaking for your own benefit. What's it to me? I'm a stranger to you.

Ivan. And if you are a stranger, madam, then don't interfere in other people's business. Leave me alone. You can see that I'm busy.

Agrafena (*after a short silence*). Treat me as you like. I'm only talking out of pity for you. Where are you going to get a dowry for your daughter? She's twenty years old, and these days no-one takes a girl without a dowry. But you have nothing here or anywhere else, just bare poverty.

Ivan. What do you mean, nothing? I have a pension, my lessons.

Agrafena. What use is your pension? What use are these lessons of yours? Do you think that's a dowry? While you are still alive, well, of course, it's enough to maintain you, but you are an elderly man; what will she do once you're gone?

Ivan. What will she do? She will teach children. She will occupy herself, madam, with the same noble work her father has done all his life ...' (ii, pp. 8/9)

It is surely significant that Agrafena's patronymic is derived from Plato, suggesting wisdom.

Likewise, in the significantly titled *Truth is Fine, but Luck is Better*, the central character (again named Platon, although this time with probable ironic intent) is another idealist, who insists on telling the truth all the time and refuses to cheat and deceive like the merchants who surround him. Once more, sticking to principles is shown to have negative consequences: Platon's insistence on telling people insulting truths, his refusal to falsify accounts or forge promissory notes leads him to a position where he has to pawn all his mother's belongings and he himself faces debtor's prison. Again, he appears oblivious to the consequences of his principled stand, as this short extract from a conversation with his mother suggests:

Platon. You understand, mama?

Zybkina. Understand what? I don't understand anything.

Platon. What he was driving at! They can't cheat themselves, so they hire others to do it.

Zybkina. Cheat whom?

Platon. The old woman, old Barabosheva. And you say I should find work!

Zybkina. Can you do this work?

Platon. Of course I can. They taught me it.

Zybkina. Would they give you money for it?

Platon. He promised 150.

Zybkina. Are we millionaires!

Platon. No, we are not millionaires, but I, mama, am a patriot.

Zybkina. You're cruel, that's what! (*Wipes her eyes with her scarf*).

Platon. What are you crying for? You should be praising me, I've managed to sell the last of our cups. (iv, pp. 288/9)

Platon's insistence on the truth is frequently ridiculed:

Platon. No, I am not afraid to speak the truth to anyone, even the most ferocious wild animal ... I would look in the eyes of a lion and speak the truth to it.

Poliksena. And it would tear you to pieces. (iv, p. 303)

And Platon himself is often made to appear ridiculous: for example, on discovering that his mother will not pay her debt, leaving him facing certain imprisonment, his response is to sit and write poetry:

Platon. What can I do? All around me is ignorance, it surrounds me in all directions, it will conquer me, conquer me! Agh! I'm going to drown myself, drown myself.

Zybkina. You won't kill yourself?

Platon. Of course I won't kill myself, that's stupid. But I'll do this, I'll do this. (*He sits at the table, takes out paper and pencils.*) ... I will write poetry. In grief such as this, educated people always turn to poetry. (iv, p. 290)

Although Platon ends the play in a positive position—he becomes chief clerk and marries the woman he loves—like Zhadov in *A Lucrative Post* before him, the idealist's success is brought about, not through adherence to ideals, but the fortuitous intervention of unexpected events, or, as the title suggests—good luck.[15]

---

[15] E.Kholodov questions whether Platon's marriage to Poliksena is indeed a happy ending. He questions the truth of Poliksena's love for Platon and asks 'can he really be happy with the daughter of Amos Panfilych and the granddaughter of Mavra

Thus we are left in a position where, rather than simply reading the destruction of idealism in Ostrovsky's plays as a criticism of social reality, it is equally possible to turn such an argument on its head, and suggest that instead of criticising the social reality, Ostrovsky was criticising the idealism itself. His dramas challenge the naivety of his characters given the grimness of real life; criticise them for dogmatically sticking to principles despite harmful consequences; or simply suggest that their ideals are little more than self-indulgent illusions and chart the inevitable disillusionment.

The Soviet critic V.Lakshin takes just this view in his analysis of the play *The Poor Bride*, which tells of a young woman forced to marry an ignorant, vulgar civil servant in order to escape poverty. Lakshin sees the play as a literary polemic which criticises the romantic idealism of the young heroine, Mar´ya. Lakshin argues that Mar´ya is attracted to the worthless suitor, Merich, because he represents the romantic 'ideal' depicted in the fashionable Romantic literature of the time. Mar´ya therefore rejects her other suitor, Khor´kov, who genuinely loves her, because he does not conform to this ideal. For Lakshin, the novelty of the play is 'the sense of the exhausted old Romantic ideal and the appeal to the sober truth of life.' Ostrovsky's message is that 'life is more cruel, more serious than it is written about in fashionable novels'[16] and he therefore punishes his heroine for her youthful ideals by having her marry the very prosaic civil servant. (M.Manheim takes a similar view of *The Poor Bride* as a play which challenges old literary forms when she notes: 'In exploring the realities of Mar´ya's world, Ostrovsky challenges the vaudeville cliché of happy marriage endings.'[17])

We are left with two entirely conflicting interpretations of the reason behind the repeating pattern of broken dreams in Ostrovsky's plays, with critics arguing that it is either the realities of society or the idealism itself which is at fault. Thus *The Ward* could be seen either to criticise society for allowing a young girl to be held hostage to the whims of her tyrannical mistress, or to criticise Nadya for failing to face up to the realities of life and for harbouring dreams that could

---

Tarasovna?' See *PSS* iv, 485.

[16] V.Ya. Lakshin, 'Ostrovskii (1843-1854)' in *PSS* i, 462-93 (pp. 478-9).

[17] Martha Manheim, 'Ostrovsky and Vaudeville' (unpublished doctoral thesis, Columbia University, 1978), 241.

never be realised. Likewise *A Lucrative Post* and *Truth is Fine, but Luck is Better* could be seen to be criticising the bribery and deception inherent in society, or to be mocking Zhadov and Platon for attempting to adhere to wholly unrealistic principles. In his reading of *A Hangover from Someone Else's Feast*, C.Manning even goes so far as to suggest that the 'samodur' merchants are the positive characters in the play. He notes that 'the schoolteacher and his daughter who spurn the suit of the well-meaning [merchant] boy are as comical as he is. They lack the wealth and the steadiness, the clear vision and the calm power of the merchant class.'[18]

As if this were not complex enough, a further weakness of the two interpretations is precisely that they fail to account for the complexity of Ostrovsky's treatment of idealism in his work. In the play *The Poor Bride*, for example, both the 'social criticism' and the 'critique of idealism' interpretations rely on the premise that the plot development of the play follows the usual pattern of destruction of idealism; with Mar'ya moving from a state of idealistic delusion in her dreams of finding a romantic love, to an acceptance of reality. Yet, on reading the play, one could argue that the reverse occurs.[19] At the beginning of the play, Mar'ya exhibits a largely realistic assessment of her situation as a poor bride: 'It's easy for mamma to say, 'Get married!' But who am I meant to marry? It horrifies me to imagine what it would be like to marry a man for whom you feel nothing but aversion. (*Reflecting*) Any old monster thinks he has the right to woo, and even considers it a kind favour, 'because she, ' he says, 'is a poor bride.' Someone or other will simply bargain for me, as if I were some kind of merchandise. "I have means, " he will say; "you have nothing. I'll take your daughter for her beauty."' (i, p. 197) And although she does treat Merich as some kind of fantasy hero, this is not due to a lack of realism, but precisely because she is aware of the reality that faces her. She appears to be using Merich as a means of escape from reality; as a fantasy figure through which she can dream of escaping a reality she is very well aware of. Even then her realism keeps breaking through in her constant fears that he might deceive her:

---

[18] Manning, 39.

[19] Eugene Bristow has noted that Mar'ya starts the play as a realistic character and then creates illusions for herself towards the end. (See Bristow, p. 24.)

Mar´ya Andreevna. You're not deceiving me, Vladimir Vasil´ich?

Merich. Oh no, no ...

Mar´ya Andreevna. You're not deceiving me?

Merich. By every oath that I know ...

Mar´ya Andreevna. There's no need, no need ... Ah, Vladimir Vasil´ich! Don't deceive me, for God's sake! You could deceive me so easily ... (i, p. 219)

Mar´ya Andreevna (*alone, leans against the door*). He's gone! Have I done the right thing? I'm both ashamed and happy. What if it is only a game on his part? (i, p. 220)

Mar´ya Andreevna ... Ah, fool, why am I crying? A man tells me right out that he'll marry me, and I cry and think up all sorts of misfortunes. (*She laughs, then falls into thought.*) But what if he doesn't? What if he doesn't? Then what? But what right have I to think badly of him: I don't even know him yet. But what's that, good God! What am I saying? I'm all mixed up. Any other woman in my place would be jumping for joy, but all sorts of nonsense creeps into my head. No, no, I won't think about anything! Vladimir will marry me!' (i, p. 248)

Indeed, her constant worry that he might deceive her suggests that she is well aware of her own self-deception in investing any faith in him in the first place.

Mar´ya's real descent into self-deception occurs once Merich has finally let her down, and she has no escape from the fate that awaits her. Rather than facing reality, she appears to slip into self-delusion. Despite all her previous concerns that Merich might be deceiving her, she states: '... How could I have known that he was deceiving me? How was I meant to know? Why should I have known? ... Why did he deceive me!' (i, p. 258). She then goes on to consciously role-play—to pretend that she is not upset and that she herself has chosen to marry the prosaic Benevolensky:

Milashin. You think to deceive me and yourself, too. What's the point? I know what's in your soul.

Mar´ya (*stamping her foot*). I'm absolutely not deceiving you; truly. I've suddenly become quite happy somehow. Let's play something or other. Ah, here are some cards! Let's play cards. (i, p. 260)

and as she plays, she '(*reflects, covers her eyes with her handkerchief and leans upon the table; then she wipes her eyes and takes the cards*): Whose go is it? Mine?' (i, p. 260)

Mar´ya's final descent into self-deception occurs right at the end of the play, when, on the day of her wedding to Benevolensky, she talks of her hopes to change and re-educate him—hopes which, many critics have noted, are little more than self-delusions. G.Vladykin, for example, states that 'Mar´ya Andreevna takes on herself a "heroic role", to re-educate and make a "human being" out of Benevolensky... the idea of "re-educating" [him] is only a form of self-consolation'[20]; while V.Lakshin notes that 'it seems the author himself does not believe in such a good outcome, and marries his heroine with cheerless feeling.'[21]

In *Talents and Admirers*, there are similar ambiguities in the message of the play. It would be easy to argue that the play criticises the patronage system, whereby the fate of actresses is left in the hands of powerful philistines such as Dulebov and Bakin, and where an actress is forced to abandon her principles of purity in order to survive financially. Yet again, the principal idealist in the play, Melusov, is often made to appear ridiculous; all the 'lovers' of art, such as Narokov and the Tragedian, are completely ineffectual; and it is the realistic Velikatov and Vasya who actually provide practical help for Negina. It is surely significant that Ostrovsky gave early drafts of the play the titles 'Dreamers' and 'Fantasists'.[22] Even at the end of the play, the message remains ambiguous. Although reality appears to have won out, as Negina leaves to live with Velikatov as his mistress, it is Melusov who is given the final, inspiring words of the play, and who is thus given victory in his spiritual battle with Bakin:

Melusov. A duel? What for? You and I are already fighting a duel, a constant duel, a never-ending struggle. I enlighten and you deprave ... So, let's fight. You do your business and I'll do mine.

---

[20] G.I.Vladykin, 'A.N.Ostrovskii' in *Sobranie sochinenii A.N.Ostrovskogo*, 10 vols, ed. G.I.Vladykin (Moscow: Khudozhestvennaya literatura, 1959-1960) I, xiv.
[21] Lakshin, 'Ostrovskii (1843-1854)', 479.
[22] See *PSS* v, 519.

We'll see who gets tired first. You'll throw in your occupation first, there's nothing very attractive in empty-headedness. You'll reach a ripe old age, and your conscience will begin to prick you. Of course, there are some with such happy natures that into deep old age they preserve the ability to fly with astonishing lightness from flower to flower, but these are exceptions. I will carry out my work until the end. But if I do stop teaching, if I do stop believing in the possibility of improving people, or if I do weakly bury myself in idleness and simply give up, then you can buy me a pistol and I will thank you for it. (v, pp. 279/80)

All this is further complicated by the suggestion that, in abandoning her ideals of honesty and purity, Negina attains what for her is an even higher ideal—the ability to go on practising her art (or indeed—the ideal of love: N.Henley puts forward a persuasive argument that Negina does not love Melusov, but is instead attracted to Velikatov[23]).

Even the play *Not of This World* presents us with a number of inconsistencies. Critics have noted that although the 'other-worldly' Kseniya is largely alienated from the real world, she takes two very worldly actions: first in marrying Vitalii against her mother's wishes, and secondly, in returning home (unnecessarily as it turns out) in order to save Vitalii from the audit.[24] To this could be added the fact that she makes a will—once more against her mother's wishes. As ever, Ostrovsky draws no definitive conclusions in the play. Both the real and ideal worlds are presented as equally valid (or false), with each having its own faults and virtues. Thus while Elokhov mocks the greed and selfishness of characters such as Barbarisov and Khoniya, Murugov mocks Kseniya's idealism, pointing out that you have to turn to literature to find examples of people who live according to her ideals, as they are impossible to find in real life:

... I will say only one thing, that the demands of Kseniya Vasil'evna are too high for us, they are not possible for us—too idealistic. Even in literature there are few examples of the kind of pure, family virtues that Kseniya Vasil'evna wishes. Who are they?

[23] Henley, *Without a Dowry*, 262-4.
[24] Hoover, 123.

> Here is an ideal couple, if you believe Ovid: Philemon and Baucis.
> But they are the creations of a poet. (v, p. 467)

And noting that you have to keep values in perspective:

> ... Imagine, a soldier needs to go to war, but his wife won't let him
> go. Well, the wife, of course, by her way of thinking, is right. But
> so is his commander when he tells him: 'If you are a soldier, then
> you should fight, and not lie on the stove ...' (v, p. 468)

The example of Snafidina, who wishes that her daughter had died as a child so that she had reached heaven while still pure, is undoubtedly another warning against idealism taken to its logical extreme.

The key to resolving this complexity lies in removing the greatest limitation presented by the critical interpretations of Lakshin and Dobrolyubov: namely, that they rely on rooting Ostrovsky's work in the narrow confines of nineteenth-century Russian literature and society. Critics traditionally seem to be trying to find in Ostrovsky's work clear-cut messages relating specifically to contemporary Russian society—in this case either a criticism of social structures and conditions, or a criticism of the romantic literature of the early nineteenth century.[25] L.Smirnova, discussing the play *A Lucrative Post*, for example, notes: 'The comedy placed before the Russian public the most sharp and real problems of pre-reform Russia.'[26] V.Sleptsov, again discussing *A Lucrative Post*, states: 'Ostrovsky's main talent as a dramatist lies in the extraordinary faithfulness with which he reproduces Russian life ... Most of his plays are concerned with resolving some peculiar question of his time. This is certainly true of [*A Lucrative Post*] which depicts the struggle of the so-called 'new generation' with the one that is passing away.'[27]

---

[25] Ironically, in *Kingdom of Darkness*, Dobrolyubov, criticising the 'confusion of opinion about Ostrovsky' among contemporary critics, states that the reason for it lies in the fact 'that a determined effort has been made to present [Ostrovsky] as the representative of a certain set of convictions.' He states that 'we do not ascribe any programme to the author' before going on to do just that in his assertion that Ostrovsky's plays are a protest against the tyranny found in the 'realm of darkness'. (See Dobrolyubov, 228 and 231.)

[26] L.Smirnova, *PSS* ii, 703.

[27] Vasily Sleptsov, 'On Alexander Ostrovsky' in *The Complection of Russian Literature*, ed. Andrew Field (New York: Atheneum, 1971), 152-5 (p. 152).

Yet as the above discussion has shown, the messages are ambiguous; there are no clear-cut resolutions. However, if you remove Ostrovsky's work from its social and historical context; if you work from the premise that Ostrovsky is not just posing the question: 'What place does idealism have in nineteenth-century Russian society?', but is taking a step back and posing the wider question: 'How do we, as human beings, reconcile our ideals with the realities of life?' then the complexity and the lack of a definitive message no longer seem so unsatisfactory. Ostrovsky is posing a question which is complex, and to which there are, perhaps, no satisfactory clear-cut answers.[28]

The specific nineteenth-century questions remain valid—both social criticism and literary polemics are clearly apparent in Ostrovsky's work—but they are revealed for what they are: simply a small part of a much wider question. Thus, in a play such as *Talents and Admirers*, Ostrovsky is not only asking the specific contemporary question—whether actresses can or indeed should maintain ideals of honesty and purity, given the difficult financial conditions they faced at the time—but also universal questions such as: should adherence to ideals take precedence over material well-being, or can one ideal (art or love) take precedence over others, such as purity. Similarly the play, *A Lucrative Post*, not only depicts the 'struggle of the "new generation"'; not only debates the rights and wrongs of the bribery inherent in contemporary society and discusses the possibility of reconciling idealism with such a reality; but also questions whether adherence to ideals should take precedence over material comfort; or whether it is right to pursue your ideals at the expense of the happiness and well-being of the people you love—much more universal concerns. It is these universal concerns which appear to have been largely overlooked in the critical analysis of Ostrovsky's work. Criticism has, in general, focused on the narrow contemporary issues at the expense of the wider picture. And in turn, it is this narrowness of focus which has led to Ostrovsky's drama not receiving the attention it deserves outside Russia.

---

[28] Compare this with V.Terras' assertion that 'the moral message of Ostrovsky's plays is simple'. [See Victor Terras, *History of Russian Literature* (New Haven: Yale University Press, 1991), 372.]

PART TWO

THE NATURE OF REALITY

The relationship between realism and idealism is merely one facet of a central concern in Ostrovsky's work: namely, the very nature of reality itself. The remainder of this study is devoted to discussion of various other elements of Ostrovsky's plays which form part of this concern with the nature of reality, with the purpose of demonstrating just how considerable a theme it is in his drama. Again, the overall aim is to demonstrate that, in general, critics have traditionally focused too greatly on nineteenth-century specifics—emphasising the veracity of Ostrovsky's portrayal of everyday life—and have neglected the wider picture. As a consequence, they have largely overlooked the universal messages in his plays, such as his concern with varying perceptions of reality and with psychological mechanisms for dealing with reality.

CHAPTER ONE

The Web of Deception

> 'How crafty and cun-
> ning it all is.' *Late Love*
> (iv, p. 50)

C entral to Ostrovsky's consideration of the nature of reality is the complex web of deception depicted in his plays. N.Dobrolyubov, describing the 'realm of darkness' which he sees portrayed in Ostrovsky's work, stated: 'Here nobody can trust one another: at any moment you may expect your friend to boast about how skilfully he has cheated or robbed you; a partner in a profitable speculation may quite easily get hold of all the money and documents and get his partner locked up in the debtor's prison; a father-in-law will cheat his son-in-law out of his dowry; a bridegroom will cheat the matchmaker; the bride will deceive her father and mother, a wife will deceive her husband.'[1]

Indeed the portrayal of deception in Ostrovsky's work is almost overwhelming in its magnitude, incorporating cheating and swindling merchants; ambitious social climbers; dishonest lovers; rich misers pretending to be beggars; and mistresses pretending to be virtuous young wards; to name but a few. As Appendix D demonstrates, deception of some kind or another occurs in all but one of the forty-one plays analysed closely in this study.[2]

---

[1] Dobrolyubov, 247.

[2] Despite the quotation from Dobrolyubov above, the magnitude of the theme of deception in Ostrovsky's plays is infrequently noted in critical analysis. I.Beasley, for example, discussing a number of plays including *The Ward, Even Wise Men Err, Easy*

The Web of Deception: *A Family Picture*

The ubiquitous nature of deception is the central theme of
Ostrovsky's very first play, *A Family Picture* (1847). Charting an
afternoon in the life of a typical merchant family—the
Puzatovs—the play depicts deception and cheating as the norm in
both business and domestic worlds. Right from the start of the play,
in the opening monologue, the young Mar'ya Puzatova, bemoaning
her fate at being kept shut up indoors all day, declares: 'Well, go
ahead! Lock us up! Tyrannize us! We'll just ask leave to go to
midnight mass at the convent; get dressed up in our best things, and
then go off to the park or Sokol'niki, or somewhere else instead!
There's nothing else for it, you have to do things on the sly.' (i,
p. 66).

Mar'ya and her sister-in-law, Matrena, go on to plan a secret
rendezvous with two admirers. The extent of the deception
involved is emphasised when the maid, Dar'ya, who is bringing
them a message from their admirers, tells how she ran into
Mar'ya's mother, Stepanida, and how she had to lie about where
she had been: 'I was running up the stairs, and Stepanida
Trofimovna was right there! I had to say I'd gone to the store for a
skein of silk ...' (i, p. 67).

The two young women continue their acts of deception when the
other family members enter. Matrena is described as kissing her
husband, Antip, 'with feigned tenderness' (i, p. 71); and when
Antip teases Mar'ya about finding her a bridegroom: 'Well-
nourished and ruddy-cheeked, you know, Masha, like me. That's
the sort of fellow to love, eh, isn't it, Masha?' she, despite her
secret assignations, responds with pretended ignorance of men:
'Well, really! And how should I know? ...' and is described as
'casting down her eyes' (i, p. 74).

Antip himself talks blithely about the cheating that goes on in
the business world. Almost his very first comment to his mother,
Stepanida, is a boast about how he 'cheated Brykhov out of a

Money, *The Forest, Wolves and Sheep, Rich Brides, Without a Dowry, A Last
Sacrifice* and *The Handsome Man*, singles out only *The Forest* and *Wolves and Sheep*
as 'concentrating on pretence and hypocrisy'. In fact, deception is a key theme in all
these plays. (See Beasley, unpublished doctoral thesis, 114.)

thousand roubles today'. Stepanida responds by stating that he himself is probably 'being fleeced on all sides', and complaining that he 'never keeps watch on his shopmen' (i, p. 69).

The widespread acceptance of deception in the merchant world is further emphasised in a later conversation in which Antip and his mother discuss the elderly merchant Shiryalov as a possible husband for Mar′ya. Antip notes that Shiryalov is 'a terrible cheat' and Stepanida responds:

> Oh, good gracious! And how is he a cheat? Tell me, please! He goes to church on all the holidays—and he's always the first to arrive. He keeps all the fasts; and during Lent he doesn't even have sugar in his tea—only honey or raisins ... and if he does deceive people from time to time, well, what's the harm in it? He's not the first to do so, and he won't be the last—he's a businessman. Why, there'd be no business without a little deception, Antipushka. It's true what they say—'no lies—no sale.' (i, p. 74)

Here, Stepanida reveals her concern with appearances. For her, cheating and deception are acceptable as long as they are hidden behind a veneer of respectability and piety. For Antip also, there is a certain 'code' of deception. With great irony, he declares that deception is important, but that there should be some conscience involved. He notes that he can be as cunning as Shiryalov, yet justifies his deception by the fact that he always tells his victims honestly afterwards: '... Take last year, for example, I caught out Sava Savich to the tune of five hundred roubles. But afterwards I said to him, 'Look here, Sava Savich, I cheated you out of five hundred. But it's too late now, mate, ' I said, 'you should keep your wits about you.' He was a bit annoyed, but we're friends again ...' (i, p. 75). Shiryalov, however, he complains, 'would deceive his own father. It's true! He looks you right in the eye, just like that. And then he pretends to be a saint!' (i, p. 75). Ironically, at this moment Shiryalov enters, and Antip demonstrates his own hypocrisy by exclaiming: 'Oh, Paramon Ferapontich! What an honour to see you!' (i, p. 76). The subsequent conversation between Antip and Shiryalov is a demonstration in hypocrisy, as both men feign friendliness and helpfulness. Shiryalov feigns piety and talks of the difficulties he has with his 'wild' son, while talking quite openly and casually about the ways in which he cheats his customers. When Antip suggests that the way to solve his problems would be to marry, which, one presumes, was always the purpose of Shiryalov's visit, Shiryalov cries: 'You're having me on!' (note that when he speaks he is described as 'looking into Puzatov's eyes', thus fulfilling Antip's accusation that he looks people straight in the eyes when lying to them). Then, with false modesty, he raises a number of weak objections to a marriage between himself and Mar´ya; and all the while is described as 'casting down his eyes' and 'casting down his eyes still further' (i, p. 83). (It is interesting to note that both he and his future wife are described as feigning modesty in this way—a link which hints at the deception that will no doubt form an integral part of their future life together.) The marriage is agreed, and Shiryalov, calling Antip his 'benefactor', invites him for further drinks at his house. As soon as Shiryalov leaves the room, all pretence at friendliness vanishes, and Antip, with a wink, declares: 'What a thieving peasant!' (the fact that he is prepared to marry his sister to such a man is indicative of the lack of compassion which Ostrovsky seems to suggest as the cause behind the commonplace deception and hypocrisy) and goes on to note: 'Only, Paramon Ferapontych [Shiryalov], as regards the dowry, who will be deceiving who isn't decided yet! My mother and I are no fools ...' (i, p. 84). Antip departs and the stage is left clear for one final act of deception: Mar´ya and Matrena, dressed in fine clothes, cross the stage on the way out to their secret assignation, stopping to note laughingly that they have told the family that they are on their way to vespers.

The overall impression created by the play is of the typicality of deception—its casual acceptance. There is much emphasis on the generality of the opinions and actions demonstrated by the characters, and great play on the sense of ease with which characters embrace deception. Mar´ya and Matrena, for example, are laughing when they leave for their secret rendezvous—they are relaxed and at ease with their behaviour. Likewise, Antip slips easily from denouncing Shiryalov, to greeting him warmly, to denouncing him again; and then heads off for a drinking spree at Shiryalov's house. All are comfortable with their deceit—it is the norm. As L.Cox notes: 'The casualness shows that to the characters these are normal, typical aspects of life';[3] while N.Dobrolyubov talks of 'the religion of hypocrisy', noting that 'Here cheating is normal and necessary, like killing in war.'[4]

The Deceiver Deceived: *It's All in the Family*

The deception portrayed in *A Family Picture* was further developed in Ostrovsky's second play, *It's All in the Family*, which again depicts the cheating and hypocrisy prevalent in the merchant world. V.Lakshin goes so far as to suggest: 'Deceit is the mainspring of the play. All the deceivers in the play expect to deceive and be deceived. Deceit is the law, tsar, religion of their life.' He describes the central character, the merchant Bol'shov, as 'a poet of deception' who 'lives for the idea of deceit'[5], while I.Esam, discussing the same play, talks of 'the leitmotif of deceit throughout the play.'[6] The play describes Bol'shov's scheme to declare himself bankrupt in order to avoid paying his creditors. Again, the ubiquitous nature of the cheating and deception is emphasised, as in Act One, Scene 11, where Bol'shov's head clerk, Podkhalyuzin, reports back to Bol'shov that the clerks are proficient in the 'usual' tricks of the trade:

> It's the usual thing. I try to have everything in order and as it should be. 'Now, lads, ' I say, 'no sleeping on the job. You keep looking out for chances for a sale; some idiot of a purchaser may turn up, or some young lady might take a particular fancy to a certain coloured pattern, and straightaway, ' I say, 'you add a rouble or two to the price per yard' ... 'And, ' I say, 'make sure you measure more naturally: pull and stretch just enough, God save us, so as not to tear the cloth. It's not us, ' I say, 'who have to wear it afterwards. Well, and if they're not keeping a lookout, then it's nobody's fault, ' I say, 'if you should happen to measure the same yard of cloth twice.' (i, p. 102)

[3] Lucy Cox, 'Form and Meaning in the Plays of Alexander N.Ostrovsky' (unpublished doctoral thesis, University of Pennsylvania, 1975), 46.
[4] Dobrolyubov, 252-3.
[5] Lakshin, *PSS* i, 468-9.
[6] I.Esam, 'The Style of *Svoi liudi—sochtemsia*', *New Zealand Slavonic Journal*, 10 (1972), 79-105 (p. 84).

In this play, the web of deceit deepens and the deceiver is himself deceived. (L.Cox discusses 'degrees of swindling—that which is done without thought (the norm) and that which is slightly riskier and therefore requires consideration.'[7]) Podkhalyuzin, to whom Bol´shov has signed over his property in order to declare himself bankrupt, double-crosses him and keeps hold of all of Bol´shov's property, refusing to pay any of his debts and leaving him in debtor's prison. Podkhalyuzin then goes on to deceive those who helped him swindle Bol´shov. In an ominous ending to the play, Ostrovsky again emphasises the prevalence of deception, leaving the audience in no doubt that the swindling will continue. Brushing aside the complaints of his victims, Podkhalyuzin turns to the audience and declares: 'Don't you believe him, everything he was saying—it's all lies. Nothing like that ever happened. Probably it was all a dream he had. But now, we are opening a little shop, so do us the favour! Send the child to us, we won't sell him short!' (i, p. 152)

The Importance of Role-Play: *At a Lively Spot*

A later play, *At a Lively Spot*, shifts the setting away from the merchant world to that of an inn on a busy travelling route. Again, the emphasis is on the deception in both the business and domestic spheres. Thus the innkeeper, Bessudny, is shown making arrangements with coachdrivers for them to stop at his inn, even if it is not a natural stopping place on their journey (Act One, Scene 1). He tells of how he gets the travelling merchants drunk in order to rob them, and talks with 'flashing eyes' about the exploits of times past: '... In the old days—so they say—such things were done along this road! It's a lively spot, as you yourselves know. Merchants would come with a string of carts, and the porters would bar the gates and without a word would cut the throats of every one of them ...' (ii, p. 558).

Bessudny is also shown arranging with a coachdriver to pretend that his coach has damaged a wheel so that the travellers are forced to stay the night (Act Two, Scene 1); and setting out to hijack and rob another carriage that he has been told is travelling through the night (Act Two, Scene 2).

---

[7] Cox, 55.

As in *A Family Picture*, the business swindler is himself being deceived at home. In *At a Lively Spot*, Bessudny's wife, Evgeniya, is having an affair with Milovidov, a frequent patron of the inn. Again, her web of deceit is full of tangles: not only is she deceiving Bessudny, but she gained the attention of Milovidov under false pretences. Milovidov was originally courting Annushka, Evgeniya's sister-in-law. However, Evgeniya told him (falsely) that Annushka was only pretending to return his love: '... 'What do you keep looking at her for, when she plays the part of the modest maiden? With others she's not so choosy—that's for you only, because she's trying to trick you into marriage. She's been telling everyone for ages: "I'm going to be a lady. Watch how I'll catch that fool!"' (ii, p. 584). So, Evgeniya is simultaneously deceiving three people—Bessudny, Milovidov and Annushka.

Ironically, in this play, the means of deception are responsible for its positive dénouement. Annushka, on discovering that Evgeniya and Milovidov are having an affair, attempts to poison herself. However, the drugs she takes are not the poison they appear to be, but the sleeping pills Bessudny uses to drug and rob his customers; thus leaving her safe and well for a joyful reunion with Milovidov.

At a Lively Spot is of further interest for the element of role-play involved in Evgeniya's deception. Although she accuses Annushka of 'playing the part' of a modest young girl, it is Evgeniya herself who is an accomplished role-player; orchestrating and playing out a scene with Milovidov in front of her husband in an attempt to distract her husband's attention from their affair (Act Two, Scene 7). Bessudny himself takes advantage of his wife's acting skills, getting her to flirt with his customers. When Evgeniya (despite the fact that she clearly relishes the task) protests: 'Oh, Ermolaich, I really don't like leading such a wild life' (ii, p. 546), Bessudny responds: 'Oh enough of that! Drop your mask! Who are you showing your piety to? You can play the fox in front of others, but I know you.' Evgeniya is then described as 'opening the door with a feigned laugh' and leaving to flirt with the customers.

Such role-playing is an integral part of the deception depicted in Ostrovsky's plays. His works teem with impoverished gold-diggers playing the part of ardent lovers (Okoemov in *The Handsome Man*, Erast in *The Heart is not Stone*, Lidiya in *Easy Money*); and greedy swindlers adopting the mask of pious benefactors (Kabanova in *The*

Storm, Ulanbekova in *The Ward*, Murzavetskaya in *Wolves and Sheep*).[8]

The False Lover: *Don't Get Above Yourself*

Thus in a play such as *Don't Get Above Yourself*, the chief deceiver is Vikhorev, an impoverished nobleman, who pretends to fall in love with a young merchant girl, Avdot´ya, in order to obtain a dowry from her wealthy father. With Avdot´ya and her family, he adopts the role of an ardent lover, making endless declarations of love:

> **Avdot´ya.** Do you love me, Viktor Arkadych, as much as I love you?
> **Vikhorev.** How can you doubt it? If you won't be mine, I will head straightaway for the Caucasus and deliberately try and get myself shot as soon as possible. You know what a good shot those Circassians are. (i, p. 294)

> **Vikhorev.** But Maksim Fedotych, I love her ... I assure you that I love Avdot´ya Maksimovna madly ... How can you doubt the honest word of a nobleman? (i, p. 306)

But his behaviour is all a façade. When he is on his own or with his friend, Baranchevsky, he reveals his true thoughts. Thus he tells Baranchevsky of his need to marry a rich bride (i, p. 289) and demonstrates his true feelings about Avdot´ya: 'Well, she's not bad-looking, and seems to be a simple kind of girl. And how terribly in love with me she is! A hundred thousand to take her, and I would be happy enough. Of course, it would be impossible to show yourself in the capital with such a wife; but here in the provinces it doesn't matter, we'd live in clover' (i, p. 295). Discussing Avdot´ya's father, Rusakov, he declares: '... it's impossible to talk to such a peasant' (i, p. 307). Even the carriage he rides around in is part of the façade—it is not his own, but Baranchevsky's.

When Rusakov refuses to let him marry Avdot´ya, Vikhorev tricks her into eloping with him, and then abandons her when he discovers that he will not receive any money. He shows no remorse for ruining her reputation, and leaves (without paying his bills) to try his luck

---

[8] N.Henley is one of the few critics to discuss in any depth the play-acting apparent in Ostrovsky's plays. He suggests that there are three types of play-actors: the 'self-seekers', the *samodurs* [wilful tyrants], and the 'histrionically obsessed'. (See Henley, 'Ostrovskij's Play-Actors, Puppets, and Rebels', 317-25.)

elsewhere: 'Once more, nothing but bad luck! Agh, to hell with it! Where will I go now? ... I've done rushing around! ... I'll have to go elsewhere ... They say that there are rich merchants in Korovaev, and it's not far away, only fifteen versts or so ...' (i, p. 316).

The Pious Hypocrite: *The Ward*

In *The Ward*, we see the first example of Ostrovsky's many 'pious hypocrites'—characters who hide their cruelty and tyranny behind a mask of kindness and piety. Here, the principal representative of pious hypocrisy is Ulanbekova. Thus her old servant, Potapych, describing the way in which Ulanbekova treats her wards, states: '... She extends her care to all. She has such a kind heart, she worries about everyone ... but the way she cares about her wards—now that is a rarity' (ii, p. 173), but then goes on to note that her kindness towards her wards is motivated by a desire to inspire envy in others: '"Let them all see the way my wards live, " she says, "I want, " she says, "them all to be envious"' (ii, p. 173).

Potapych describes the lectures Ulanbekova gives her wards when she decides to marry them, reminding them of the insignificance of their station, as 'such touching sermons, ... and delivered with such feeling, even she herself is in tears' (ii, p. 174), when her behaviour is, in reality, extremely cruel. Likewise, we learn in Act Two that Ulanbekova's 'good deed' for the worthless Negligentov—ordering the Chief of Police to appoint him head clerk—means that a truly 'good man' will be forced out of his job. Yet, with typical sanctimoniousness, Ulanbekova states: 'I don't think I have ever done anyone any harm' (ii, p. 180). Similarly, Ulanbekova's disgust at Negligentov's behaviour rests not on his drunkenness itself, but on the fact that he dared to turn up drunk at her house: '... If he suffers from such a weakness, then, at the very least, he should have attempted to hide it from me. He can drink where he wants, only I don't want to see it! I would then know, at least, that he respects me!' (ii, p. 187). Her concern with appearance—the façade of respectability—is made doubly clear.

Ulanbekova's 'poor relation', Vasilisa Peregrinovna, is another 'pious hypocrite'. She, however, does not have Ulanbekova's power, which makes her especially spiteful. She is extremely bitter about the powerlessness of her position as a dependant of Ulanbekova's, and takes every opportunity to poison the atmosphere and cause trouble for others, an attitude thinly veiled by flattery. As she states in Act One, Scene 5:

> How I suffer in this world. (*She angrily snatches up a flower and picks off its petals.*) If only I had the power, then they would all have to watch out! They would get what's coming to them! But here I go, simpering in front of the mistress like a fool! ... what a life! ... (ii, p. 178)

The play teems with numerous examples of Vasilisa's hypocrisy. In Act Two, Scene 2, she flatters her 'benefactress', talking of her 'angelic heart' (ii, p. 180), and her 'gentility' (ii, p. 181), before upsetting her by suggesting that people complain about her actions. Later in the same scene, she praises Leonid:

> ... God has given you a son for joy and comfort. And we all rejoice in him. Just like the sun itself he seems to us, so kind, so merry, so tender! (ii, p. 182)

before going on to suggest that he is chasing the peasant girls. And it is the snooping Vasilisa who, again under a veneer of piety, tells Ulanbekova of Nadya's meeting with Leonid:

> **Vasilisa.** How I pity you, dear benefactress! You do not expect joy for yourself in this world; you shower everyone with kindness; and how do they repay you? This world is full of depravity ... my tears overflow, my heart bleeds, dear benefactress, that you are treated with such disrepect! In your own home, you aren't respected! ... (*She glances around in all directions and sits on the bench beside Ulanbekova.*) I had finished, dear benefactress, all my evening prayers to the creator of the heavens, and I went out to have a stroll in the garden; ... and what did I see there, kind benefactress? I don't know how my legs supported me! Lizka was running about the gardens with a depraved air, searching for her lover, and our little angel, the master, was out on the lake in a boat, and Nad´ka, also with a depraved air, was grasping him by the neck with her hands and kissing him ... (ii, pp. 200/1)

The Pious Hypocrite: *Wolves and Sheep*

The character of the pious hypocrite reappears in *Wolves and Sheep*, a play which again has deception as its overriding theme. It charts the ploys by which the deceivers (the 'wolves'—principally Murzavet-skaya, Glafira and Berkutov) cheat their victims (the 'sheep'—princi-pally Kupavina and Lynyaev). Here the chief role-player is Murza-vetskaya, who, like Ulanbekova, is a powerful landowner who adopts the role of a pious believer while cheating and manipulating the people around her. From the outset of the play, her exploitation of other people and the guise of religious piety behind which she masks it, is made clear. The play opens with the arrival of a crowd of her estate workers who have come to demand long-overdue payment for their work, and shows the butler, Pavlin, fending them off on the premise that today, a religious holiday, is not the day to be bothering Murzavetskaya with mundane, 'worldly vanities' such as money: 'What would you like her to do on a church holiday, and in the morning as well; is this the time to deal with such vanities? At such a time the mistress likes quiet and doesn't want to be disturbed by anyone, especially about money. You think about it: when she comes home from the cathedral, sits down to meditate and raises her eyes to the heavens, what do you think is in her soul at such a time?' (iv, p. 116)

Murzavetskaya's entrance is marvellously theatrical. Preceded by a footman who 'opens both the folding doors and remains standing on the left of the entrance', Murzavetskaya herself then enters. De-scribed as 'wearing on her head a black lace kerchief, which, like some kind of veil, half-covers her face', she passes through the room 'without looking at anyone'. Glafira follows two steps behind her, her 'eyes lowered to the floor', and behind her come two 'poor relations' (iv, p. 118). Yet despite the pious image presented, the watching village head notes—almost respectfully—that the stick Murzavet-skaya leans on is the same one she used to beat him with when he was one of her serfs.

As Act One unfolds, we watch as Murzavetskaya extorts money from her neighbour, the rich but naive widow, Kupavina, using forged letters; and we see how she sets in motion a plan to bully Kupavina into marrying her alcoholic fool of a son, Apollon, so that she can gain control over Kupavina's estate. The role of a pious benefactor is carefully maintained throughout. Thus when Pavlin tells her of the workers who have come to ask for their wages, she dismisses such worldly concerns: 'I don't even know how much money I've got, or whether there is any money at all—and I consider it a sin to root about for it. When it's needed—that is to say, when I want to give it to them—then the money will be found, I'll just have to grope about in the air around me. That's the sort of miracle that happens to me' (iv, p. 126). The money does, of course, 'miraculously materialise', when she cheats it out of Kupavina, claiming that Kupavina's late husband had promised to donate a thousand roubles for orphans. Again, Murzavetskaya pretends a lack of interest:

Murzavetskaya. What's that you're giving me?
Kupavina. The money.
Murzavetskaya. I don't like to touch it even. It's somehow disgusting to me to hold such an abomination in my hands.
Kupavina. You should at least count it.
Murzavetskaya. Well, there's no need for that! It's not my money, there's no need for me to dirty my hands with it. If there isn't enough, then it's not me you'll be deceiving, but the orphans...
Kupavina. Then where shall I put it?
Murzavetskaya. Oh, put it on the table, in the Bible. (iv, p. 137)

As soon as Kupavina has left, Murzavetskaya does indeed count the money, pockets half, and puts the rest back in the bible for Pavlin to find 'miraculously'.

The pious façade is even maintained in front of her fellow deceivers. When Chugunov, the 'court clerk' she employs to aid her in her schemes, presents her with the forged letter in Act One, she feigns shock and reluctance: 'I'm helping the poor, and for them, it is acceptable to act against one's conscience a little—that's no great sin; but you, you would be happy to get up to such tricks for your own profit' (iv, p. 132)—her own profit is, of course, exactly what Murzavetskaya herself is interested in. (She feigns a similar reaction in Act Five when Chugunov again presents her with false documents: 'Why should I look [at them], the devil helps you.' ... 'How could it not be the devil's work? Would a man think up such wickedness?' (iv, p. 191).)

Act One concludes with another show of piety as Murzavetskaya 'repents' her sins:

Murzavetskaya (*lifting her eyes to the heavens*). Ah, I'm damned, damned! (*To Glafira.*) Glafira, I'm damned. What are you looking at me for? Yes, it's true, I'm damned, what did you think? It seems

I will never be able to atone for my sins today. I deceived a silly
woman; it's as if I deceived a little child. I shall not have dinner, I
shall fast and pray on bended knee. And don't you have dinner
either, fast with me! Come on, let's go to the chapel at once! You
too, you too ... (*She stands up.*)
Glafira leads her by the right hand.
Lead me! (*She walks as if all the strength has gone out of her.*) I
have sinned, I'm damned, I have sinned.' (iv, p. 139)

Her repentance does not, however, prevent her from continuing to
deceive in the Acts to follow. (I.Beasley describes this behaviour by
Murzavetskaya as 'brilliant hypocrisy', suggesting that the 'self-im-
posed fast is more probably in the interest of economy than piety,
since Glafira is obliged to share in it.'[9])

The characters who surround Murzavetskaya are prepared to
maintain the façade. Some, like Kupavina, are simply naive; but most
are well aware of the true situation, yet are happy to let it go unchallenged: Lynyaev, out of laziness; Glafira because she is adopting
similar tactics herself; and Pavlin and Chugunov out of both fear and
an understanding that it is in their own best interests—as Murzavetskaya notes to Chugunov in Act One:

Murzavetskaya. ... you're afraid of me, you know that I could get
you pushed out of your cushy job and chased out of the town—
your crimes aren't small, you know. Then you'd have to go begging for some job as a district clerk. It wouldn't take me long, you
know, I could do it right away. (iv, p. 127)

In many ways, their society seems to depend on the deceit—it is
accepted as the norm. This is turned to his own advantage by Berkutov, who deceives people with their full knowledge and complicity. As
Lynyaev states in Act One, Scene 10: 'The wolves devour the sheep,
and the sheep humbly allow themselves to be devoured' (iv, p. 134).

Glafira is another character in *Wolves and Sheep* who masks her
true character behind a veneer of religious piety. When we first encounter her, in the stage-managed 'grand entrance' of Murzavetskaya
mentioned above, she is described as dressed in 'a plain, black woollen
dress', walking two paces behind Murzavetskaya, with 'her eyes
lowered to the floor' (iv, p. 118). She appears again at the end of Act

---

[9] Beasley, unpublished doctoral thesis, 185.

One (again, she is described as standing with 'her eyes lowered to the floor' (iv, p. 138)) when Murzavetskaya sends her over to stay with Kupavina for a few days to act as a spy and ensure that Kupavina has no intentions to marry Lynyaev. Glafira seems very willing to do this, and when Murzavetskaya warns her not to cast her own eyes at Lynyaev, she declares demurely: 'My dreams are of a different nature ... I dream of a convent cell,' adding: 'I don't think of earthly pleasures' (iv, p. 139).

In Act Two, Glafira initially maintains her pious façade. Yet on learning that Kupavina has no intention of marrying Lynyaev she declares: '... Enough of playing this comedy!' and talks of the 'foul role' (iv, p. 151) she has been playing in front of Kupavina. She admits that she is determined to catch Lynyaev, stating: 'My clothes, behaviour and sermons are all a mask' (iv, p. 151). She talks of how she wears such clothes solely because she has no fashionable ones: '... Plain, black clothes are at least original and attract attention to you. Smiling and casting eyes at people are much more effective in such dresses ...', but notes that she 'will go mad' if she has to go on wearing them much longer (iv, p. 152). When Kupavina asks why Murzavetskaya does not find a husband for her, Glafira immediately puts her finger on the motivations behind Murzavetskaya's behaviour, noting that Murzavetskaya would only permit a marriage where she herself could gain control of the husband's wealth: 'She and I see through one another, and she knows well that if I succeed in marrying then she won't see me again' (iv, p. 153). She goes on to express her thanks to Murzavetskaya: 'she taught me cunning, how not to waste a single word, how to have no shame in striving for what you want. She taught me that a sanctimonious hypocrite can get away with treating people unceremoniously, even rudely, by passing it off as frankness and simplicity ...' (iv, p. 153).

Glafira's capture of Lynyaev is a delightful exercise in deception. First she lulls him into a false sense of security with her pious ways and declarations of desire to enter a convent; then she suggests it would be an amusing pastime to pretend to be in love with one another; and finally, she declares that their pretended love has become real for her—a poor, innocent, naive girl, destined for the convent—and 'in despair' she clings to his neck until they are caught in this compromising position and he is forced to agree to marry her.

Their conversations are full of irony as Glafira, lulling Lynyaev into a false sense of security, talks of all the tricks she would employ if she were trying to capture a husband—yet all the discussion of her 'hypothetical ploys' is itself part of an actual plan to ensnare Lynyaev into marriage. This is, of course, compounded by Ostrovsky's use of dramatic irony since the audience knows full well what Glafira is doing; only the unfortunate Lynyaev is left in the dark.

Other characters in the play practise deception on a more minor scale. Chugunov, for example, who aids Murzavetskaya in her deceptions by providing her with false documents and trumped-up legal charges, is doing very well out of 'managing' Kupavina's estate—as Pavlin notes in Act One, Scene 2: 'You're obviously not doing too badly out of it: you've had a house built, you've acquired some horses, and you've got money too, so they say ...' (iv, p. 117). Yet in comparison with Murzavetskaya, he is a minor player, and does not seem particularly practised or comfortable in his deception. When, for example, in Act Two, Scene 1, Kupavina naively gives him a blank bill of exchange, he seems almost afraid to take it, and even then uses it to claim only a small amount of money. Likewise, Goretsky, Chugunov's nephew and the man who forges documents for him, is another minor player. He is merely concerned with making money to go drinking at the fair with, and is prepared to sell out his uncle for very small sums of money.

In a typical twist, the deceiver is deceived, when Berkutov, the most accomplished 'wolf' in the play, appears out of the blue in Act Four. He ends the play having seized all of Murzavetskaya's spoils—gaining Kupavina and her estate; and, perhaps most importantly of all, gaining control over Murzavetskaya, Chugunov and Goretsky themselves. He achieves this, not (as might be expected) by publicly exposing their schemes, but by turning their deceptions to his own advantage, while allowing them to maintain their façade of respectability.[10] Thus, when he first appears in the play in Act Four,

---

[10] Ostrovsky hints at Berkutov's eventual success in his name, which, as M.Hoover notes, has the literal Russian meaning of 'a golden eagle'. She states that this is a bird capable of killing a wolf and suggests that he 'drives off the wolf Murzavetskaya in order to seize her prey' (see Hoover, p. 98). Ostrovsky made much use of the Gogolian practice of giving his characters significant names, key examples of which will be noted throughout this study. (The significance of Kseniya and Vitalii in *Not of this World* and Platonovna in *A Hangover from Someone Else's Feast* has already been

he tells Lynayaev that he does not believe that Murzavetskaya's letters are forgeries, stating that Goretsky purposely slandered himself for money, and noting: 'In my opinion, in your society Murzavetskaya should stand above suspicion. A society where everyone regards everybody else as a criminal can hardly be a good one' (iv, p. 176). He goes on to surprise Kupavina by berating her for not settling Murzavetskaya's [false] claims against her earlier, and suggesting that her only option is to marry Apollon.

In Act Five, when Berkutov goes to visit Murzavetskaya, he flatters her and asks for her assistance in getting elected as Chairman of the Rural Council, before casually mentioning the forged documents, suggesting that she herself must have been deceived by Chugunov and Apollon: 'You have such a loving heart, you probably don't even suspect their villainy.' ... 'They have forged promissory notes from the late Kupavin; it was done yesterday ... I suspect your nephew, of course, for I can't suspect you' (iv, pp. 194/5). Thus, he allows Murzavetskaya to save face, while holding her completely in his power. He repeats the process with Chugunov and Goretsky.

The play ends with Murzavetskaya publicly appearing to remain in control: Berkutov declares to the assembled company: 'I have only been here a short while, but I have already been able to realise the full value of this rare woman. I hope that the local people always treat Meropia Davydovna with the deepest respect. We should set an example to others of how one should respect and revere old age' (iv, p. 205); and he 'allows' her to 'order' him to marry Kupavina. Yet behind the scenes the balance of power has shifted completely. Ostrovsky's refusal to give the play a traditional dénouement of deception exposed and the triumph of virtue reinforces even more strongly the falsity on which his characters' lives are based.

Role or Reality?: *The Forest*

One of Ostrovsky's acknowledged masterpieces, *The Forest*, is another play which centres on a wealthy landowner playing the role

---

discussed.) Further details of the use of names in Ostrovsky's plays can be found in V.A.Filippov, 'Yazyk personazhei Ostrovskogo', in *A.N.Ostrovskii—dramaturg*, ed. V.A.Filippov (Moscow: Sovetskii pisatel´, 1946), 122-31 and E.G.Kholodov, 'Chelovek i ego imya', in *Masterstvo Ostrovskogo* by E.G.Kholodov (Moscow: Iskusstvo, 1967), 196-205.

of a religious benefactress. Once again the central role-player, Gurmyzhskaya, spouts religious and moral platitudes, while masking her true character. Thus she claims not to be interested in money: '... Gentlemen, do I live for myself? All that I have, all my money, belongs to the poor ... I am merely the cashier of my money, its owner is every poor man, every unfortunate' (iii, p. 255); yet does all that she can to avoid paying her debts, and later openly states: 'You wouldn't believe, my dear, how I hate to part with money' (iii, p. 299). Similarly, she brings a young man, Bulanov, to her estate because she is herself attracted to him, yet she claims that he is there as a suitor for her niece, Aksinya, and continually emphasises this to neighbours and friends: 'So, now, gentlemen, I am at peace. You know my intentions. Although I'm above suspicion, should you find evil tongues wagging, you can explain how things are' (iii, p. 56) '... She already has a suitor, he lives here with me. Perhaps in the town they are saying some kind of nonsense, but you understand, he is her suitor' (iii, p. 262).

Similarly, she talks in public with great affection of her only surviving relative—her nephew—and states that she wishes to draw up a will to leave him well provided for when she dies (iii, p. 257). Yet as Aksinya has noted earlier, she is busy selling the estate because: 'She doesn't want there to be anything left for her heirs. Money can be given away to strangers' (iii, p. 241). Gurmyzhskaya has treated her nephew harshly, but yet again, excuses her behaviour with a moral justification:

> ... I brought him up to join the army. When his father died, he was left a young boy of fifteen, with hardly any fortune. Although I was young myself, I had strict ideas about life and I raised him according to my own method. I prefer a simple, stern education, a 'copper penny' training as it's called; not because of stinginess, no, but on principle. I'm sure that simple, uneducated people live the happiest lives ... I, Gentlemen, am not against education, but I'm not for it either. Corrupted morals are caused by the two extremes: ignorance and over-education; good morals come from in between the two ... I wanted this boy to experience for himself the harsh school of life; I prepared him for a position as a junker and left him to his own resources ... I sometimes sent him money, but I must confess, little, very little. (pp. 257/8)

In this play, however, the emphasis is on the role-playing itself. Gurmyzhskaya's long-lost nephew is in fact a provincial actor named Neschastlivtsev. He and a fellow actor, Schastlivtsev, visit Gurmyzhskaya's estate, adopting the role of a colonel and his manservant. In the course of their visit, the two 'actors' quickly reveal the falsity of the 'real' characters on the estate. The 'real' people are role-playing far more than the 'actors', and for far less noble reasons. (V.Lakshin notes that the actions of Neschastlivtsev and Schastlivtsev reduce the whole way of life of the landowners into a 'rudely playing farce'[11], and states that 'in front of us is a "comedy within a comedy", where the "noble" heroes are clowns, and the actors are the heroes.'[12]) In his famous speech at the end of the play, Neschastlivtsev reverses the role of the 'actors' and the 'real characters':

> Comedians? No, we are artists, noble artists—you are the comedians. If we love, then we love truly, if we don't love, then we quarrel or fight; if we help, then it is with our last hard-earned penny. And you? All your life you chatter about public welfare, about love of mankind. And what have you done? Whom have you fed? Whom have you comforted? You comfort only yourselves, you amuse only yourselves. You are the comedians and the clowns and not we. (iii, p. 337)

L.Cox, discussing *The Forest*, notes that 'the paradox underlying the play is that those who play roles in real life, that is behave as hypocrites, would not be able to act in the theatre. The reason for this is that the prerequisite for being an actor is the capacity to feel deeply.'[13] She notes that Gurmyzhskaya adopts her mask for reasons of self-interest, whereas Neschastlivtsev adopts his role in order to protect his aunt's feelings: he knows that actors are looked down upon in society, and does not wish to embarrass her. This is echoed by I.Zohrab, who notes that Gurmyzhskaya 'plays a role to conceal her meanness, her lack of real feeling for her dependents and fellow human beings ... Neschastlivtsev plays a role because he cares about the feelings of others and has the capacity to feel deeply ... He goes through life as if he were playing his tragic parts, helping the

---

[11] V.Ya. Lakshin, 'Tri p'esy A.N.Ostrovskogo', in *Groza, Les, Bespridannitsa A.N.Ostrovskogo* (Moscow: Khudozhestvennaya literatura, 1964), 5-19 (p. 13).
[12] Lakshin, *PSS* iii, 488.
[13] Cox, 170.

humiliated and injured and exposing pretence and greed.'[14] (However, the play also includes some hints that Neschastlivtsev is motivated by shame at his poverty—as indicated when he refuses to take the money his aunt owes him.) Certainly it is significant that it is Aksyusha, the one truly positive member of Gurmyzhskaya's household, who is deemed worthy of joining a theatrical troupe. Yet similarly, it is interesting to note that Petya, her lover and another largely positive character, also sees fit to fall back on play-acting. When he suggests to Aksyusha that they should run away together and Aksyusha asks what they should do if they happen to meet any acquaintances, Petya immediately suggests adopting a role: 'Then you promptly close one of your eyes, and you've become one-eyed; they won't recognise you' (iii, p. 271). He tells of how he escaped recognition on another occasion:

> ... I'll tell you of something that really happened. Dad sent me to Nizhny on business and told me to waste no time. But in Nizhny I found some friends who persuaded me to ride to Lyskovo. What could I do? If they found out at home, there'd be trouble. So, I put on someone else's coat, tied something around my face and went. On the steamer, straightaway, I met an acquaintance of dad's. I don't hide from him, you know, I walk past him boldly, while he watches. Then I see that he's coming over. 'Where are you from?' he says. 'Myshkino, ' I say, '—though I've never been there in my life.' 'You look familiar somehow, ' he says. 'That's not unusual, ' I say; and then, you know, I just walk on. He comes up to me in the same way a second time, then a third. Finally I got angry. 'Your face looks familiar to me too, ' I say. 'Weren't we in prison together in Kazan?' ... he couldn't get away quick enough ... (iii, p. 271)

He is a further example of a 'real' person acting a part.

The paradox is deepened further by the fact that, despite the sincerity of his motives, it is Neschastlivtsev who appears theatrical. He makes bold dramatic gestures and continually quotes lines from dramatic works, most frequently from those of Shakespeare and

---

[14] Irene Zohrab, 'Problems of Translation', 58-9.

Schiller. In contrast, the hypocritical landowners do not immediately appear to be play-acting.[15]

Interestingly, *The Forest*, a play which compares 'real life' with 'art', is one of the most artfully constructed of Ostrovsky's plays. M.Hoover notes that it contains 'perhaps the most artful of Ostrovsky's endings; not only does the actors' plotline come full circle when they leave on foot as they came, but the lives of the other two couples are enshrined as money passes from hand to hand until it too ends up where it started.'[16]

A similar example of role reversal—where supposedly 'real' characters out-act professional actors—occurs in *Talents and Admirers*. Here the 'real' character, the mysterious Velikatov, enters the world of the actors and skilfully charms them, seeming to know just the right thing to say to each character. None of the other characters appear to know much about him, and their debates about what kind of man he is are always left unresolved. Even at the end of the play his true character remains a mystery. You are left with the impression that he is giving a far better performance in the real world than the actors in the play give on stage.[17]

The Master Role-Player: *Even Wise Men Err*

The most accomplished role-player of all, however, is to be found in *Even Wise Men Err* (1868). The entire play is a damning indictment of the hypocrisy endemic in Moscow high society, as the social-climbing Glumov attempts to deceive his way to a position of

---

[15] Irene Zohrab has also noted this paradox. See 'Problems of Translation', 59.

[16] Hoover, 90. V.Lakshin also emphasises the circular passage of money in the play. See *PSS* iii, 487.

[17] The enigmatic nature of Velikatov has led to conflicting interpretations of his character. I.Beasley, for example, sees him as a positive character, and discusses him in glowing terms: 'Although he loves Sasha, his feeling for her is something greater than the mere desire of possession. He wants to give her every chance for a full and beautiful life, where her talent can develop unhindered by the cares of poverty and the petty squabbling of a provincial theatre.' (See Beasley, unpublished doctoral dissertation, 355.) Others have been less generous: Nemirovich-Danchenko wrote in *Russkii kur′er* on 23 December 1881 that he is 'Glumov with money, a Glumov of the merchant class' [see *PSS* v, p. 522], whilst Revyakin notes: 'Velikatov is insincere, false, from beginning to end' [see A.I.Revyakin, *Istoriya literatury XIX veka*, II, (Moscow, 1963), 336].

wealth and high standing. Role-play is central to Glumov's deception. He discovers people's weaknesses and then adopts a role accordingly—each calculated to ingratiate him with the person concerned. Thus with Mamaev, 'The Newest Instruction Manual' (iii, p. 11), he plays the role of a fool in need of advice; with Manefa, he plays the role of a pious benefactor; with Mamaeva, that of a diffident lover; with Gorodulin, that of a free thinker and irreverent social commentator; with Krutitsky, that of an admiring reactionary; and with Turusina that of a pious and superstitious man.

Glumov is aided in his schemes by his mother, Glumova, who is also an accomplished role-player. She plays the part of a foolish but grateful hanger-on with Mamaev and Mamaeva, 'innocently' flattering them, and praising her son, painting a picture of him as an innocent, naive little angel, dazzled by Mamaev's brilliance and Mamaeva's beauty.

The net effect of Glumov's deceits is to expose the role-playing and hypocrisy prevalent throughout society. The 'victims' of Glumov's deception are eager to accept his acts and flattery, however improbable they may seem, as they are all engaged in similar behaviour themselves. Thus we see the pious and superstitious Turusina who acts the role of a generous benefactress, despite, or perhaps because of, the references to her somewhat less than moral past; Krutitsky, who is prepared to accept Glumov's fulsome flattery, and who, together with Gorodulin, is prepared to claim authorship and credit for works he did not write; Mamaev, who goes so far as to instruct his nephew to pay court to his wife in order to ward off other potential admirers; Mamaeva, who is prepared to accept the improbable love of a young nephew; and Manefa, 'a half-drunk peasant woman' (iii, p. 78), who passes herself off as a psychic. And all the while, the above characters are feigning friendship with one another, while readily making disparaging remarks about one another behind each other's backs: Krutitsky refers to Turusina as a 'sanctimonious hypocrite' (iii, p. 56), Mamaev refers to Krutitsky as 'not much of an intellectual' (iii, p. 33), and Krutitsky states of Mamaev: 'He says he's clever, but he's an absolute blockhead' (iii, p. 54). As Glumov states in the final scene of the play: 'What was it that offended you about my diary? Did you discover anything new about yourselves? You say the same things about each other all the time, only not to their faces. If I'd read out to each one of you privately what was written about the others, you'd have applauded me' (iii, p. 79).

Examples of hypocrisy in the play are almost too many to mention without quoting the entire play. They make for a number of delightfully comic passages, and Ostrovsky exploits to the full the device of dramatic irony. Perhaps there is no better example than in Act Two, Scene 7, when Mamaev, who has previously berated Glumov for teaching his mother to be a hypocrite (iii, p. 18), advises him to flatter Krutitsky. Glumov, who is doing exactly that, responds with mock innocence: 'Uncle! What sort of lessons are you teaching me?' to which Mamaev responds: 'Flattery is a bad thing; but to do it a little every now and then is permissible' (iii, p. 33). Mamaev then goes on to suggest to Glumov that he pay court to his wife, again unaware that Glumov is already doing precisely that. Glumov's mock innocence makes for great comedy:

> **Mamaev.** ... What sort of relationship have you established with your aunt?
>
> **Glumov.** I've been well brought up, you don't have to teach me respect.
>
> **Mamaev.** Now, now, don't be silly. She's still quite young, and pretty, it's not your respect she needs! Do you want to make her your enemy?
>
> **Glumov.** I don't understand, uncle.
>
> **Mamaev.** If you don't understand, then listen, and learn! And thank God that you've got someone to teach you. Women won't forgive a man who doesn't notice their beauty.
>
> **Glumov.** Yes, yes! You're right! That had gone clean out of my mind!
>
> **Mamaev.** Indeed, young fellow! Well, although there's only a distant connection, you're a relative none the less, so you have more freedom then a mere acquaintance. You can, occasionally, as if out of absent-mindedness, give her unnecessary kisses on the hand; make eyes at her. You can do that, I take it?
>
> **Glumov.** Make eyes?
>
> **Mamaev.** Oh, what are you like, sir! Look, like this. (He rolls his eyes upwards.)

Glumov. Oh surely not! What are you doing! I can't possibly do that.

Mamaev. You'll soon learn if you practise in front of a mirror. Yes, and you should sigh now and then, with a kind of languid expression. These sorts of things all tickle their egos.

Glumov. I am most humbly grateful to you. (iii, pp. 33/4)

Another fine comic passage occurs in Act Three, when the superstitious Turusina talks of being unable to trust humans, as only the 'oracle' tells the truth. She is unaware that the 'oracle' (Manefa) and her superstitious hangers-on have been bribed by Glumov. She compounds her mistake in Act Five when she declares: 'It's our custom these days to believe in absolutely nothing, it's quite the fashion. All I hear is 'Why do you allow that Manefa woman into your house? She's a fraud!' Well, I'd love to invite all those unbelievers here today, just to see what kind of a fraud she is! I'm so pleased for her, she'll be all the rage now, and have a large clientele. Moscow should be grateful to me for finding such a woman, I've done the town a great service' (iii, p. 74). Of course, just moments later, to Turusina's dismay, Manefa is indeed revealed as a fraud.

As elsewhere in Ostrovsky's works, there is constant emphasis on the ubiquitous nature of deception and role-playing. At one point in Act Two, Scene 7, Glumov, playing the role of a free thinker, delights Gorodulin by talking about the role-playing required to be a civil servant: 'Don't think, unless you're ordered to. Laugh, whenever your boss fancies he's cracked a joke. Do all the thinking and work for your boss, while at the same time convincing him with all the humility you can manage that it's all his—oh, me, you say, I'm stupid, it was all done as you yourself were pleased to command...' (iii, p. 31). In Act Three, Scene 2, Krutitsky warns Turusina of how easy it is to deceive do-gooders, giving an example of an acquaintance of his who took in two 'pilgrims' from the street, only to discover that they were infamous forgers; and in the following scene, Gorodulin warns her against trusting in so-called 'fortune-tellers', telling her of a fortune-teller who was exiled to Siberia for poisoning someone with a 'love-potion'. Turusina responds by declaring: 'I would never have expected it! It's easy to make a mistake. You simply can't live in this world (iii, p. 45).

It is, of course, the final indictment that, even after the exposure of Glumov's schemes, the play ends with the other characters discussing his reinstatement into society:

Krutitsky. Well, whatever you say, gentlemen—he has a good head on him, all the same. He must be taught a lesson; but in a little while, I think we might bring him back into the fold again.
Gorodulin. Oh, no doubt about it.
Mamaev. I agree.
Mamaeva. I will take it upon myself to achieve it. (iii, p. 79)

Deception is a crucial element of Ostrovsky's plays. His dramas overflow with examples of cheating, hypocrisy, pretence and role-playing—only a fraction of which have been outlined above. As this study progresses, it aims to demonstrate that this theme, together with an interest in the relationship between realism and idealism, and a number of other, closely-related motifs, forms a crucial element of an even larger preoccupation apparent in Ostrovsky's work: the nature of reality itself.

CHAPTER TWO

The Superficiality of Appearance

> 'We are poor physiognomists.' *A Last Sacrifice* (iv, p. 373)

C losely related to the deception and hypocrisy prevalent in Ostrovsky's plays, and central to its success, is another little-noted element of his work: the superficial nature of appearance. Deception is, of course, all about 'seeming'—things not being as they first appear—and the acceptance of a veneer of respectability advocated by characters such as Stepanida in *A Family Picture* or the 'pious hypocrites' of *The Ward* or *Wolves and Sheep* demonstrates the centrality of the 'superficial' to the characters in Ostrovsky's plays. When the Gossip in *A Last Sacrifice* claims: 'you can recognise the dubious people straight away', the significantly named Observer replies: 'No, you cannot. We are poor physiognomists. People read in the newspapers: "So-and-so was arrested for forging cheques; so-and-so disappeared and there proved to be two hundred thousand roubles missing in the treasury; so-and-so shot himself." And you will hear his friends say: "But I had supper with him only yesterday, and we played preference for penny stakes. And I went out of town with him and I didn't notice anything peculiar"' (iv, p. 373). It is such concern with outward appearance which allows Glumov's victims in *Even Wise Men Err* to be so easily taken in, not only because of his cleverness at deceit, but because they themselves are willing accomplices. They do not look beyond the image presented to them, the image they wish to see. As L.Cox notes, theirs is a world where 'shadow is appreciated more than substance, words more than action'.[1]

---

[1] Cox, 99.

In *Even Wise Men Err* the characters' concern with outward appearance is posted early in the play. In Act Two, Scene 2, for example, Mamaeva talks of how Glumov was always going to be a success in society because of his good looks: 'Believe me, people will always help out a handsome young man and give him the means to live well, simply out of compassion. If you see a clever man poorly dressed, living in some squalid apartment, going about in nasty cabs, it doesn't startle you, you don't find the sight offensive. In fact that's how it should be, poverty suits clever men, there are no obvious contradictions. But if you see a handsome young man poorly dressed—that's painful, it shouldn't happen ...' (iii, pp. 23/4). It is a theme that Ostrovsky repeats with almost obsessive regularity throughout his work (see Appendix E). In *The Heart is not Stone*, for example, Ol´ga and Apollinariya express their horror at Vera's use of headscarves:

> **Ol´ga.** And who goes out wearing headscarves these days! Even shopkeepers' wives have long since been wearing hats.
> **Apollinariya.** Nowadays merchants' wives behave like real ladies. They don't want to be inferior to any foreign women—in appearance. (v, pp. 85/6)

And later Apollinariya complains at church: 'There are very few people here, there's no-one to look at and no-one to show yourself off to. No-one here is going to notice how you're dressed.' She dismisses Vera's more pious response: 'It's all the same to me, I don't come for that' with the calm acceptance that: 'We are sinful people. We come to church to look at people and show ourselves off.' (v, p. 109).

In *A Lucrative Post*, Yusov emphasises the importance of neat penmanship over content (ii, p. 43) and Belogubov notes: 'I even deny myself food so I can be neatly dressed. When an official is neatly dressed, his superiors always take notice' (ii, p. 43). In *A Hangover from Someone Else's Feast*, Andrei talks about the difficulty in attracting women without the right looks and accomplishments: 'If you know French and have the right walk, then you can dare ... that means that whatever you see—the hawk in the sky, the pike in the sea—they are all yours' (ii, p. 16). And in *Truth is Fine, but Luck is Better*, there is an amusing scene in which Baraboshev and his mother demonstrate their determination to maintain appearances in the eyes of their neighbours:

Baraboshev. ... Old Pustoplesov next door is also on the look-out for a son-in-law.

Mavra. I know, dear.

Baraboshev. We need to take care that we are not discrediting ourselves in comparison with him. I asked him: 'Who do you have in view?' 'A factory-owner, ' he says. I think: 'That means we're level pegging, he hasn't got one up on us.' Only in time I hear from him quite a different tone. The other day we were sitting in the pub, drinking madeira, then some kind of Lafite, 'Chateau La Rose'—it's a new kind, it softens your mood and produces pleasant thoughts. Only we started talking again about having a factory-owner as a son-in-law. 'You give her away to a good business, ' he says, 'you need that sort, but I've changed my mind.' 'Why?' I ask. 'You will see, ' he says. And that very evening I meet him, sitting in a carriage. He bows so proudly and looks pointedly at his companion. I look—it's a colonel! With the best appearance and parading about in front of everyone ... How I remained standing I don't know. The wine I drank from grief! There wasn't any 'Chateau La Rose', but madeira makes you feel better all the same... You tell me, mama, is that an insult or not?

Mavra. Of course it's an insult! It's an insult just in itself!

Baraboshev. He bowed, and squinted at this colonel, just like this. 'Take that, Baraboshev, ' he says, 'you appreciate this!'

Mavra. He's stabbed us, dear, stabbed us!

Mukhoyarov. Now he thinks he's on a par with a colonel, and you're on a level with dirt.

Mavra. Until this happened it was impossible for him to rise above us ... You didn't ever let him get in front of us in anything.

Baraboshev. And we won't this time either. Loosen your purse strings, mama. We'll prepare a dirty trick.

Mavra. And what trick is that?

Baraboshev. Mr Colonel is coming to see them at seven o'clock, and they'll all be there, watching at the window with their eyes skinned, half an hour in advance! ... so ... at quarter to seven, who will approach our porch, but—a general! We'll give them something to look at!' (iv, pp. 271/3)

Concern With Appearance: *Poverty is No Vice*

A concern with outward appearance is, almost without exception, shown to have negative consequences. In *Poverty is No Vice*, for example, concern with appearance is the overriding theme of the play, which contrasts the superficiality and hypocrisy of Gordei Tortsov and Afrikan Savich with the honesty and kindheartedness of Mitya, Pelageya, Lyubov and Lyubim. Here, Gordei Tortsov is the character most concerned with appearances. His ambition and desire to keep up with the fashions lead to cruelty towards his family and employees, and even to a willingness to sacrifice his daughter in marriage to the debauched, elderly Afrikan. When we first hear of Gordei (whose name, significantly, means 'pride') in Act One, Scene 1, we learn from Egorushka that he is in a rage, because his brother Lyubim has 'shamed him in front of the whole town', by joining the beggars at the cathedral door (i, p. 329). We next hear of him in Act One, Scene 3, when Pelageya describes how Gordei has become involved with Afrikan Savich, as he believes that 'no-one here is worth keeping company with, they are all scum, all peasants, and they live like peasants; but he [Afrikan] is a Muscovite ... and rich' (i, p. 331). She decribes how he has got caught up with the modern fashions—even trying to get her to wear a bonnet; and complains that he is refusing to think of finding a husband for Lyubov, again because no-one in the town is good enough.

Gordei eventually enters the action in Act One, Scene 7, and his concern with appearances to the exclusion of all else is immediately made apparent. He ridicules Mitya's poetry, describing it as 'nonsense'; he rubbishes Mitya's desire to educate himself and states that he would do better to buy a new coat, as he disgraces them all with his shoddy clothes: 'If you can't make yourself look decent, stay here in your kennel; if you've got nothing, then don't dream about yourself! He writes poems, wants to educate himself, yet he goes about looking like a factory worker! ... Fool! ... Don't you dare show yourself upstairs in that coat!' (i, p. 336). (Note the contrast here with Pelageya, who in Scene 3 came down to see Mitya specifically to invite him to join them that evening to 'play games with the girls, sing songs' (i, p. 330).)

In Act Two, Scene 6, Gordei enters the house with Afrikan while the others are having a party, and he again shows his concern with appearance and desire to appear up-to-date and fashionable in the eyes of others: 'Who are these scum! Clear out! (*to his wife*) Pelageya! Welcome our guest. (*Quietly*) ... you've done for me! ... I've told you so many times: if you want to have a party, hire musicians and do it in style' (i, pp. 356/7). He rubbishes Pelageya's madeira and orders champagne for Afrikan; and then in Scene 8 goes over to Mitya and exclaims: 'Why are you here? Is this your place? You've really got above yourself!' (i, p. 358).

The full extent of Gordei's concern with appearances is revealed in Act Two, Scene 10, when he announces his decision to marry Lyubov to Afrikan, despite her obvious horror and Pelageya's protests: 'Now look, woman, I've been telling you for ages how sick I am of living in this town, where at every step you see nothing but boorishness and ignorance. That's why I want us to leave here and settle in Moscow. But we won't be among strangers there, we will have our son-in-law, Afrikan Savich' (i, p. 360). He dismisses Lyubov's protests: 'You, you fool, don't understand how lucky you are. In Moscow you'll live like a lady, you'll ride about in carriages ... you'll live in full view, and not in these backwoods ...' (i, p. 361).

In Act Three, Scene 8, Gordei again boasts to Afrikan of how superior he is to the others in the town: 'No, you tell me this: isn't everything in order? In another place, you'd find a young man in a coat or a maid serving at table, but I have a butler in cotton gloves. He's trained, this butler, he's from Moscow, he knows all the right ways to do things: where to sit who, what to do. But at other houses! They're all gathered in one room, they sit in a circle and sing peasant songs. It's all very jolly, of course, but I consider it so low, there's no style to it ... Oh, if only I lived in Moscow or Petersburg, I would soon pick up all the fashions' (i, p. 371).

Gordei's aspirations to grandeur are crushed in Act Three, Scene 12, when Lyubim provokes Afrikan into saying what he really thinks of all Gordei's 'fine style': 'So this is the way things are done in your home! You've set a new fashion: where guests are insulted by drunkards! Heh, heh, heh! "I will go to Moscow, " he says, "they don't understand me here." In Moscow fools like that are laughed at. "Dear son-in-law, dear son-in-law!" Heh, heh, heh! Beloved father-in-law! No, you're mistaken if you think I'll let such insults go for nothing. No, you'll come and bow before me, beg me to take your daughter' (i, p. 374).

Gordei, insulted by Afrikan's words, comes to his senses and agrees to marry Lyubov to Mitya.

Concern With Appearance: *Late Love*

Late Love is another play which emphasises the destructive power of concern with appearance. Here, both the principal hero, Nikolai, and the principal villain, Lebedkina, fall victim to a concern with appearance. For Nikolai, it leads to ruin and a life of debauchery and debt, whereas Lebedkina's obsession with appearances leads her to cheat and deceive.

Again, the importance attached to appearance is demonstrated right from the start of the play, as Shablova talks about the confidence a fine appearance gives people: 'A poor person with character, for heaven's sake! That really would be a miracle! It's because he hasn't any decent clothes, that's all. If a person doesn't have decent clothes, then he acts shy, rather than hold fine conversation ... Take us women, for example, why is it that a high-class lady is so confident about talking in company? It's because her clothes are all in order, one fits with the other ... the colours match, the patterns fit. It strengthens her spirit ...' (iv, p. 10)

Shablova goes on to discuss Lebedkina, describing her as 'a lightweight, spoilt woman, who relies on her beauty. She's always surrounded by young men and she's accustomed to everyone obliging her. She even considers people lucky to serve her' (iv, p. 10); and noting: 'Oh, she's a great lady in appearance, but if you look a bit closer she's quite simple-minded. Caught up in debts and love-affairs, she even sends for me to tell her fortune from the cards. I spin her some nonsense or other and she cries and laughs like a little baby' (iv, p. 11). We learn that Nikolai is in love with Lebedkina, and that despite his poverty, he spends all his (and thus, all his family's) money on courting her:

Nikolai is a proud man, he doesn't want to look any worse than all
the others who play the dandy round at her place from morning till
night, so he's ordered himself a good outfit from an expensive
German tailor, on credit (iv, p. 10) ... it's a crying shame for a poor
man to chase after a rich lady, and even more so to be wasting his
money on it. How's he meant to keep up? Over at her place you
get such colonels and guardsmen and the like, that you can't find
the words to describe them. You look at them and the only thing
you can say is 'Ah, my God!' Why, judge for yourself, one of these
colonels drives up to the porch behind a pair of horses with traces,
lets his spurs or sabre fall in the entrance hall, one passing glance
over his shoulder at the mirror, a shake of his head and then
straight to her in the drawing room. And, you know, she is only a
woman, a weak creature, a fragile vessel, just one sudden look up
into his eyes and it's all boiling passion. (iv, p. 11)

In Act Three Nikolai himself describes how he has been destroyed by
his attempts to maintain appearances:

... I imagined that I was the best lawyer in Moscow, I lived very
extravagantly. After life as a poor student, suddenly I had two or
three thousand in my pocket; well, I lost my head. Dinners and
drinking bouts, I became lazy, and there was no serious work, and
at the end of the year, it turned out that I had no money, and my
debts, although not large, were not small. And that is when I did
what was so unforgivably stupid, what is now destroying me ... I
thought that I should not give up this lifestyle, that I should not
lose my acquaintances. I borrowed a huge sum of money at great
interest, paid off my trifling debts, and began to live as
extravagantly as before, in expectation of future fortune ... I
thought that I would get a big case ... but I didn't. I spent the
money, and the debts weigh like a noose round my neck ... (iv,
p. 42)

When Lebedkina enters the action, we learn that she too is consumed
by a need to maintain appearance. When Shablova tells her that she is
going to have to pay off one of her debts, Lebedkina declares: 'But I
don't want to pay. The winter season is near and you know my
expenses: opera, balls—the news from abroad will be coming in
soon, and one of my gloves is torn ... all decent people borrow for the
winter, and you tell me to pay ... I need the money for myself... look

at this hat ... is there anything special about it?' (iv, pp. 31/2). Lebedkina, however, is prepared to deceive in order to maintain appearances. She has forged her dead husband's signature on a promissory note, yet has no intention of paying the debt. Instead she persuades Nikolai to exploit Lyudmila's love for him and ask Lyudmila to steal the promissory note from her lawyer father. She states that this is a test of his love for her; and promises to give him money in return, thus offering a way out of his own debt. When Lyudmila does procure the note for Nikolai, and he in turn gives it to Lebedkina, the extent of her capacity for deception is revealed. Rather than giving him the promised money, she callously burns the note. Ironically, however, her concern with outward appearance is her downfall. We learn that Nikolai only gave her a copy of the promissory note. He produces the real one and Lebedkina is forced to pay her debt. The message of the play is summed up neatly with Nikolai's words: 'You should have looked more carefully' (iv, p. 57). (It is indicative of the widespread failure to understand the full complexity of Ostrovsky's drama that this—one of the most telling statements in the play—is omitted from the only English-language translation of the work.[2] Ostrovsky himself clearly felt that this was one of the most important points in the play. When F.Burdin complained that this was the play's 'biggest mistake' as 'it is obvious that Nikolai is deceiving Lebedkina'[3], Ostrovsky felt concerned enough to respond that 'in my opinion, this is in no way obvious', noting that 'if an actor plays this scene with a sarcastic tone and a mocking smile, then it is he who is making the mistake, and not I.'[4])

It is of further interest to note that in this, a play which warns about the dangers of superficial appearances, part of Lebedkina's deception involves disguise. When she comes to procure the promissory note from Nikolai, she enters, dressed in plain clothes, her head covered with a scarf:

Shablova. Varvara Kharitonovna! I didn't recognise you. Why are you sneaking about so?

---

[2] See *The King of Comedy*, tr. and ed. by J.McPetrie (London: Stockwell, 1937).
[3] A.N.Ostrovskii and F.A.Burdin, *Neizdannye pis'ma*, ed. N.L.Brodskii (Moscow-Petrograd: Gosizdat. , 1923), 180.
[4] See *PSS* iv, 496.

> **Lebedkina.** I am in a hired carriage. It isn't wise to come to this part of town in my own. People are so inquisitive: who is coming, to see whom, and why ... I didn't want anyone to know that I have been here today.' (iv, p. 47)

And when she leaves she reminds them:

> **Lebedkina.** Remember, Felitsata Antonovna, I haven't been here today, you haven't seen me ... I left my carriage close by, near the zoo. I'll have a stroll, and in ten minutes or so I'll return ...
> ...
> **Nikolai.** How crafty and cunning it all is! (iv, p. 50)

The superficial nature of appearances, with the suggestion of false appearances, of 'seeming', of things not being as they first appear, is another significant feature of Ostrovsky's plays and another important element in his concern with the nature of reality.

CHAPTER THREE

Blindness to Reality

> 'Just don't be blind,
> don't be blind!' *We All*
> *Have our Cross to Bear*
> (ii, p. 414)

C losely related to Ostrovsky's exploration of the superficial nature of appearances is another dominant theme of his drama, and one which, yet again, has largely been neglected in critical examination of his work: blindness to reality. Indeed, one of Ostrovsky's central criticisms of his characters' obsession with superficial appearance seems to be that it causes them to be blind to the true nature of the characters and events which surround them.

Blindness to Reality: *A Young Man's Morning*

A close reading of Ostrovsky's drama throws up numerous examples of plays where a concern with outward appearance leads to blindness to reality. In one of his very early sketches, *A Young Man's Morning*, for example, a concern with appearances is the primary theme of the play, which depicts a morning in the life of Nedopekin, a young man obsessed with appearances and keeping up with the fashions. Nedopekin's concern with appearances is emphasised immediately. The play opens with the arrival of Nedopekin's aunt's clerk, Sidorych, who has come to invite Nedopekin to his aunt's house the following evening. Ivan, Nedopekin's manservant, insists that Nedopekin will not attend:

Your lot are just rusaks[1], you know. On weekdays you eat all day
from the same plate, and at eight o'clock you go to bed. It's only
on a nameday or a holiday that you loosen the purse strings a bit.
But us, you see how we live? Look! (*He gestures around him.*) See
what it's like! See what it's like, my friend! Yes, and we haven't
even touched on the company. What sort of company do they get at
your place? No-one with any kind of education or politics. Yours is
no place for us, my friend. Why do you think he respects me so
much? Because I know the right way to do things. I, my friend,
have served with all the best people. I served at General
Simevich's for two years, and I've served at a councillor's. So I
should know. He always asks me: 'Tell me, Ivan, how was it done
at the General's?' 'Well, ' I say, 'like this and like that.' (i, p. 154)

Ivan goes on to talk about how obsessed with fashion Nedopekin is:

I've never seen a man who imitates the fashions so much. At the
moment he gets up at two o'clock; but if you told him that these
days the gentlemen are getting up when the cock crows, well, then
he too would start getting up at daybreak.
    And how he watches the fashions, it's simply hilarious to watch
him. He'll be out on a walk, or at the theatre, and he'll see someone dressed a certain way, or walking a certain way, and he'll
change immediately; he comes right here and practises in front of
the mirror. (i, p. 155)

As the play progresses it becomes increasingly obvious that
Nedopekin's concern with appearances has left him blind to the true
nature of the people around him. Scene after scene demonstrates the
ease with which his friends and servants are taking advantage of him,
eagerly exploiting his determination to keep up with the fashions and
inability to see beyond the superficial. (V.Lakshin talks of him
allowing his friends to put 'dust in his eyes'.[2]) Even in the first scene,
when Ivan boasts to Sidorych about their standard of living and offers
him endless books, cigarettes and cigars, it becomes apparent that
Ivan himself does little but help himself to his master's cigars and sit
and read all day; as the houseboy, Grisha, complains: 'And what has

---

[1] 'Rusak' is a colloquial word meaning 'a plain and simple Russian man'. It is intended
here to be derogatory.
[2] Lakshin, 'Ostrovskii (1843-1854)', 474.

he done? He's been reading *The Northern Bee* all morning!' (i, p. 156).

When Lisavsky enters in Scene 2, the pattern established by Ivan is repeated, as Lisavsky throws himself into an armchair and examines the books. He asks where the copy of *Readers' Library* is, and Ivan responds that Lisavsky has probably taken it himself and not returned it. Lisavsky is then described as 'taking a cigar and putting two more into his pocket' (i, p. 156). After reading for a short while, Lisavsky notices that the sleeve of his tailcoat has worn through, and he immediately responds by noting: 'I think Senechka [Nedopekin] has a spare one ...' and asking Ivan to bundle up Nedopekin's green tailcoat for him. Ivan, however, refuses, stating that a winter coat Lisavsky once borrowed came back entirely worn out: 'You take this and that from the master, but I still haven't seen as much as a ten-kopeck piece from you ... You just shout: give me this, give me that. I've lived with the best people, you know, and I never saw those sort of manners' (i, p. 157).

Scene 3 sees the arrival of two young men who stand on the doorstep, one arguing that he cannot take advantage of the hospitality of a stranger, the other saying: 'These days you've got to look at it from a philosophical point of view: he feeds you well, the wine's good—what more do you need? There's no need for good breeding and manners ...' and later noting: 'You can borrow money from him' (i, p. 158). The Second Young Man protests: 'Think about the sort of roles we'll be playing', while the First Young Man declares: 'No roles of any sort! We'll just eat and drink and that's that' (i, pp. 158/9). The First Young Man eventually suggests that the Second go to Le Chevalier, a nearby restaurant, and wait for him to bring Nedopekin there; the two of them will then get acquainted and Nedopekin will treat them to dinner. At this, the Second Young Man loses his qualms completely: 'Well, that's a different matter altogether, that won't be at all awkward' (i, p. 159), and he leaves for the restaurant. Scene 4 sees the entrance of Nedopekin himself, and his involvement in the action demonstrates even more clearly the extent to which his concern with appearance has left him blind to reality. The scene shows Nedopekin talking to the First Young Man about how he reads long into the evening, how he subscribes to all the latest journals, writes poetry and wishes to learn how to sing. The

First Young Man expresses his surprise that Nedopekin reads Russian translations of all the French novels, remarking that surely it would be better to read them in the original—with which Nedopekin immediately agrees. He then skilfully goes on to suggest that he could introduce Nedopekin to a certain 'man of letters'—'the most clever chap'—and that if Nedopekin went to dinner at Le Chevalier that evening, he would introduce them. Nedopekin replies that he will attend without fail, thus ensuring the Two Young Men their free dinner (i, p. 160).

Scene 5 illustrates yet more emphatically Nedopekin's desire to keep up with the trends, and the clever exploitation of this by his acquaintances. The scene opens with Nedopekin (having quickly picked up on the new fashion described by the First Young Man) asking Lisavsky how quickly he can teach him French. When Lisavsky asks why, Nedopekin replies: 'What do you mean, why? So as to read French books, of course. You don't read in Russian! Ha, ha, ha! Who reads Russian! No, my friend, you can't deceive us.' (i, p. 160). Lisavsky then sets about tricking Nedopekin out of his green tailcoat. Perhaps inevitably, he begins by praising Nedopekin's appearance: 'Listen, Senechka! You're a good-looking man, you know. My God, you're good-looking. You don't know your own worth. Look at yourself. You are the ideal man! Apollo! An absolute Apollo!' (i, p. 160). (Nedopekin responds to this praise by going to stand in front of the mirror and smiling.) He then, however, goes on to note: 'Only Senya, don't be angry! But you've got no dress sense, ' pointing out: 'That green tailcoat you wear, it's simply disgusting!' (i, p. 161). Nedopekin, of course, immediately denies ever wearing the green coat, protesting that he could order a hundred new tailcoats if he wanted and thus has no need of the green one. Hearing this, Lisavsky again orders Ivan to parcel the coat up for him—this time successfully. Not content with stopping there, Lisavsky goes on to ask Nedopekin if he has had breakfast yet. Nedopekin replies that he doesn't want any, to which Lisavetsky expresses horror, noting that all decent people have breakfast at one o'clock. Of course, Nedopekin, keen to keep up with the fashions, immediately orders breakfast. Finally, Lisavsky asks Nedopekin if he will be going to the theatre today and when Nedopekin replies 'of course' and asks Lisavsky to get him a ticket, Lisavsky asks Nedopekin for the money for two tickets, noting that he should, naturally, accompany Nedopekin (i, p. 164).

The Scene ends with Nedopekin preparing to go out. He is described as putting on his coat and hat, then taking a stick, and 'walking up and down in front of the mirror' (i, p. 164)—again emphasising his concern with appearances.

In Scene 6, the full nature of Nedopekin's folly is revealed. In his absence, his uncle and second cousin come to visit (the 'rusaks' of Scene 1), and through them we learn that Nedopekin is heavily in debt and lives on credit secured by his mother's fortune. His uncle, Smurov, is disgusted by the way Nedopekin lives, criticising the apartment: 'How stupidly he's decorated this place! He's hung a pier-glass! (*Laughs*) Various books! ...' (i, p. 165) and the ridiculous clothes and pretensions of Grisha and Ivan. The play ends with Smurov stating that he is going to tell Nedopekin's mother to publish a notice in the newspapers that she will no longer pay any of Nedopekin's debts.

Blindness to Reality: *All Good Things Come to an End*

While not employing quite the same exaggerated satire of *A Young Man's Morning*, a much later play, *All Good Things Come to an End*, again demonstrates the link between a concern with appearance and blindness to reality. Here, it is the 'samodur' merchant, Akhov, who is, in a manner reminiscent of Gordei Tortsov in *Poverty is No Vice*, deeply concerned with appearances. Akhov is desperate to be afforded the respect and servility from others he thinks is due to him because of his wealth. In Act One, Scene 7, he berates Kruglova for receiving him while his nephew and assistant, Ippolit, was in the house: 'But just consider, will you, how could he and his master be in the same room? Supposing I'm talking away to you, and perhaps I want to joke around with you a bit. Is he supposed to listen in with his mouth wide open? In all his life he's never heard anything from me but orders and abuse. How's he meant to stay in awe of me after that? He'd say, 'Our master talks just as much nonsense as every one else does.' I don't want him to know that!' (iii, p. 350); and he goes on to tell her: 'It's absolutely essential for you to show me the greatest respect. I should receive extra-special respect compared with other people' (iii, p. 351). In Act Two, Scene 7, when courting Agniya, he tries to tempt her with a vision of the luxury she will live in as his wife: 'You, for example, are a poor girl, but all the same, you wish to live. Well, now, how can you do it like a lady? Maybe you'd like a cloak, or a hat of some kind, or to ride with fine horses in a fashionable carriage?' (iii, p. 366); and again in Act Three, Scene 2, when he sends Feona to Agniya with a present, he tells her: 'Tell them that they ought to appreciate it! Perhaps they won't appreciate it, so you should tell them that I bought it, wasted a lot of money on it, so that they know ... I do grudge the money if it's taken carelessly, without the right kind of appreciation. Perhaps they will value it in their hearts, but if they don't show it, then it's just the same as if they haven't appreciated it at all' (iii, p. 374).

A similar concern with appearance at the expense of reality is evident in his dealings with Ippolit. Throughout the play (in a manner reminiscent of the Puzatovs in *A Family Picture*), Akhov makes it clear that he considers cheating and deception perfectly acceptable so long as it remains undetected. In Act Three, Scene 3, he even berates Ippolit for not stealing from him: 'Don't you know the Russian proverb, 'Steal, but cover your tracks'? ...' (iii, p. 377); and later in the same scene, he is happy to sign a false reference 'just for the look of it':

Akhov. What's this paper? What's it for?
Ippolit. It's a reference.
Akhov. What do you mean, a reference?
Ippolit. It's like this: it says that I, living at your house as a clerk, learned the business in detail and conducted myself honestly and nobly—even beyond the call of duty!
Akhov. All that is written here?
Ippolit. It's all written there. And that I received a salary of two thousand a year.
Akhov. When was this?
Ippolit. It's just for the look of it. Then, if I go to another place ...
Akhov. Ah, it's to deceive people? Well, so what! That doesn't matter—it can be done!
Ippolit. And that at the end, in return for my working hard beyond the call of duty, I received a reward of fifteen thousand ...
Akhov. Also for the look of it?
Ippolit. No, this is for real.

Akhov. What do you mean, for real? I'd have thought five hundred roubles was more than enough?
Ippolit. No, all of it, the full amount.
Akhov. No, my friend, you can't try that on with me! (iii, p. 379)

When Ippolit finally forces Akhov to give him the full amount, Akhov again is concerned with maintaining a façade of respect, ordering Ippolit to bow down to his feet in thanks. When Ippolit refuses, Akhov declares: 'This recalcitrance of yours is even harder for me than the fifteen thousand!' (iii, p. 380). As in the earlier play, Akhov's concern with appearances makes him blind to reality. He cannot even begin to conceive that the impoverished Kruglova could refuse him as a husband for her daughter, Agniya. She, however, is well aware of the reality behind the life of luxury he describes to Agniya:

Agniya. If only you had heard him: he promised me mountains of gold!
Kruglova. He's a master at talking about mountains of gold, but no doubt he didn't say anything about tears, about how much his late wife cried?
Agniya. No, he didn't say a thing.
Kruglova. Well that's something worth hearing. She didn't dare to cry at home, so she would go to other people's houses to cry. She would get herself together as if she were going out visiting, and then she would drop in on this person or that, and have a good cry. Sometimes she would come to me, throw herself on the bed and cry for three hours or so, so that I couldn't bear to look at her ... (iii, pp. 368/7)

The discrepancy between Akhov's grossly inflated opinion of himself—his constant demands for respect and honour—and the reality of the other characters' opinion of him, provides much of the humour in the play. Akhov constantly fails to see that he is being mocked. His courtship of Agniya in Act Two, Scene 7, is a delightful case in point. Akhov boasts of wealth and power, and impresses on Agniya the financial benefits of having a rich, elderly husband. She responds that it all sounds 'Very jolly!' but then adds: 'And then, it's even more pleasant to think that in a year or two, your husband will die—he won't have two centuries to live—and you will be left a young widow with money and the full freedom to do whatever your heart desires' (iii, p. 367). Akhov, of course, passionately denies this possibility, and Agniya, with mock servility, placates him by asking his forgiveness and promising to remember that 'it's the young that die first' (iii, p. 367).

Ironically, when Kruglova and Agniya refuse Akhov, preferring Ippolit instead, Akhov believes they must be joking with him, and repeatedly demands that they 'Drop the mask!' (iii, p. 385). When the truth finally sinks in, he goes to leave, but immediately returns, fearing for the effect on his reputation: 'But no, wait! You've made a fool of me! How am I meant to look people in the eyes now? What will decent people say of me?' (iii, p. 388). As in his dealings with Ippolit, he again makes an attempt at a face-saving gesture, demonstrating beyond doubt his concern with appearance:

> **Akhov.** Here, listen to this! In order to stop the talk that you, lowly people, have scored off me, we'll put out a story that I'm marrying off Ippolit ... After the wedding we'll have such a dinner at my house the like of which has never been heard. I'll get all the flowers from Fomina and the others, and we'll put them in all the rooms. There'll be two bands, one in the house and one out on the balcony for spectators. Waiters in lace-up shoes. Won't that make an effect? ... The bride and groom will come from the church pulled by six grey horses, and as they reach the gates—stop! They won't drive through the gates! Immediately the porters will come out with brooms and they'll sweep their path up to the steps. Don't worry, it'll be clean, they'll have swept it before the bride and groom get there, it'll just be for show! And I will stand on the balcony with the guests and I'll forgive you and promote you into my good books, and you'll mingle with all the guests at my house as an equal! (iii, pp. 388/9)

Note the emphasis on things being done 'for effect' and 'for show'.

Blindness and Deception: *Don't Get Above Yourself*

In *A Young Man's Morning*, concern with appearance, leading to a blindness to reality, acts as an aid to deception. Ostrovsky returns to this theme in *Don't Get Above Yourself*, where Avdot'ya falls victim to the deception of Vikhorev.[3] Avdot'ya is blind to reality, believing

---

[3] See p. 42.

in Vikhorev's love for her, despite warnings to the contrary. As ever, her blindness to reality is the result of a concern with appearance—Avdot´ya is attracted to Vikhorev because of the image he presents. In Act Two, Scene 2, she talks of 'how handsome he is', noting that 'as soon as I saw this beauty, my heart missed a beat. Well, I thought, he'll be trouble. But he was so tender, as if on purpose, and said such wonderful things' (i, p. 300); and in Act Three, Scene 1, she declares to Vikhorev: 'How handsome you are! I've never seen the like ... just as if you'd been painted!' (i, p. 313).

Avdot´ya is aided in her blindness to reality by her aunt, Arina, who is, again, overly concerned with appearance. Thus she dismisses the honest and loyal Borodkin as a suitor for Avdot´ya, declaring: 'It's unpleasant for me to see it. Well, what sort of match are you for her? What sort of match are you for her? With your beard and your lack of education?' (i, p. 297). She refers to him as 'dregs' (i, p. 302) and 'bearded rubbish' and calls her brother, Rusakov, an 'ignorant peasant' (i, p. 321). In contrast she sees Vikhorev as 'an educated man', noting: 'He's a man of the capital, he's lived in Moscow, amongst the nobility' (i, p. 308).

Arina is indeed as blind to reality as Avdot´ya. When Avdot´ya declares: 'Surely he [Vikhorev] doesn't love me because of money?' Arina adds: 'Do you really think that such a fine-looking man could be such a schemer? He is absolutely not as mercenary as you think' (i, p. 310). Even after Avdot´ya's abandonment by Vikhorev, Arina declares: 'Who would have known that would happen? It never even entered my head.' (i, p. 323).

Throughout, the blindness of the women is contrasted with the realism of Rusakov and Borodkin, who see through Vikhorev's deception and constantly warn Avdot´ya that he is deceiving her. Rusakov sets the scene in Act One, Scene 3, when he declares:

> You can't trust a girl to choose for herself! It's well known that when it comes to this sort of thing, girls are just stupid ... they are always being deceived! Any kind of empty head—God forgive me—turns up and fawns all over them, and then, well, the girl's in love. Should I just hand her over? No, that's not the way to do it. Let me like the fellow. I'm not going to give her to someone she likes, I'll give her to someone I like. Yes, I'll watch him for a year, study him from all angles. Who can believe a girl? What has she

seen? What does she know? ... But I, my friend, haven't lived sixty years in this world for nothing. I've seen all sorts of people. You won't catch me napping. (i, p. 287)

It is Rusakov who tells Vikhorev that he does not believe in his protestations of love:

> **Vikhorev.** I assure you that I love Avdot´ya Maksimovna madly.
> **Rusakov.** I don't believe you.
> **Vikhorev.** How can you not believe me?
> **Rusakov.** I simply don't believe you, and that's that.
> **Vikhorev.** How can you doubt the honest word of a nobleman?
> **Rusakov.** What do you love her for? She is a simple girl, uneducated, and not at all your match. You have relatives, acquaintances, who would all laugh at her as if she was a fool. She would become unutterably repulsive to you ... (i, p. 306)

And it is he who warns Avdot´ya that Vikhorev is only interested in her for her dowry: 'He needs your money, you silly! He is only deceiving you, he will swindle you out of your money and chase you out after a week' (i, p. 309).

Borodkin also warns Avdot´ya that Vikhorev is only interested in money, stating: 'his sort learn their speeches—they say one thing and think another. It's plain to see that he needs your money; otherwise he would find himself a different bride' (i, p. 300).

Blindness and Deception: *The Handsome Man*

Perhaps Ostrovsky's strongest warning of the danger of taking things at face value comes in one of his very last plays, *The Handsome Man*, which is again dominated by the theme of concern with appearances. The theme is introduced in the opening scene of the play when Zhorzh and P´er discuss the 'odd fellow' who turned up last year:

> **Zhorzh.** Don't you remember what an odd fellow turned up last year? He was all dishevelled—his hair uncombed, frock-coat covered in fluff, his boots all dirty. He drank champagne mixed with kvass. He couldn't hold cards in his hands, but gathered them all together. (v, p. 283)

Despite the man's odd appearance, Zhorzh goes on to note:

I saw him later in Petersburg, in Livadyi street, drenched in perfume, his hair all curled. It turns out he knows all the operetta artists, he sings songs as well as they do. (v, p. 283)

Thus already the idea is introduced of things not always being as they first appear. This theme is continued in Scene 2, when Lotokhin tells Sosipatra of his difficulties in saving his female relatives from financial ruin when they fall in love with handsome men. The men are only ever interested in his relatives for their money, but they constantly fail to accept that good-looking men can be dishonest:

... Do you really think that such a fine-looking man could be such a schemer? That never happens, never! I assure you that this is an exception. A man who is handsome also has a noble soul, it is always that way, always, always! ... (v, p. 287)

It continues again in Scene 4 with the argument between Oleshunin and Apollinariya over whether women should pay attention to a man's inner or outer qualities (it is significant to note that there is general agreement with Apollinariya's viewpoint—that external qualities are of most importance). Apollinariya is obsessed by male beauty. She is shocked by Oleshunin's suggestion that women should not pay attention to a man's outward appearance, stating more than once that he says 'terrible things':

Apollinariya. It's terrible what he says. He says that a woman shouldn't pay attention to a man's outward appearance, shouldn't pay attention to his beauty! ... (v, p. 300)

She bemoans her fate at being married off by her parents before she had become aware of male beauty:

... I was young, I had seen little of people and still hadn't learned to distinguish men by their appearance, by their outward behaviour... well, of course it was going to happen, and it did happen, I matured and developed an understanding of male beauty, but by then, gentlemen, I was no longer free, I no longer had the ability to choose ...

But all the same, I had eyes; it wasn't as if I lived behind the walls of a nunnery. I saw handsome men, I saw them with great pleasure. Well, gentlemen, I was human, a woman, how could I not be tempted by the thought that if I had been free, then that

handsome man could have been mine, and that one, and that one?...
(v, p. 293)

Sosipatra describes her as 'crazy about male beauty' (v, p. 324) and at the end of the play, it is Apollinariya who is used to suggest that nothing much will change. She ends the play by marrying the young, empty-headed, but handsome, Zhorzh.

Zoya has been brought up by Apollinariya to be similarly obsessed with male beauty—her marriage to the handsome man of the title, Okoemov, was orchestrated by Apollinariya. It is Zoya whose illusions are shattered during the course of the play. She begins the play completely blind to reality, believing that she and her husband live in a state of mutual love and bliss. Her very first words in the play are:

> Why do you concern yourself with my husband? Leave us in
> peace. No-one can interfere with our serene happiness ... (v,
> p. 291)

Yet the extent of her misconception is quickly hinted at. In the very next scene Oleshunin describes her as a '... blind woman ...', and goes on: '... She doesn't see that he [her husband] fell out of love with her long ago ...' promising that 'I will soon open her eyes, she will see clearly what kind of man her beloved spouse really is' (v, p. 295).

People are often warning Zoya to look at life more clearly. In Act Two, Scene 5, Lupachev warns her that '... your rosy view of life will cause you certain disillusionment and much suffering' (v, p. 305). He tells her that 'It's time for you, Zoya Vasil´evna, to come of age ...' pointing out that '... beauty is a glittering toy, but only children grab at toys' (v, pp. 305/6). He also warns her that '... in the eyes of a stranger, your marriage has the appearance of a business deal' (v, p. 307). Zoya, however, refuses to believe him. At the end of the above conversation with Lupachev, she states that '... it is better to be disillusioned and to suffer, than never to believe in people' (v, p. 307); and in the very next scene tells Lotokhin how much her husband loves her, talking of their 'passionate mutual love; in a word, complete happiness' (v, p. 309). Her concern with outward appearance at the expense of reality is further emphasised when she tells Lotokhin how everyone envies her for having such a handsome husband. She talks of how Okoemov turned up and 'blinded everyone here' (v, p. 309); how she 'fell in love with him at first sight' (v, p. 309); all the while blithely discounting Lotokhin's concern as to why, if everything is going so well, they are in such financial trouble and selling their estate so cheaply.

Zoya begins her rather rude awakening to reality at the end of Act Two (Scene 8), when Okoemov tells her of his debts and his plans that they should divorce to enable him to marry a rich woman—it is interesting to note that at this point he too tells her that '... the time has come for you to look at life more seriously' (v, p. 312). This is compounded when she learns that not only must she and Okoemov part, but that she must pretend to be unfaithful to him so that he can obtain a clean divorce. Yet at this stage she still believes in his love for her and assures herself that they will get back together when he has paid off his debts. At his threat that she will never see him again if she does not agree, she eventually concurs with his plan. Her final awakening to reality comes at the end of Act Three (Scene 7), when, after she has gone through the trial of her feigned love for Oleshunin, Okoemov treats her with extreme callousness and suggests that she should marry Lupachev. It is noteworthy that here, at her moment of revelation, Zoya is described as taking Okoemov by the face and 'looking penetratingly at him'. It is as if she is actually 'seeing' the true Okoemov for the first time. She finally sees beyond the outer beauty.

Susanna is another character who is completely taken in by male beauty. She is also forced to face reality in the course of the play. Susanna is first heard of in Act One, Scene 8, when Lotokhin receives a letter from her begging him to sell her Bryakhimov estate. She has rejected Lotokhin's favoured suitor, 'an intelligent, practical man', and has instead '... found my ideal ... he is young, clever, educated, and so handsome, oh so handsome!' (v, p. 298). In order to marry him, however, she needs a 'great deal of money'. Given the scene set previously by Lotokhin in his earlier conversation with Sosipatra (Act One, Scene 2), the audience is left suspecting that Susanna will be deceived in her new love. This suspicion is proved correct at the beginning of Act Three, when we learn that Susanna's 'ideal' is in fact Okoemov—Zoya's husband.

Susanna's concern with appearance (often at the expense of reality) is made clear throughout the play. When she arrives at the hotel in Bryakhimov, Lotokhin's servant, Akimych, is overwhelmed by the amount of luggage she has brought with her, describing her room as looking like 'a whole shop' (v, p. 317). As she tells Lotokhin of her latest love, she breaks off in the middle of their conversation to go and look in the mirror and asks: 'So, uncle, do I please?' (v, p. 318). In Act Four, Scene 2, Sosipatra states that Susanna has spent three hours at her toilette that morning; and when she tells Susanna about Oboldueva, the millionairess merchant's daughter, Susanna's first response is to ask 'is she pretty?' (v, p. 340). On learning that Oboldueva has a disfiguring facial birthmark, she is very distressed for her and cannot understand why the young men of the town should still want to pay court to her. Like Apollinariya and Zoya, Susanna is unable to believe that Okoemov could do anything deceitful; it is only when she comes face to face with his dishonesty (in the scene where she herself pretends to be Oboldueva) that she finally faces up to reality.

Oleshunin initially appears to be unconcerned by appearance. As noted above, Apollinariya often complains that '... he says that women shouldn't pay attention to a man's appearance, but to his inner qualities ...' (v, p. 291); and it is Oleshunin who notes that Zoya is a 'blind woman' and vows to 'open her eyes'. Yet despite this apparent disregard for outward appearance, Oleshunin is as concerned with appearance as any other character in the play. Of all the main protagonists, it is he who is most concerned with how he appears in the eyes of others. His attacks on male beauty occur largely as a result of his own lack of good looks. He is very proud and egotistical, he believes himself to be superior to his rivals and wants to show them that this is the case. When, in Act One, Scene 4, Oleshunin asks what is so special about Okoemov, Apollinariya's rebuff: 'Oh, my God! Well, look, go and talk to the man! What's the matter with you! Either you haven't got eyes, or you think very highly of yourself?' (v, p. 291) is ironic, precisely because Oleshunin does think highly of himself. All this makes him a very easy target for Okoemov's fake flattery in Act Two, Scene 3:

Oleshunin (*squeezing Okoemov's hand*). Thank you! You understand me! I don't like to boast about myself, I want only to be viewed justly. I tell you openly, I have read Plutarch's biography ... and I find it strange that people value him so highly. All his features, I find in myself, only I haven't yet had the opportunity to show it.' (v, p. 302)

Likewise, he believes in Zoya's feigned love for him, not because he himself genuinely loves her, but because it would increase his status in the eyes of others:

Zoya. Weren't you surprised? Please, sit down. (*She sits in an armchair.*)
Oleshunin. For pity's sake! What's there to be surprised about? (*He sprawls on the divan in a very free-and-easy manner.*) I know my own worth, Zoya Vasil′evna. How can such gentlemen as P′er and Zhorzh understand me! Just because they allow themselves to play stupid jokes! No, I don't have any pretensions to be like them, they are too trivial. If only they could see me now! (v, p. 331)

As Sosipatra says in Act Three, Scene 3: 'He doesn't need love, just for everyone to know that he is loved' (v, p. 322).

Lupachev's concern with appearances limits itself to a desire to own Zoya for her beauty:

What a fine woman! And look who she has around her! A diamond like that should have a much finer setting! She found herself a good-looking husband, and she's glad! What kind of happiness can that greenhorn give her! She needs a rich man, not a handsome one. (v, p. 290)

He is the prime mover behind the action of the play—it is he who encourages and aides Okoemov in his plans.

P′er and Zhorzh act as indicators of the ubiquitous nature of concern with appearance within society. They too will become worthless 'handsome husbands' like Okoemov. The pervasive nature of this concern with appearance is also shown in the fact that there is general agreement with Apollinariya's viewpoint in her argument with Oleshunin in Act One, Scene 4 (note that Apollinariya tells Oleshunin: 'You won't change life' (v, p. 290)) and (perhaps more dangerously from the point of view of the 'educator' Ostrovsky)[4] in the fact that the disfigured Oboldueva has been deprived of education to avoid exposing her ugliness to teachers and governesses. Interestingly, those characters who show no concern for appearance are labelled as somehow strange or alien. Lotokhin is repeatedly described as an 'odd fellow' and Sosipatra is described in the *dramatis personae* as someone who 'conducts herself independently and completely freely, not restrained by custom'.

Okoemov is also distinguished from the others as the 'handsome man' in question. He himself is not unduly concerned by appearance—as his willingness to marry Oboldueva shows. He simply exploits his good looks to his advantage—it is, as he himself states, his one talent. He appears cold and callous—an empty shell; yet the play makes it clear that he has the capacity for redemption. He too is a victim of his society's concern with appearance.

On a final note, it is significant that much of the deception in the play again involves disguise—such as Susanna dressing up as Oboldueva—and role-playing—such as Zoya's staged infidelity with Oleshunin. Again, the dangers of concern with appearance and the warnings that things may not be as they initially seem are central to the work.

The Blind Idealist: *Rich Brides* and *Guilty without Guilt*

Many of the plays discussed above depict blind-to-reality characters forced to face up to reality in a manner reminiscent of Ostrovsky's treatment of the theme of realism and idealism. And indeed, such blindness to reality is closely connected with the kind of self-delusion that appears in Ostrovsky's exploration of the earlier theme. His characters are often blind to the true nature of events because of their insistence on inaccurate or unrealistic perceptions of reality. They, like Glumov's fools in *Even Wise Men Err*, are not only the victims of deception, nor simply the victims of an involuntary inability to see beyond superficial appearance; they are the victims of their own capacity for self-delusion. Their own wishes and desires lead them to

---

[4] Ostrovsky believed very strongly in the importance of education and saw the theatre as a tool for education as well as entertainment. He stated: 'The domestic repertory ... is a great thing for the ... public: it will reveal ... what is good, what is kind in the Russian person, what he must cherish and educate in himself.' (See Bristow, 17.)

see only what they want to see. As L.Cox, discussing *Even Wise Men Err*, suggests, blindness to reality is 'not necessarily involuntary. It is, in some characters, a deliberate, wilful refusal to let the truth interfere with a sense of self-esteem.'[5]

Thus in a play like *Rich Brides*, for example, we are presented with Tsyplunov, a character who maintains a highly idealistic view of women. He idolises them, placing them on pedestals, and then succumbs to seemingly inevitable disillusionment when they fail to meet his expectations. Early in the play, with bitter despondency, he complains to his mother: '... I have loved more than once in my life; but you yourself know why I haven't married. Every time my love ends, withers with bitter disillusionment, or still worse, they simply deceive me' (iv, p. 218). His mother, with contrasting practicality, points out: 'And always you yourself are to blame, because you never trouble yourself to have a good look at the women you favour with your love, you imagine all kinds of virtues in them which they don't have, and expect things that they can't give' (iv, p. 218). 'You create in your imagination a non-existent goddess, and then you are angry when you don't find her in reality. You, poor creature, not only can't forgive, but are even ready to insult a good woman if she is not the same as the pale, lifeless template that you create in your idle imagination' (iv, p. 219).

In the course of the play, Tsyplunov becomes reacquainted with a young woman, Belesova, whom he had known when she was a child, and whom he had then admired for her 'childish purity'. She has now become a beautiful young woman and Tsyplunov falls deeply in love with her, delighting in how 'now, in my imagination, the child and the woman have merged into a remarkable combination: childhood purity, somehow showing through the luxury of female beauty' (iv, p. 220) and ascribing to her all kinds of virtues, amongst which the chief are chastity and childlike purity. The use of the words 'in my imagination' is not, of course, without significance, and we soon learn that Belesova is not simply the ward of her travelling companion, but also his mistress. As so often in Ostrovsky's plays, Tsyplunov's illusions come crashing down around him.

[5] Cox, 100.

The scene in which Tsyplunov confronts Belesova with his
knowledge of her true status resounds with significance:

> **Belesova.** If you think that I am the guiltless child that you knew
> before ...
> **Tsyplunov** (*clutching his head*). Yes, I thought that you were just
> as pure ...
> **Belesova.** Then you are mistaken ... I should confess ... that I am
> not a child.
> **Tsyplunov.** Why did you let me go on thinking you were still an
> innocent girl? It was the one thing I loved about you.
> **Belesova.** You didn't ask anything about it. You only told me that
> you loved me ...
> **Tsyplunov.** But in my dreams you were pure, there were rays of
> goodness shining around you ... You cheated me.
> **Belesova.** It would be better to say that you cheated yourself.
> **Tsyplunov.** No, you cheated ... with your angelic face, the same as
> it was before ... it lies, you should cover it up with make-up, use
> rouge, so that it doesn't deceive ... it is wonderful, it has such light,
> charm. But there should be some kind of screen ... a long tail, a
> special hairstyle ... these would be the little signs by which lovers
> of bartered beauty would know your goods ... Why kill me again?
> I've already been killed, killed by you ... your blow straight to the
> heart! You have killed my love, that was the dearest thing to me in
> the world, and without it ... (*he clasps his chest.*) Without it, there
> is no life either! (*Falls unconscious into an armchair*). (iv,
> pp. 248/9)

Thus we see how Tsyplunov's own belief system—his idealisation of
women—has led him to accept unquestioningly outward appearance—'You didn't ask anything about it.' Moreover, his concern with
outward appearance has led him to assume that beauty equates with
goodness and virtue, and he complains that Belesova should have
some outward 'sign' by which he could perceive her inner nature.

With typical complexity, Ostrovsky does not leave things there,
but adds a further dimension to his exposure of the superficial nature
of appearances. Having noted that things are not always as they
initially appear, and that beauty does not always equate with virtue,
Ostrovsky goes on to point out that vice is not clear-cut either. We
learn that as a poor ward, Belesova was raised with little understanding of morals. Indeed, her guardian raised her with almost the sole

intention of making her his mistress: 'All that I needed to maintain appearances, to conduct myself skilfully—I was taught in detail. But what is honourable or dishonourable you hid from me ... Your silly wife tried, with all her might, to develop in me pride, extravagance, vanity; and how she rejoiced in her success; never suspecting that it was all for you, that she acted to the benefit of your lascivious thoughts. After such an upbringing, it was not difficult for you to seduce me ...' (iv, p. 237). (Note that again the emphasis is on appearance—'all that I needed to maintain appearances...'). Belesova expresses her desire to change her ways, to learn how to live virtuously, and Tsyplunov and his mother agree to help her. Significantly, she indicates her desire to start over by changing her outward appearance—she dresses simply, sells her goods, and moves into a plain, simply-furnished dacha. Tsyplunov declares: 'In these wonderful features I again see the childlike purity and clarity and the angelic expression' (iv, p. 261). Thus the question of whether Tsyplunov has learnt his lesson is, once again, left unresolved.

A link between blindness to reality and idealism appears again in *Guilty without Guilt*. Here, Act One of the play is almost a microcosm of the destruction of idealism usually found in the course of an entire Ostrovsky work. The idealistic and kind-natured Lyubov is deceived by her lover of four years and father of her son. Lyubov's blindness to reality is demonstrated almost immediately when, in Scene 1, she is shown refusing to believe the rumours that her 'friend', Taisa, acquired her sudden wealth by becoming the mistress of a rich, old gentleman—despite all the evidence to support it. She is also shown referring to Taisa as her 'friend', although Anna, her serving-maid, who is much more realistic than Lyubov, points out that Taisa has not been to see Lyubov in over a month, and that Lyubov only found out about Taisa's forthcoming marriage through a seamstress.

Anna goes on to point out the difficulties Lyubov will have in finding a husband, despite her education and gentle birth, because of her poverty. Lyubov naively dismisses her concerns, protesting that she will somehow get rich and get married; and then, referring to her lover, Murov, suggests that she may get married without needing to get rich first. In response, Anna states prophetically that today's men 'are very alluring at first, but often go on to make good deceivers' (v, p. 357). When Lyubov asks how she knows this, Anna protests: 'Do you think I can't see what happens in this world! ...' (v, p. 357)—thus emphasising the fact that Lyubov herself is unable to see reality.

In Scene 2, during her conversation with Murov, Lyubov's blindness to reality is made even more apparent as she blithely accepts Murov's explanations for his bizarre behaviour. Thus, she notes that he always comes very early to see her, as if he was afraid of being seen, yet accepts his response: 'Of course I'm afraid, only not for myself, but for you. It's very simple, I don't want ugly things said about you' (v, p. 358). When Lyubov points out that the best way to avoid gossip would be to stop hiding their relationship and marry, Murov comes up with a number of objections to their marriage, all of which come as a complete surprise to Lyubov: 'All this is news to me; I have known you for four years and you haven't said a word to me about it' (v, p. 358). When she presses him as to his intentions, Murov at first protests: 'Ah, don't ask me, please! It makes my head spin' (v, p. 358); and then, 'embarrassed', states: 'Well, now what ... well, you know what they are ... how could I, in my position ... It's my duty ...' Lyubov takes this as confirmation of the honour of his intentions towards her, replying: 'Well, yes, yes! I hope that you know your obligations well.' She then, revealingly, goes on to say: 'It's impossible for me to doubt you, otherwise it would be such a trial, such a trial ...' (v, p. 359).

Murov's suspicious behaviour continues when he goes on to talk obliquely about the possibility of their son, Grisha, being without a father, and then becomes very agitated when Lyubov talks of Taisa and her forthcoming marriage—although he protests that he does not know Taisa. His agitation increases when Taisa is seen approaching the house to visit Lyubov. Frightened, Murov demands to be hidden, insisting: 'She mustn't see me here' (v, p. 363); and even Lyubov shows surprise at his behaviour, reminding him that he had said that he did not know Taisa, and describing his reaction as 'strange'. Her final words, however, show that she remains blind to the reality of the situation, as she ends the scene protesting: '... only, I don't understand' (v, p. 363).

Lyubov's awakening to reality comes in Scene 3, when she discovers that Murov is in fact Taisa's fiancé. The scene is full of irony as Taisa, talking of her future husband, notes: 'I don't believe a word he says; it's impossible to believe in him' (v, p. 364). When she shows Lyubov a photograph of her fiancé, thus revealing to Lyubov that he is Murov, Lyubov responds with shock and pain, which she explains away as the result of leaning on a pin on the table (thus Lyubov herself is quickly forced into her own deception). Her new-found realism is demonstrated when Taisa asks her how she likes the look of her future husband; Lyubov responds with the significant: 'I don't know what to say. Appearances are so deceiving' (v, p. 365). Taisa's reply again resounds with unwitting irony: 'Yes, that's true. But if he deceives me, then it will be the worse for him.' The scene ends with Lyubov described as 'staring fixedly at the bedroom door' (v, p. 365), behind which Murov is hiding (thus once again the stage directions imply seeing clearly for the first time) and when Murov emerges she tells him to get out.

Blindness, Deception and Idealism: *We All Have our Cross to Bear*

We All Have our Cross to Bear, a rather bleak drama which tells of a deceived husband who kills his cheating wife in a fit of jealousy, is a prime example of how deception, idealism, and a concern with appearances all intermingle to cause blindness to reality.

Blindness is one of the central themes of the play—emphasised by the fact that it is one of the few Ostrovsky plays to have a physically blind character, Arkhip—and numerous characters in the play are shown to be blind to reality. Krasnov, the cheated husband, for example, maintains almost until the very end of the play his blind belief in Tat'yana's good, kind nature, and in her love for him.

Tat'yana herself is also blind to reality—she fails to see the honesty, kindness and genuine love of the peasant Krasnov, prefer-ring instead to believe in the false love of the aristocratic Babaev. She is encouraged in this by Luker'ya. In Act Three, Part 1, Scene 1, when Tat'yana is complaining about Krasnov's 'vulgar, peasant' treatment of her, Luker'ya states: 'How can he not seem loathsome after such behaviour on his part. Especially when you compare the two of them. This admirer of hers [Babaev] has manners, he does everything as it should be done' (ii, p. 426).

Tat´yana herself does not always seem to be entirely taken in by Babaev's behaviour. She is constantly exhorting him not to deceive her, scoffs at his plans to take her away with him and, at the end of Act Two, runs out on him, telling him to leave. It is Luker´ya who comes back to set up another meeting with Babaev, and indeed it is she who sets up all the meetings between them. Given that Tat´yana states on more than one occasion that life with her husband was bearable before Babaev reappeared—in Act Four, Part 1, Scene 3, she says: 'But it is all your fault, Valentin: it's because of you that I don't stay at home. If it were not for you, then I would have managed to live with my husband somehow' (ii, p. 442)—it could be argued that she and Krasnov might have successfully made a life together, if not for this outside interference by Luker´ya.

Tat´yana's blindness is very closely linked to her concern with appearance. She cannot see beyond the 'peasant exterior' of Krasnov to his true inner qualities, and she is attracted by the outward 'nobility' of Babaev, again ignoring the falseness of his inner nature. In contrast, Afonya is the character who can 'see all'—although his clear-sightedness is perhaps provoked by jealousy and pride, as suggested by his conversation with Arkhip in Act One, Part 2, Scene 1:

> **Afonya** ... Before, Lev loved me and you much more.
> **Arkhip.** That is why you are full of hatred! That is why—you're jealous.
> **Afonya.** No, I'm not jealous. Is Lev blind? Does she deserve him? Why does he act like a slave in front of her? It insults me that he slaves for her. (ii, pp. 400/1)

It is Afonya who is constantly pleading with Krasnov not to be blind (note the 'Is Lev blind?' in the above quotation.) He tells Arkhip that he 'sees and hears all': 'You know, grandfather, I see everything, hear everything; she can't hide from me, the shameless hussy. Lev gives her a silk dress and scarf, but she and her sister are laughing between themselves, calling him a fool' (ii, p. 401); and he accuses Tat´yana of blinding Krasnov: 'You've blinded him, blinded him' (ii, p. 408). In Act Two, Part 1, Scene 3, he warns Krasnov to watch Babaev, again crying: 'Just don't be blind, don't be blind!' (ii, p. 414). In Act Three, when Tat´yana and Luker´ya involve Arkhip in their deception of Krasnov, it is Afonya who warns: '... Don't believe

them, grandpa, they are tricking you' (ii, p. 429); and when Tat´yana
has left for her final, fateful meeting with Babaev, Afonya turns on
Luker´ya, crying: 'I know where she has gone. You are the devil.
You have cheated Lev. Yes, I've seen through you with my own
eyes: you have fire in your eyes, devil's fire,' and goes on to exclaim:
'What a man to deceive, right before his eyes!' (ii, p. 439).

Significantly, Afonya is often shown in the company of the blind
Arkhip—perhaps to emphasise even further his ability to 'see' reality.
Thus in Act One, Part 2, Scene 1, when Arkhip regrets his loss of
sight, Afonya responds by stating that while Arkhip regrets his
blindness, he himself is tired of seeing.

As always in Ostrovsky's plays, those who are most blind to
reality are also those who are most concerned with appearances.
Thus, Luker´ya and Tat´yana are constantly shown to be concerned
with how things look. Luker´ya is again the prime mover. When she
first goes to meet Babaev, in Act One, Scene 4, she states that her
reason for seeing him is: '... I want terribly to prove to this town what
sort of high-class acquaintances we have' (ii, p. 394). (It is interesting
to note that, given this motivation, the entire plot, ending in
Tat´yana's death, then rests on Luker´ya's desire to give the town an
impression of high social status. Thus once again, Ostrovsky depicts
most forcefully the negative consequences of concern with appearance.[6]) Luker´ya is greatly distressed by having to admit that
Tat´yana has been forced to marry a petty shopkeeper: 'Agh, really,
you simply couldn't imagine how embarrassed I am about having to
admit this family connection. Well, in short, our circumstances were
such that she was forced to marry a shopkeeper' (ii, p. 397). And
although she admits that for 'one of his sort' Krasnov is a good man,
who loves her sister dearly, works hard and keeps a good home, this
is soon dismissed: 'but his manners are terrible, and his conversation
embarrasses us greatly. He is quite, quite not the man I would have
wanted for Tanya. Judging by her beauty and the way people look at

---

[6] I.Beasley has noted the influence of Luker´ya on Tat´yana's behaviour, but states that
it is 'unclear what her aims are'. Although she refers to the suggestion in the play that
Luker´ya has an idea of 'dazzling the townsfolk with her acquaintances' she soon
dismisses this to propose that Luker´ya acts out of spite towards Krasnov; for material
gain; and even out of jealousy towards Tat´yana. She thus fails to recognise the
overwhelming concern with appearances emphasised in the play. (See Beasley,
unpublished doctoral thesis, 166.)

her, she should be driving around in a carriage. But for the sake of a crust of bread she was forced to marry a peasant. And in front of others, it's simply so embarrassing for us' (ii, p. 397).

At the start of Act Two, Part 1, Scene 1, while preparing for Babaev's visit, Luker´ya enters with a table-cloth she has borrowed from the neighbour because 'ours is terribly poor' (ii, p. 407); and she is keen to ensure that Tat´yana looks her best, commenting on her headscarf: 'Well, here, you see, like I told you, wear it like that: that scarf suits you much better' (ii, p. 407).

In Act Two, Part 1, Scene 2, when Krasnov brings his sister and brother-in-law home, just as Luker´ya and Tat´yana are expecting Babaev, they bemoan their embarrassment: 'Well, we must confess, you cut us up. So embarrassing, so embarrassing!' (ii, p. 409). They spend the whole of Babaev's visit acutely ashamed by the boorishness of Krasnov's behaviour, and when it is over, their concern at the impression he must have caused is again acute:

> **Tat´yana.** Agh, Lusha, what a disgrace! What must he think of us!
> **Luker´ya.** Yes. Soon, he'll be going to Petersburg and a fine impression of us he'll give them! (ii, p. 417)

(It is noteworthy that Tat´yana's concerns, perhaps understandably, are directed at what Babaev—the man she loves—might think, whereas Luker´ya is again concerned by the opinion of the wider community.)

Krasnov is also concerned with appearance. He emphasises Tat´yana's beauty, and is aware of the status she brings him in society: 'What a wife you are! Who else has such a wife! You are the envy of the whole town ...' (ii, p. 435). However, like Tsyplunov in *Rich Brides*, Krasnov's blindness to reality rests largely on his idealistic assessment of Tat´yana's virtues. He believes that he should be grateful that someone of her standing and education should have deigned to marry him. (I.Beasley notes that 'Krasnov desires in [Tat´yana] a curious ideal of happiness.'[7])

In contrast, Afonya shows little concern with appearance. He notes in Act 1, Part 2, Scene 1: '... others like to dress well, but to me it's all the same. I'll wear a homespun coat, so long as it's warm' (ii, p. 399).

---

[7] *Ibid.*, 165.

Finally, it is significant to note that the deception in the play is once more tied up with the concern that outward appearance causes blindness to reality. Tat´yana distracts Krasnov from her affair with Babaev by role-playing—pretending to be in love with him—and again, Krasnov is happy to accept her deception—the appearance of love—because this is what he wishes to believe. (It is no doubt significant that Tat´yana and Luker´ya involve the blind Arkhip as an unwitting aid in their deception, thereby emphasising the blindness of Krasnov.) Likewise, the deceiver, Tat´yana, is herself deceived by the insincere Babaev because of her concern with outward appearance— her willingness to accept his outward pretence of love. Thus, with rather cruel irony, given the play's bleak dénouement, both husband and wife fall victim to the same cause.

Blindness to reality, closely related to a concern with outward appearance and deception, is a key—if little-noted—element of Ostrovsky's drama. As Appendix F shows, the examples of blindness to reality discussed above are only a fraction of the instances which appear in his plays. Blindness to reality occurs either because a character is being deliberately deceived or because he or she is avoiding reality in some way: concentrating on outward appearance or upholding unrealistic ideals, deluding him- or herself. It is perhaps a testament to Ostrovsky's preoccupation with this theme that the word 'samodur', which he coined to describe his tyrannical mer-chants and landowners—characters who are traditionally accepted as the keystone of his work (V.Lakshin places 'samodurstvo' 'on a par with Turgenev's nihilism and Goncharov's Oblomovism'[8])—has the literal meaning of 'self fool', implying a propensity 'to fool oneself'.

---

[8] Lakshin, 'Mudrost´ Ostrovskogo', 6.

CHAPTER FOUR

The Language of Deception

> 'I told you, don't believe
> even what you can see
> with your own eyes.' *Not
> of this World* (v, p. 471)

Anotable feature of *We All Have our Cross to Bear* is the constant use of language relating to blindness and vision. Thus the 'blind-to-reality' Krasnov is constantly warned against blindness ('Is Lev blind then?' [*Brat neshto slep?*] (ii, p. 401)); 'Just don't be blind! Don't be blind!' [*Tol'ko ne bud' slep! Ne bud' slep!*] (ii, p. 414); whilst Tat'yana is accused of having blinded him ('You were the reason why he went blind' [*Da on oslep ot vas, oslep*] (ii, p. 408)). In contrast, Afonya can 'see everything' and Krasnov's sister, Ul'yana, catching Tat'yana on her way to a secret meeting with Babaev, notes that she 'isn't blind' ('I haven't gone blind yet, thank God' [*Ya eshche, slava bogu, ne oslepla*] (ii, p. 440)).

A similar emphasis on words connected to vision and blindness occurs in another play devoted to blindness to reality and superficial appearances: *The Handsome Man*. Thus Zoya is a 'blind woman' [*slepaya zhenshchina*] (v, p. 295) with a 'rosy view' [*s rozovymi vzglyadami*] (v, p. 305). She 'does not see' [*Ona ne vidit*] (v, p. 295), but 'the time has come when she should look at life more seriously' [*nastupaet vremya, kogda dolzhna vzglyanut' na zhizn' ser'ezno*] (v, p. 305). Likewise, Okoemov 'blinded everyone here' [*oslepil zdes' vsekh*] (v, p. 309) and has a 'contemptuous view of women' [*prezritel'nyi vzglyad na zhenshchinu*] (v, p. 324). (Okoemov's very name comes from the word *okoemkost'*, meaning 'eye capacity'.) Once more, in contrast, the practical, realistic Lotokhin is described as a man who has 'seen sights' [*vidali vidy*] (v, p. 289), and is frequently connnected with seeing: 'When I see ...' [*Kak uvizhu*] (v, p. 288); 'As you look around' [*Glyadish´, glyadish´ krugom*] (v, p. 288). Such phrases are not, in themselves, necessarily surprising, yet Ostrovsky's plays are full of words relating to vision—seeing, blindness, eyes, watching—which, given a concern with deception and blindness to reality, seem more than mere coincidence. It is, perhaps, a curious side-effect of the unchallenged acceptance of Ostrovsky as a purely realist writer, that critics have largely failed to notice the paradox inherent in this 'realist's' frequent use of significant words, images and (as we shall see later) symbols. This oversight is even more strange given the commonly attested importance of words and images as a key to understanding character and ideas in Ostrovsky's work. Ostrovsky's use of significant (and therefore artificial) names has already been noted[1] and numerous critics have discussed the importance of key words and images in Ostrovsky's plays as a means of understanding characters and ideas. R.Peace, for example, emphasises the importance of the words *volya* (will; freedom) and *serdtse* (heart) in an understanding of *The Storm*.[2] N.Kashin, E.Kholodov and L. and V.Uspensky have all discussed the importance of words in an understanding of Ostrovsky's drama.[3] Similarly, I.Esam has made a number of interesting observations about the use of imagery in Ostrovsky's plays, noting the 'imagery relating to gardens, trees, birds and beasts' in *The Forest*[4] and the animal, food and body imagery in *It's All in the Family*.[5] All this is further compounded by the playwright's own emphasis on the meaning of words: Mudrov in *Difficult Days* notes: 'there are words, there are, madam, which have a secret meaning hidden in them; and hidden so deeply that a weak mind ...' (ii, p. 466). Given this context, Ostrovsky's use of 'seeing' words cannot fail to resound with significance.

---

[1] See p. 49, note 10.

[2] R.A.Peace, 'A.N.Ostrovsky's *The Thunderstorm*: The Dramatization of Conceptual Ambivalence', *Modern Language Review*, 84 (1989), 99-110.

[3] See N.P.Kashin, 'O yazyke A.N.Ostrovskogo. Nablyudeniya i zametki', in *A.N.Ostrovskii— dramaturg*, ed. by V.Filippov (Moscow: Sovetskii pisatel´, 1946), 78-132; E.G.Kholodov, *Masterstvo Ostrovskogo* (Moscow: Iskusstvo, 1967), 430-52; and L.Uspenskii and V.Uspenskii, 'Ostrovskii-yazykotvorets', in *A.N.Ostrovskii: Sbornik statei i materialov*, ed. A.L.Shtein (Moscow: Vserossiiskoe teatral´noe obshchestvo, 1962), 184-265.

[4] Irene Zohrab (née Esam), 'Problems of Translation', 56.

[5] I.Esam, 'The Style of *Svoi liudi— sochtemsia*'.

Ostrovsky's 'blind-to-reality' characters are often associated with words indicating a lack of vision. Avdot´ya in *Don't Get Above Yourself* is often associated with being unable to see: '... without him I feel sick, I can't make my eyes see anything' (i, p. 296), 'I can't look at anyone' (i, p. 300), 'You've lived all your life in this town and haven't seen anyone' (i, p. 302), '... she hasn't seen the world' (i, p. 306), 'I've never seen the like' (i, p. 313), 'my eyes became dark, dark' (i, p. 313), and she is frequently described as covering her face (thus shrouding her vision): 'She raises her scarf to her eyes' (i, p. 294), 'She covers her face and moves away' (i, p. 294), 'She covers her face with her hands' (i, p. 315). Similarly the idealistic Ivan in *A Hangover from Someone Else's Feast* is connected with an inability to see. When Agrafena talks to him of the benefits of marrying Liza to a rich merchant's son, he declares: 'I don't see anything but ignorance' (i, p. 9); and he is described as 'raising his eyes to the ceiling' (i, p. 10); Liza talks about how the merchants 'laugh practically into his eyes' (i, p. 13); and in Act Two, Scene 2, when Nastas´ya and Nenila talk of how Ivan has ruined his daughter, they ask: 'Where are his eyes?' (i, p. 27). In *Without a Dowry*, the deceived Larisa declares: 'I've become blind' (v, p. 34). And in *Guilty without Guilt*, Kruchinina, when talking of her dreams that her son is still alive, is described as 'Covering her face with her hands' (v, p. 377); and 'Hiding her eyes with her hands' (v, p. 378).

In contrast, realistic characters are associated with clear vision. Rusakov, for example, in *Don't Get Above Yourself*, notes: 'I've seen all sorts of people, you won't catch me napping' (i, p. 287). He talks of having guarded and protected Avdot´ya ['I took better care of you than of my own eyes' (i, p. 309)]. Meanwhile Agrafena in *A Hangover from Someone Else's Feast* responds to Ivan's 'I don't see anything but ignorance' with the words: 'But I see' (ii, p. 9); and for her, Liza's marrying Andrei is an 'obvious thing' ['vidimoe delo' (ii, p. 18)].

Much of Ostrovsky's 'seeing' language is used ironically. Thus in *Wolves and Sheep*, the 'all-seeing' Murzavetskaya accuses the completely undeceiving Kupavina of trying to 'pull the wool over my eyes' (iv, p. 135); while the blind-to-reality Kupavina declares: 'I've got eyes, haven't I?' (iv, p. 143). In *Without a Dowry*, the blind-to-reality Larisa accuses others of not being able to see the 'true worth' of the deceiving Paratov: 'How can you be so blind! Sergei Sergeich ... is the ideal man' (v, p. 22). Similarly, in *The Handsome Man*, the blind-to-reality Apollinariya protests that 'I have eyes' and asks indignantly: 'Well, what? Am I blind, is that it?' (v, p. 300); and Oleshunin, another self-deceiving character, declares that he will open Zoya's eyes to reality: 'But I will soon open her eyes' (v, p. 295). (There is a double irony here: as a leading player in the infidelity drama set up by Okoemov, Oleshunin does indeed play a part in Zoya's process of awakening, but not in the way he had envisaged.) In *Even Wise Men Err*, the self-deceiving Mamaeva is described as 'wearing out her eyes' (iii, p. 11) when staring at Glumov at the theatre, although she does not really 'see' him and is easily taken in by his deceptions. Likewise when she tells him that she 'can see in his eyes' that he is in love with her (iii, p. 36) she is again 'seeing' what she wants to see, not the reality of the situation. In Act Two, Scene 4, Glumova talks to Mamaeva of how Glumov has been 'blinded by his benefactors' (iii, p. 25), when in reality it is the Mamaevs who are blind to Glumov's true nature; likewise in Scene 6, when Gorodulin states of Glumov: 'Allow me to cast an eye over this phenomenon; then I could tell you definitively what he is fit for, and what sort of position it will be possible to recommend him for' (iii, p. 30), he too is incapable of seeing the 'true' Glumov. In the fortune-telling scene in Act Three (Scene 5) there is much talk of 'seeing visions', all of which are false. However, by far the greatest irony in the play comes at the end of Act Five when, after Glumov's exposure, Krutitsky turns to Mamaev and states: 'You know, I noticed there was something funny about him straightaway ...'; Mamaev responds: 'So did I—there's something about his eyes' (iii, p. 79). In reality, of course, they saw nothing at all, and it cannot be insignificant that Ostrovsky chooses this moment to highlight Glumov's eyes.

In *We All Have our Cross to Bear*, when Krasnov talks of his jealous suspicions regarding Babaev, he states that his 'eyes become clouded' and that he walks 'without seeing' (ii, p. 433). Thus, ironically, at the very point when he is indeed seeing the truth, he believes that his vision is clouded. And in *A Young Man's Morning*, Ivan is constantly exhorting others to 'see how we live!' when in reality their grand way of life is little more than an illusion—it is all based on credit.

Ostrovsky's deceivers are often shown trying to hide their eyes. In *A Lucrative Post*, both Yulin´ka and Kukushkina are deceivers, and both are described as 'covering their eyes'. Yulin´ka 'covers her eyes with a handkerchief' in Act Two, when, trying to get Belogubov to marry her quickly, she ironically accuses him of deceiving her (ii, p. 67). Later in the same scene, she extends her hand for Belogubov to kiss, 'not looking at him' (ii, p. 67). When Zhadov asks Kukushkina for Polinka's hand in marriage, Kukushkina, although desperate to get Polinka married, declares: 'I must confess that it's painful for me to part with her. She's my favourite daughter ... she would have been a consolation in my old age ... but God be with her, take her ... her happiness means more to me' and is then described as 'covering her face with her handkerchief'. She goes on to note: 'No, bringing up daughters is a thankless task! You raise them, hold them close to you, and then you give them away to a stranger ... you're left alone like an orphan ... It's terrible!' and once more: 'She covers up her eyes with her handkerchief' (ii, p. 70).

In *Wolves and Sheep*, the deceiving Murzavetskaya is frequently described as 'raising her eyes to the heavens', while Glafira is described as having 'her eyes lowered to the ground ...' Glafira is particularly linked with eyes. Apollon's first words to her are: 'Cousin, favour me with your gaze! Ah, what eyes! I'd give up everything for a glance from such eyes' (iv, p. 121); Murzavetskaya warns her not to 'cast her eyes' at Lynyaev; and she herself tells Kupavina of the effectiveness of 'casting eyes' when wearing dowdy, black clothes. When Lynyaev and Glafira are pretending to be in love, Lynyaev initially protests that he does not know what to do, saying: 'Are you asking me to praise your eyes?' (iv, p. 168). (He has previously warned of the dangers of the 'languid eyes' of unmarried women (iv, p. 134)). Just before the hapless Lynyaev is finally caught by Glafira, he talks of how wonderful it is to be a bachelor; to be able to 'close your eyes' and sleep whenever you wish; and how on 'opening your eyes' your first thoughts are that 'you are your own master; you are completely free' (iv, p. 185). Yet when Lynyaev does open his eyes, it is to see Glafira hanging on his neck 'and staring him straight in the eyes'. In the Scene which follows she is described as 'closing her eyes' or 'opening her eyes' on four different occasions (iv, pp. 185/6).

A *Family Picture* has the deceivers Mar´ya and Shiryalov both 'casting down their eyes'. In *The Forest*, Karp warns Bulanov about the deceiving Gurmyzhskaya by noting: 'You just watch her eyes all the time!' (iii, p. 254). And in *At a Lively Spot*, Anna warns the travelling merchants that Bessudny's eyes 'are beginning to gleam, and no good comes from that' (ii, p. 563). Evgeniya notes that Bessudny has 'eyes like the devil's. When he glares with them, it's as if someone were gripping your heart' (ii, p. 567). In contrast, Zhadov, reaffirming his belief in honesty at the end of *A Lucrative Post*, declares: 'I want to preserve for myself the precious right of looking people straight in the eye, without shame, without secret pangs of conscience' (ii, p. 110).

Even Wise Men Err, with its emphasis on role-playing, has a particularly high use of the word *vid* (sight, vision, view; look; appearance, impression). Thus, Glumov 'pretends to be busy' ['Delaet vid, chto zanimaetsya rabotoi' (ii, p. 13)]; he 'adopts a pious expression' ['s postnym vidom' (ii, p. 19)]; Mamaeva talks of poverty removing that 'triumphant look' ['pobednyi vid' (ii, p. 24)] which is so becoming in a young man; Krutitsky is described as adopting a 'serious expression' ['s ser´eznym vidom' (ii, p. 55)]; and he goes on to dismiss Mamaeva's sudden 'headache' (brought on by the discovery that Glumov is planning to marry Masha), noting: 'You look perfectly healthy' ['u vas vid takoi zdorovyi' (ii, p. 59)].

In the discussion of *The Handsome Man* and *Guilty without Guilt* above, it was noted that at the moment when the 'blind-to-reality' characters face up to reality, they are described as 'looking penetratingly' or 'looking fixedly' at their deceivers, as if finally 'seeing' clearly for the first time.[6] This is a feature which occurs repeatedly in Ostrovsky's plays, which often seem to build up to a climax when the deceived or blind characters suddenly 'see'. Thus in *A Last Sacrifice*, Yuliya, who finally realises the extent of Dulchin's deception when she receives an invitation to his wedding to Irina, is described as 'rubbing her eyes with her hand and reading again', as if finally seeing clearly. Her immediate reaction is to declare: 'I only want to see him. I must look into his eyes. I want to see what his eyes

---

are like now' (iv, p. 394). Similarly, in *Without a Dowry*, when Paratov admits to Larisa that he has deceived her, and is to be married to someone else, she cries:

> Look at me!
> (*Paratov looks at her.*)
> 'Your eyes shine bright, like heaven's light.' Ha, ha, ha! (*She laughs hysterically.*) Get away from me! (v, p. 76)

Again, attention is drawn to a deceiver's eyes. At the end of *The Heart is not Stone*, when Vera tells Potap that she will remarry after his death, he threatens to kill her and then: '*Looks into her eyes*', and—as if suddenly seeing the light—says that she should be able to live as she likes, considering all that she has borne from him while he was alive (v, p. 144). And *Incompatibility of Character* ends with Pol 'sitting down and staring fixedly' (ii, p. 168) at his self-deceiving mother, before attempting to convince her of the reality of their situation. He, too, is attempting to force her to look at reality.

Often, 'looking into the eyes' is used as a means of determining whether someone is speaking the truth. Thus Apollinariya in *The Heart is not Stone*, who cannot believe that Vera is as pious as she makes out, declares: 'We need to keep an eye on her, surely there's an 'orphan' of some sort' ... 'Look her in the eyes. I never believe the quiet ones. You know the proverb: still waters run deep' (v, pp. 91/2). Gurmyzhskaya in *The Forest*, trying to determine whether Bulanov is speaking the truth, cries: 'How do you know? Look into my eyes, look!' (iii, p. 321). In *Guilty without Guilt*, when Kruchinina is trying to learn the truth from Arina about what happened to her son, she is described as 'kneeling before her, and looking straight into her eyes' (v, p. 378). And at the end of *We All Have our Cross to Bear*, Krasnov asks Tat´yana to look him directly in the eyes and tell him whether she has been deceiving him: '... you look me straight in the eye and tell me what you have done to me' (ii, p. 447).

In *The Storm* and *The Ward*, two plays which have as their focus questions of freedom and a desire for escape, the use of 'seeing' words is connected to a sense of being watched and, as such, they are linked to the characters' lack of freedom. Thus in *The Storm*, in Act Two, Scene 2, Varvara talks of Tikhon's trip as an opportunity for him to get out of his mother's sight (ii, p. 229). In Act Three, Part 1, Scene 3, Boris talks of how everyone is always watching you in this town (ii, p. 240). And it is interesting that when Katya dreams of flying in Act Two, Scene 8, she dreams of flying 'unseen' (ii, p. 234). E.Kholodov has noted how 'Katerina's drama is completed before the eyes of the town. She confesses her betrayal to her husband in front of the people. People watch as she hurls herself from the precipice into the Volga.'[7]

In *The Ward*, in Act One, Scene 1, Nadya complains of how the mistress has a 'constant watch over us' (ii, p. 171); in Scene 3, Gavrilovna again uses the phrase 'they keep a close watch' (ii, p. 175); and in Act Three, Scene 3, she complains: 'But all she does is shout: watch, watch the girls!...' (ii, p. 195). In this play, Vasilisa is often linked to 'seeing' words—and it is her spying, her watching for others' misdemeanours, which gives her power. Her very first words in the play are 'I saw you, my friend, I saw you' (ii, p. 177); and it is interesting that when Ulanbekova accuses her of deliberately trying to cause upset (Act Two, Scene 2), Vasilisa responds: 'May my eyes burst!' (ii, p. 181)—as if losing her eyes would be her worst punishment.

Words and phrases connected to seeing are, of course, a common part of everyday phraseology. But if, as the previous chapters have argued, Ostrovsky had a particular interest in the theme of deception—the idea of things not being as they seem, of people failing to look beyond the superficial and 'see' things as they truly are—then the frequent use of words connected with seeing and blindness, often occurring at crucial points in his plays, does indeed take on a greater significance.

---

[7] E.G.Kholodov, 'A.N.Ostrovskii v 1855-1865 godakh', *PSS* ii, 675.

CHAPTER FIVE

The Psychological Level: Escape from Reality

> '"Seems." Yes, that's man.' *The Heart is not Stone* (v, p. 114)

S o far, this study has striven to demonstrate that the themes of deception, a concern with the superficial nature of appearance, and blindness to reality are central to Ostrovsky's drama. Apart from deception, these themes have been little-noted in traditional critical discussion of Ostrovsky's work (and even deception is infrequently mentioned). M.Manheim, for example, describes Ostrovsky's favourite themes as 'the position of women, the rise of the new class in Russia and the decay of the old one, the criticism of authority, the dignity of art, the dignity of man'[1]; whereas M.Hoover sees the important concerns in Ostrovsky's work as 'the theme of capitalism' and 'the theme of the woman sold in marriage'[2]; and I.Beasley also highlights the 'theme of money' and cites 'the degrading position of women as another favourite theme'.[3] Once again, all three critics concentrate on themes which have their basis in the specifics of nineteenth-century Russian society—a view emphasised by G.Vladykin when, expressing the traditional Soviet interpretation of Ostrovsky's work, he states that 'the main conflict in [Ostrovsky's] work is between the wealthy and the unfortunate, the oppressed. His best works are a passionate protest against the social system.' He goes on

---

[1] Manheim, 322.
[2] Hoover, 35.
[3] Beasley, *Slavonic and East European Review*, 610.

to cite the central themes of Ostrovsky's work as 'the power of money and family despotism'.[4]

Even where themes such as deception, blindness to reality and superficiality of appearance are discussed, it is often in relation to the context of mid-nineteenth-century Russian life. Certainly critics who concur with the 'social criticism' interpretation of Ostrovsky's work can, and do, see such elements in his plays as further examples of the grim social reality of the time. Thus the prevalence of deception in his work reflects the cheating and corruption inherent in nineteenth-century Russia, while concern with appearance and blindness to reality reflect the frivolity of society and the lack of proper education. L.Cox, discussing the widespread deception in *It's All in the Family*, sees its cause as 'social determinism' and notes that 'the final impression given by the play is that no change is possible in the world ... because the characters ... are automatons, mechanically acting on the basis of the prevalent external standards and devoid of any inner values which are strong enough to cause them to even question seriously, much less begin to withstand the "general conditions of life".'[5] Discussing the hypocrisy in *The Forest*, she notes that 'the title 'The Forest' is taken for granted by most critics as symbolic of Russia'[6]; while she sees *Even Wise Men Err* as criticising a 'society where a clever outsider cannot be valued in his own right, but has to use deceptive means'.[7] Some critics have even gone so far as to complain that the characters of Neschastlivtsev and Schastlivtsev in *The Forest* detract from the real subject of the play which they cite as a social study of the landed gentry, thus completely overlooking the significance of role-play in the work.[8]

However, if you apply the same principle that was employed in the section on realism and idealism; if you take a step back from the 'there and then' and remove the social and historical context; you are again left with a much more universal reading of Ostrovsky's work. His web of deception, self-delusion and blindness-to-reality are, indeed, closely drawn universal human psychological reactions. At

---

[4] Vladykin, 'A.N.Ostrovskii', v.

[5] Cox, 73.

[6] *Ibid.*, 169.

[7] *Ibid.*, 100.

[8] See J.Patouillet, *Ostrovski et son théâtre de moeurs russes* (Paris: Plov-Nourit et cie, 1912), 270.

certain points in our lives, we all deceive, role-play, delude ourselves and see only that which we wish to. As Apollinariya states in *The Heart is not Stone*: "'Seems." Yes, that's man. What he needs, so he seems: where he needs to be submissive, so he seems submissive. Where he needs to be lively, so he is lively. Where he needs to cry, he cries; and where he needs to dance, he dances. Every man, if not a fool, is a swindler, and every swindler has his profit' (v, p. 114).

What Ostrovsky is depicting are escape mechanisms—means of avoiding or escaping from a reality which his characters find unpleasant or unbearable. As such they relate closely to the exploration of the relationship between realism and idealism in his plays, acting as a means of reconciling the gulf between the real and the ideal. And the means of escape he employs are not limited to nineteenth-century Russia, but are universally recognisable.[9]

Avoiding Reality: The World of Fantasy

The psychological element of Ostrovsky's work is demonstrated by the overwhelming emphasis on daydreams and fantasy present in his plays. We saw in *The Poor Bride* that, by the end of the play, Mar´ya had retreated into a world of self-delusion.[10] She believed, without any basis in reality, that she could change and re-educate Benevolensky. In order to make the reality of her marriage more bearable, she retreats into a world of fantasy. Such retreat into fantasy worlds is a common feature of Ostrovsky's drama. His works are full of characters who dream of escaping or changing their current circumstances. Some of these characters were met with earlier in the

---

[9] Many of the mechanisms employed by Ostrovsky are recognised psychological behaviours. Role-play, for example, is widely accepted as the basis for much social interaction and, at a more extreme level, can also be seen as evidence of psychological disorder [Frank A.Johnson, for example, describes the schizoid personality as someone 'who looks upon himself as a collection of roles rather than a self'. See 'Some Problems of Reification in Existential Psychiatry: Conceptual and Practical Considerations' in *Theories of Alienation: Critical Perspectives in Philosophy and Social Sciences* ed. by R.Felix Geyer and David R.Schweitzer (Leiden, 1976), pp. 77-102 (p. 92).] Similarly 'coping mechanisms' such as fantasy, denial, self-deception and self-justification are widely acknowledged psychological behaviours. Useful studies include: Eric Berne, *Games People Play: The Psychology of Human Relationships* (London: Penguin, 1968) and Elliot Aronson, *The Social Animal*, 5th edn (New York: W.H.Freeman, 1988)

[10] See p. 28.

section on realism and idealism: Nadya in *The Ward*, for example, who dreams of finding a good husband; or Zhadov in *A Lucrative Post*, who dreams of a world where 'bribetakers fear the court of society, more than the court of law' (ii, p. 110). There are numerous further examples. In *It's All in the Family*, for instance, Lipochka daydreams of going to dances and meeting handsome men:

> How pleasant these dances are! Very good indeed! What could be more delightful? You go to the assembly, or to someone's wedding. You sit down. Naturally, you are dressed all in flowers, like a doll or a picture in a magazine. Suddenly a young man comes dashing up: 'May I have the pleasure?' Well, you see, if he's a man of understanding, or someone from the military, then you accept, and lowering your eyes a little, you answer: 'Of course, with pleasure!' Ah! ...' (i, p. 86) I picture it to myself: suddenly a soldier is courting me, suddenly we have a ceremonial betrothal, candles burn everywhere, there are waiters in white gloves. I, naturally, am in a tulle or gauze dress. Then suddenly they begin to play a waltz—oh, how confused I am in front of him! Agh, what shame! Where will I put myself? What will he think? He'll say: 'What an uneducated little fool!'... (i, pp. 86/7)

Meanwhile, in the same play, Podkhalyuzin dreams of marrying Lipochka:

> What fantasies crawl into a man's head! Of course, Olimpiada Samsonovna is an educated young lady; and you could say there's no-one on earth like her. But that young man won't take her now; he'll say: 'Give me money!' and where are they going to get it from? ... I'll go and bow down to Samson Silych ... Why shouldn't he give her to me? I'm a man, aren't I? ... And besides, Samson Silych has entrusted his house and shops to me, I can threaten not to give them back ... (i, p. 109)

On both occasions their daydreams are a means of escaping the harsh realities of their lives. For Podkhalyuzin, his dreams are a means of escaping his life as the downtrodden clerk of a tyrannical master, whereas for Lipochka, marriage is an escape route from her position as the daughter of an uncultured 'samodur': 'Oh, if you knew, Lazar Elizarych, what my life here is like! For Mama there are seven Fridays in the week, and Papa, when he isn't drunk, just keeps quiet, but when he's drunk then he'll beat you as soon as look at you.

How's a cultivated young lady meant to bear it? But if I could marry a nobleman, then I could leave this house and forget all about it ...' (i, p. 135).

Similarly, in *Poverty is No Vice*, Mitya's dreams of love for Lyubov are a means of escape from reality. In Act One he frequently bemoans the difficulties of his life, before 'sinking into thought' and talking of Lyubov and his love for her. He uses his dreams of love as a way of avoiding the realities of his life.

In *Guilty without Guilt*, Kruchinina's daydreams about the past are a means of escaping from her believed reality that her son is dead. In Act Two, Scene 3, she talks of her 'strong imagination' (v, p. 376): 'It means nothing for me to transport myself seventeen years into the past, to imagine that I am sitting in my apartment, working. Suddenly I feel lonely, I grab my shawl and rush off to visit my son; I play with him, talk to him. I can imagine him so vividly' (v, p. 376). She notes: 'I am a strange woman, my emotions have complete control over me; their power is so great that they often lead to hallucinations' (v, p. 377). And when Dudukin suggests that she should take treatments to cure her hallucinations, she replies: 'I don't want to be cured. I enjoy my illness. It is pleasant for me to conjure up the image of my son, to talk to him, to think that he is alive. Sometimes I sit with such fear and trembling, expecting him to appear in front of me' (v, p. 377). The play is full of somewhat heavy-handed irony, as Dudukin reminds her that her dreams are just that—dreams—and that if her son should suddenly materialise in the flesh, he would not be the angelic little boy she remembers but 'a great hulking fellow like Neznamov, unshaven, stinking of cheap cigarettes and brandy' (v, p. 377). Later in the same scene, she again daydreams of her little boy, exclaiming: 'There, there he is, how I see him now!' (v, p. 378) just as Neznamov enters. At the end of the play, it emerges that Neznamov is indeed her long-lost son.

Larisa in *Without a Dowry* is another character who sinks into daydream as a means of avoiding the reality of her position. Like Nadya and Lipochka before her, her dreams are of escape. Forced into a humiliating engagement to the foolish Karandyshev, she pleads desperately with him to make arrangements for them to leave for the country (her constant refrain: 'To the country, to the country' will be echoed some years later in Masha's cries of 'To Moscow, to

Moscow' in Chekhov's *Three Sisters*). She notes: 'For a long time now I've looked at everything around me as if seeing it in a dream ... I must leave, tear myself away from here ... I want to walk through the woods, to pick berries and mushrooms ...' Her mother responds: 'So that's why you've got yourself a little basket! I understand now. You could get yourself a straw hat with a wide brim as well. Then you'll be a shepherd girl' (v, p. 34). Thus Larisa's desire for escape is reflected on three different levels: she has removed herself from reality—her 'real' life is 'like a dream'; she wishes for physical escape also—to go 'to the country'; and she wishes to construct for herself a new reality—to play the role of a 'shepherd girl'.

Ultimately, Larisa's means of escape from the realities of life is death. This is also the final escape route for another notable dreamer—Katya in *The Storm*. *The Storm* is full of characters who dream, and most of their dreams are quickly shown to be futile. Thus, Kuligin talks of his dreams of writing poetry but notes that 'they [the townsfolk] would eat me, swallow me alive' (ii, p. 215). He also dreams of discovering perpetuum-mobile: 'The English would give a million for it; I would use all the money for improving society, for supporting the people' (ii, p. 216); yet this too will never be realised. When Boris asks: 'Have you any hope of discovering perpetuum-mobile?' Kuligin replies: 'Without fail, sir, I have only to acquire some money for my model.' Yet in Act Four, Scene 2, he is shown failing to secure ten roubles from Dikoi to erect a sundial on the promenade. As Boris goes on to say: 'It's a shame to disillusion him! He has his dreams and is happy' (ii, p. 216).

Katya, however, is by far the most significant dreamer. As before, her daydreams all revolve around freedom, the desire for escape. In Act One, Scene 7, she talks of how she wishes she could fly: '... You know, I sometimes think that I am a bird. When you stand on the top of a hill, then you so long to fly' (ii, p. 221). She talks of her life before she was married—how they used to go to church; how their house was always full of pilgrims and beggars: 'I lived with nothing to grieve over, as free as a bird ... It was such a good life!' When Varvara points out that they do the same sort of things here, Katya replies: 'Ah, but here it is all seems to be forced' (ii, p. 221)—again, the concern is with freedom, free will.

Katya states that when she used to go to church:

> It was just as if I had entered paradise, I didn't see the people around me, I wasn't aware of the passage of time, or of the service ending ... And you know, on sunny days, such a column of light came down from the cupola and the smoke mingled with it, just like clouds, and it was as if I saw angels flying and singing among these clouds ... And what dreams I had, Varen´ka, what dreams! Either golden temples, or fantastic gardens, and invisible voices singing, and the scent of cypresses, and hills and trees, not at all like ordinary ones, but like those painted on icons. And always as if I was flying, flying through the air. (ii, pp. 221/2)

Again, Katya's dreams involve removal from reality. When she was in church she 'didn't see the people' around her; she was 'unaware of the passage of time'; and the trees and hills in her dreams were not like 'ordinary ones, but like those painted on icons'. Katya goes on to say: 'I still have dreams sometimes, but not very often and not the same kind' (ii, p. 222). She talks of her sense of fear and dread, her belief that she is going to die soon:

> I get a dream creeping into my head that I can't escape from. I try to think, but I can't gather my thoughts; I try to pray, but I can't. I babble words, but my mind is full of something else - it is as if the devil is whispering in my ear; and always about such terrible things. And sometimes I imagine things that make me so ashamed of myself ... At night I can't sleep, it is as if there is some kind of murmuring whisper: someone talks to me so caressingly, so sweetly, it's as if a dove is cooing. I don't dream of the trees and hills of paradise, like before, Varya; but of someone embracing me so passionately, and leading me somewhere, and I go with him, I go ... (ii, p. 222)
>
> And the thought comes to me that if I had my way, I would set out along the Volga in a boat, singing, or in a troika, with somebody's arms embracing me ... (ii, p. 223)

In Act Two, Scene 8, Katya wishes that she had children, and then again talks of escape: 'It would have been better if I had died when I was little. I would look down on the earth from heaven, and would take pleasure in everything. Or I would fly about unseen wherever I wished. I would fly down into a field and flit from cowslip to cowslip, blown by the wind, like a butterfly. (*Becomes lost in thought*)' (ii, p. 234).

Katerina's love affair with Boris is, of course, a fulfilment of her fantasy, a momentary escape from reality. Interestingly, their initial meeting in the ravine is closely linked with dreaming. Whilst waiting for Katerina to arrive, Boris exclaims: 'It is precisely as if I was dreaming!' (ii, p. 245); and on parting, Katerina's last words to him are: 'Tell me what you dream about tonight!' (ii, p. 248).

In the discussion of *The Ward* it was noted that during her love scene with Leonid, Nadya seemed to fix her eyes on him to the exclusion of all else, as if she were trying to avoid reality and live out her dream of love and happy marriage.[11] A similar phenomenon occurs in *The Storm*, which has an interesting use of 'seeing' language. Throughout the play, Katerina is frequently described as having her eyes closed, lowered, or as covering her face. Thus in Act One, Scene 9, she is described as 'screwing up her eyes' (ii, p. 224); in Act Two, Scene 2, she is twice described as 'lowering her eyes' (ii, pp. 227 and 228), and then 'lowering her eyes still further' (ii, p. 228). In the next Scene, Katerina is described as 'lowering her eyes to the ground' (ii, p. 230); and in Scene 4, as 'covering her face with her hands' (ii, p. 231). In Act Four, Scene 3, Varvara tells Boris that Katya 'dares not lift her eyes to her husband' (ii, p. 253). It is as if she cannot bear to face the reality of the world around her and instead lives in her dream world, seeing her visions.

In contrast, when Varvara gives Katya the key at the end of Act Two—thus enabling her to meet Boris—Katya cries: 'I would die just to see him' and 'come what may, I will see Boris' (ii, p. 235). Boris too emphasises his wish just to see Katya. In Act Three, Part 1, Scene 3, he says: 'If only I could just have one glimpse of her' (ii, p. 240). When Katya first comes to meet Boris, she keeps her eyes lowered. She is described as 'covered in a large white shawl, her eyes lowered to the ground' and initially she refuses to raise her eyes. Her decision to give in to her love for him is marked by the words 'She raises her eyes and looks at Boris' (ii, p. 246), and later in their conversation she declares: 'I was lost as soon as I saw you' (ii, p. 247). After Tikhon returns, Katya seems almost to become obsessed with seeing Boris again. Varvara describes her as 'wandering about the house as

---

[11] See p.18.

if looking for something. Her eyes like a madwoman's' (ii, p. 253). And in her final meeting with him in Act Five, she states: 'That was all I needed, to see you again' (ii, p. 262), and then repeats: 'That's it, well, and now I've seen you.' When Boris goes to leave she cries: 'Stop, stop! Let me look at you one last time' and is described as 'gazing into his eyes'; and as he walks away she is described as 'following him with her eyes' (ii, p. 263). Again she appears to be concentrating on Boris—her fantasy figure, the embodiment of her dreams—to the exclusion of reality. After Boris—her living dream—has left, she 'becomes lost in thought' about her final dream—that of a 'pleasant grave under a tree, warmed by the sun, watered by the rain, covered with soft, silky grass and colourful flowers' (ii, p. 263).

Perhaps the greatest dreamer of all, however, is Bal´zaminov, the comic hero of three plays, one of which is even entitled *A Holiday Dream before Dinner*. Bal´zaminov is a consummate dreamer. A poor, rather stupid civil servant, he is constantly dreaming and daydreaming of a different reality, one in which he is wealthy, a person of high standing in society. He spends his time trying to make his dreams a reality by chasing after rich women. The importance of dreams is emphasised right from the start of the first play, *A Holiday Dream before Dinner*:

> **Bal´zaminov.** I forgot to tell you what a dream I had! ... Here, suddenly I see that it's as if I was riding in a wonderful carriage, and dressed very well, with taste—a black waistcoat, mama, with fine gold stripes—there were grey horses, I was travelling alongside a river ...
> **Bal´zaminova.** Horses mean lies, and a river—a conversation.
> **Bal´zaminov.** Listen what happened next, mama. Here, I dream that the driver pushes me, all in my new clothes, and there I am, straight into the dirt.
> **Bal´zaminova.** Dirt, that means wealth.
> **Bal´zaminov.** And what dirt, mama! Brrr ... and then I ... am in those clothes ... dirty all over. So my heart stood still! Wearing new clothes, imagine it!
> **Bal´zaminova.** That means gold. It means that you are going to come into great wealth.
> **Bal´zaminov.** Only if it comes true! I've had so many dreams like that: ones where I have lots of money, where I'm dressed so well, then I wake up and things are nothing like that at all. Once I dreamt

I was a general! How happy I was! No! I've given up believing in dreams. (ii, p. 115)

The emphasis on dreams goes on to increase in intensity and the last play of the trilogy, *You'll Find what you Seek*, overflows with references to dreams and dreaming; all of which highlight Bal´zaminov's attempts to avoid reality. Thus, even before Bal´zaminov enters the action, we learn that he is constantly sleeping—thereby blocking out reality: 'He sleeps easily, no other business is more important to him' (ii, p. 346). When he comes on stage it is to complain that Matrena, the cook, has disturbed a most wonderful dream: 'Matrena woke me up in the most interesting place! ... I was walking through a garden; a woman of incomparable beauty was coming to meet me and she says: 'Mr Bal´zaminov, I love and adore you! ...' And then, as if for a joke, Matrena goes and wakes me up. What a nuisance! Couldn't she have waited a bit longer? I would have been very interested to see what happened next. You wouldn't believe, mama, how much I want to finish that dream. Perhaps I should go back to sleep? Yes, I'm going to sleep, though very likely I won't dream it.' (ii, p. 348). Again, he is avoiding reality and concentrating on his dream world although, interestingly, he makes some attempt to bring that dream world into the real one, noting: 'What a nuisance! In my kind of business it's very important to have dreams like that, it could have been some kind of prophecy' (ii, p. 348). Later he talks of his dream of joining the army: '... you just imagine it, mama, all at once I am an officer, I'm swaggering down the street—yes, then I would swagger—suddenly I see a girl sitting at the window, I twirl my moustache ...' (ii, p. 349). And he then again emphasises how he uses his dreams to avoid reality. When his mother asks: 'And what are we meant to live on while you're off becoming an officer?' he responds: 'Ah, my God! I forgot about that, it went clean out of my head' (ii, p. 350).

Bal´zaminov places great importance on his dreams: 'That dream... if only it had gone on—damn that Matrena!—but I can expect something good to happen all the same. That dream ... mama, is highly significant, yes, highly!' (ii, p. 350). And even Bal´zaminova gets caught up in the importance of dreams, having a very vivid one herself by which she sets great significance. The full extent of Bal´zaminov's daydreaming is made clear in Picture Three, shortly before he succeeds in realising his dream and marries a rich widow:

Bal´zaminova. How dark it's got, I'm going to order the fire to be lit.

Bal´zaminov. Wait, mama! There's no need for a fire, it's better in the dark.

Bal´zaminova. What's better about sitting in the dark?

Bal´zaminov. You can dream better in the dark, mama. It is possible to dream by firelight, but you have to screw up your eyes. In the dark you can do it just like this, with eyes open. At the moment I can picture everthing just as I would like it to be. I can get a perfect picture of myself either in a coach or a garden. But as soon as you bring in the candle, then I see straight off that in reality I am sitting in a poor room with terrible furniture ... and everything just fades away. Yes, I look at myself and I see that I am absolutely not how I see myself in my dreams.

Bal´zaminova. What are you like in your dreams?

Bal´zaminov. In my dreams, mama, I imagine that I am tall and well-built, with dark hair.

Bal´zaminova. Well, yes, that is better of course.

Bal´zaminov. Here, mama, I will describe to you what I imagine: at the moment I seem to be sitting in a hall by the window, in a velvet dressing gown. Suddenly my wife approaches...

Bal´zaminova. Well, what happens then?

Bal´zaminov. 'Darling, ' she says, 'let's go out for a walk.'

Bal´zaminova. And why not go out, so long as the weather's good.

Bal´zaminov. The weather is excellent, mama. I say: 'Go and get dressed, darling, and I will come in a minute. Valet!' The servant comes in. 'I'm getting dressed, ' I say, 'go and get the light blue cloak with the velvet lining!' I don't really like him, mama, he has a funny smile, sort of offensive, as if he's laughing at me ... (ii, pp. 379/80)

The Bal´zaminov plays are farces. They contain much slapstick comedy and humour as the hapless Bal´zaminov chases after his dreams, yet despite this, they are grounded in a universal psychological reality. As M.Manheim notes, much of the humour in the plays derives from 'the perception of ourselves as as foolish as the characters. All of us, like the hero, dream when we cannot change reality.'[12] Similarly, the intensification of dreaming throughout the trilogy is psychologically true. Bal´zaminov 'dreams more and more as he meets defeat after defeat' until the last play, when he 'is by now dreaming more than he is living in reality'. 'This clown-hero is made sympathetic, his yearnings and deficiencies linked to our own, his resilience in the face of defeat a pattern of hope. Mitya Bal´zaminov ... is not only a vaudeville clown, but a human being.'[13]

Avoiding Reality: Crossing Class Boundaries

A significant feature of the dreams of escape depicted in Ostrovsky's plays is the desire to cross class boundaries. Many of the dreamers in his plays fantasize about escaping their present reality by rising in rank and moving into a higher class. Thus Lipochka in *It's All in the Family* dreams of marrying an officer or a nobleman. She complains at her mother for sending away one of her suitors, noting: 'He was no merchant!' (i, p. 88), and later declares: 'I won't marry a merchant, not for anything! ... No, no, find him where you like, but get me a nobleman!' (i, p. 93). The principal theme of *Don't Get Above Yourself* is, as the title suggests, a warning against Avdot´ya's dreams of crossing ranks and marrying a nobleman. Similarly, the clash between Krasnov and his wife in *We All Have our Cross to Bear* arises, to a large extent, out of the characters' dreams of bettering themselves. For Tat´yana and Luker´ya, their dreams of acquaintance with 'nobles' such as Babaev have as their basis the desire for escape from the unpleasant 'peasant' reality in which they find themselves. So their memories of the time they spent at Babaev's mother's house were of an 'earthly paradise!' (ii, p. 395). Ironically, while Babaev admires Tat´yana as a 'simple girl', for Krasnov she is the embodiment of his dreams of bettering himself and his family. Consequently he bestows on her precisely those qualities of nobility and education which she admires and aspires to in Babaev. (Krasnov refers to his wife using the formal 'vy'—further evidence that he considers her to be of higher social status.) It is surely not without significance that, when Krasnov is finally awake to Tat´yana's deceit,

---

[12] Manheim, 226.
[13] *Ibid.*, 267, 274, 276.

Ostrovsky has him say: 'Did I only dream of those beautiful days?' (ii, p. 447).

An Old Friend is Better than Two New Ones is another play which has dreams of crossing class boundaries at its centre. Olin´ka daydreams of life married to Vasyutin, a wealthy titular counsellor. In turn, his mother wishes him to marry an educated noblewoman in order to improve his status still further: 'In everything I do, I try to ennoble him a little ... Now he will marry an educated noblewoman, and everything will be done quite differently in this place' (ii, p. 287). The character of Pulkheriya, who has indeed managed to marry above her rank, and who is determined to look down on her former friends and acquaintances, highlights further the obsession with rank at the heart of the play.

Strikingly, dreams of crossing class boundaries are always couched in terms of appearance. The characters dream of the trappings of high rank—the clothes they will wear, the carriages they will drive around in. Thus Olin´ka boasts: 'How I will dress then! I won't need to learn taste, I'm a dressmaker myself' (ii, p. 269). And her mother tells Pulkheriya: 'Yes, wait a little and we will show you! My daughter and I will be dressed to kill, and will drive around in our carriage and horses' (ii, p. 309). Lipochka, in her dreams, is 'naturally in a tulle or gauze gown' (i, p. 86). She concentrates on the appearance of her 'dream' admirers:

> ... it's best of all to dance with army men! Ah, charming! Wonderful! Their moustaches and their epaulettes, their uniforms, and some of them even have spurs with little bells. Only it kills me that they don't wear their sabres. Why do they take them off? God, it's strange! They themselves just don't understand how much more charming they'd look! If they just looked at their spurs, the way they jingle, especially when some uhlan or colonel is showing off—it's a marvel! ... (i, p. 86)

And Podkhalyuzin finally persuades her to marry him by concentrating on appearance:

> ... But if you should marry me, Olimpiada Samsonovna, here's my promise: you'll go about in silk dresses, even at home. And when you go out visiting, and to the theatre, then we shan't dress you in anything but velvets. As for hats and cloaks, we won't look at what's usual for the gentry, but will get you the finest ever! We'll

get horses from the Orlov stud. (*Silence.*) And if it's my looks you have doubts about, then I'll dress just as you want. I'll wear a dress coat, and trim my beard or even cut it right off, whatever's the fashion. It's all the same to me. (i, p. 134)

Bal′zaminov's fantasies all involve appearance. In *A Holiday Dream before Dinner*, he talks of life after marrying his dream rich bride: 'Here's what: firstly, I would have made for myself a pale blue cloak with a black velvet lining. You need only imagine, mama, how well pale blue suits me! Then I would buy myself a grey horse ... and I would ride all over Zatsepa ...' (ii, p. 114). In his day-dreams in *You'll Find what you Seek*, he is wearing 'a velvet dressing gown', he calls the valet and cries: 'go and get the light blue cloak with the velvet lining' (ii, p. 380)—again the emphasis is on externals such as clothes and carriages.

The reason for this emphasis on the external relates to Ostrovsky's concern with the superficial nature of appearance. Ostrovsky makes the dreamers couch their fantasies of crossing class boundaries in terms of the external trappings of wealth in order to demonstrate that underneath they will remain the same as they have always been. Despite all her dreams of becoming a cultivated lady, Lipochka will remain the daughter of an ignorant boorish merchant: 'she writes like an elephant crawling on its belly; with both French and the piano, it's a bit here and a bit there, and there's nothing much at all; well, and when she starts to dance ...' (i, p. 117). Even when she and Podkha-lyuzin seem to have realised their dreams—they appear in Act Five dressed in all the latest fashions and living in a luxurious apartment—their rise in rank is little more than an illusion. Underneath, they remain the same uncultured merchants they have always been.

Similarly Tat′yana's and Luker′ya's dreams in *We All Have our Cross to Bear* serve only to emphasise how far removed they are from their aspirations. Despite their condescension towards Krasnov and his family, they themselves are from the petty middle-class. Their father was a minor clerk. Afonya and Ul′yana are constantly accusing them of putting on airs and of being no better than they are themselves. More tellingly, Babaev also distinguishes between Tat′yana and his 'own sort': '... women in general like to suffer, it's in their character; ... of course, that doesn't apply to Tanya. She seems to be overjoyed that I've come. I was talking about women of our rank' (ii, p. 402).

Ironically, the very nature of these characters' dreams of social climbing—their concern with the appearance of wealth—shows how rooted they are in their social class. K.Derzhavin notes: 'From the offended Bal´zaminov's stories of the 'uncouth' stall-owners and his complaints about the 'ignorance' that rules in Zamoskvorech´e comes not protest, but dreams of having a pale-blue cloak with a velvet lining, like a symbol of petty-bourgois life-affirmation... Bal´zaminov is one of the most complete pictures of petty-bourgeois vulgarity and the triviality of the petty-bourgeois world outlook in our literature.'[14] And L.Cox concurs: 'Bal´zaminov's dreams are the ultimate indication of his inability to transcend. Even in his subconscious, at his deepest imaginative level, his ideal is trite, a cliché.'[15] Typically, Cox sees this as yet another example of Ostrovsky criticising the prevailing social reality: 'For in Bal´zaminov's striving for something higher which is in itself vulgar and banal, can be seen how the vulgar atmosphere reduces aspirations to banality.'[16] Yet the argument that the attainment of the dream is often as illusory as the dream itself certainly has some force. When, after finally capturing his rich bride, Bal´zaminov declares: 'I am now not Bal´zaminov, I am someone quite different' (ii, p. 388), his words are full of irony. Bal´zaminov's transformation, as with Lipochka and Podkhalyuzin in *It's All in the Family*, Olin´ka, Vasyutin and Pulkheriya in *An Old Friend is Better than Two New Ones* and even Gordei Tortsov in *Poverty is No Vice*, will be limited to the wearing of a new set of clothes. The inner character remains unchanged.

Avoiding Reality: Fantasy Role-Players

The fantasists described above use the act of dreaming as their escape mechanism. They momentarily escape from the realities of life by sinking into reverie and dreaming of a different, better reality. Some characters, however, bring fantasy into the real world, adopting a

---

[14] K.N.Derzhavin, 'A.N.Ostrovskii', in *Russkie dramaturgi XVIII-XIX vv.*, ed. B.Bursova, 3 vols (Leningrad-Moscow: Iskusstvo, 1962), III, 75-163 (p. 97).
[15] Cox, 91.
[16] *Ibid.*, 93.

fantasy persona in real life. Indeed, a significant number of Ostrovsky's characters seem to get so wrapped up in their fantasy roles that they appear to believe that those dreams are indeed reality. Bal´zaminov slips momentarily into this state in *You'll Find what you Seek* when, having been deceived by Luk´yan and Raisa, he declares: 'I was all in a fog. It seemed to me that if she loved me and agreed to elope with me, then a carriage would appear all by itself and I would take her to our house.' Bal´zaminova asks: 'To this apartment?' and Bal´zaminov responds: 'You won't believe how it was, mama. I imagined that we had our own house, a stone one, on Tverskoi' (ii, p. 386). Mar´ya in *The Poor Bride* looks in danger of slipping into such a state when she talks of re-educating Benevolensky. Similarly Larisa in *Without a Dowry* slips into a fantasy world when she talks of playing the shepherdess.

Such characters are often deceivers. However, they differ from the role-players discussed earlier in 'The Web of Deception', as their role-playing does not appear to be conscious. Rather than entering into role-play deliberately—as a specific means to a specific end—they appear to adopt their roles involuntarily, as a means of reconciling the conflict between their inner dreams and desires and the realities of their position in life.

Ippolit in *All Good Things Come to an End* is one such fantasy role-player. A meek and timid clerk (as often with Ostrovsky, this name—which derives from the mythological Greek hero, Hippolytus—resounds with irony), he is mocked for his cowardice by his own fiancée, Agniya: 'Shame on you, shame on you for being so cowardly!' (iii, p. 350) and she refers to him as a 'little boy' (ii, p. 362). Faced with losing Agniya or demanding the salary owed to him by his 'samodur' uncle and master, Akhov, Ippolit disappears to get drunk and suddenly reappears adopting the role of a romantic hero. Whilst under this guise, he confronts his uncle and threatens to kill himself unless his uncle gives him the money to which he is entitled. With no sign of any conscious deliberation, Ippolit drops his weak and cowardly persona and instead adopts the melodramatic tones and gestures of a world-weary romantic hero. Thus in Act Three, Scene 1, he tells the housekeeper, Feona, that his previous melancholy was due to 'love, extraordinary love' (iii, p. 370); and he berates her for trying to advise him: '... What have you seen of the world? About a yard around you! I know everything about this business. What understanding have you of life or love? None at all! Have you got any education or any of these fine feelings? What have you got in you? Ingrained habit, that's all! And you are trying to tell me how to live, ... although I have reached the full ripeness of age and everything!' (ii, p. 372). He finishes the scene with a melodramatic declaration of impending doom:

> **Ippolit.** It is all over! Good-bye forever!
> **Feona.** Surely you don't really want to leave us?
> **Ippolit.** And even so, my eyes will close on life, and my heart will cease to beat!
> **Feona.** What are you talking about? You're not making any sense!
> **Ippolit** (*shaking his head, sorrowfully*). Black raven, why dost thou hover over my head!
> **Feona.** Good God! Are you in your right mind?
> **Ippolit.** It is all over! Good-bye forever!
> **Feona.** Ah, Apolitka, Apolitka, you're a good lad, but why do you put on such airs? Why are you saying such crazy things, assuming such an air of importance?
> **Ippolit.** This is beyond your understanding. There are people who are dull and stagnated; but others wish to be higher in their thought and feelings.
> **Feona.** You may have left the stupid folks, but you haven't caught up with the clever ones, so you're left dangling!
> **Ippolit.** Well, all right then. Let me know when uncle wakes up. It is all over! Good-bye forever! (iii, pp. 372/3)

Ippolit continues his role during the meeting with his uncle in Act Three, Scene 3:

> **Ippolit... .** Despair alone is acting in me now. I was a man, but soon I will become one with the earth. What use is money, you can't take it with you!
> **Akhov.** It's true you can't take it. Only I think it would be a better arrangement if I just tie you up now.
> **Ippolit.** It's too late to bind me now!
> **Akhov.** No, I think it's just the right time.
> **Ippolit.** You are mistaken.
> **Akhov.** Really? And what are you going to do?

Ippolit (*taking the knife from his pocket*). Here you are right now! One strike ... (*he indicates his own throat*) and I'm dust!
Akhov (*in fright*). What are you doing, you scoundrel? What are you doing! (*He stamps his feet.*)
Ippolit. My eyes will close forever and my heart will cease to beat!
Akhov. I'll get you! I'll get you! (*Stamping.*)
Ippolit. How can you frighten me, uncle, when I myself find no joy in living? My hope has died, my love is over—that means everything is finished! Ha, ha, ha! I will now sacrifice my life so that people will know what a tyrant you are to your own kinsfolk. (iii, p. 378)

Ippolit's role-playing is made clear by the constant references to him 'not being himself'. In the extract quoted above between Ippolit and Feona, Feona asks: 'Are you in your right mind?' and talks of Ippolit 'putting on airs'; and indeed when she first sees him at the start of Act Three, she declares: 'It's as if you ... weren't in your right mind?' (iii, p. 371). When talking to his uncle in Act Three, Scene 3, Ippolit himself says: 'Excuse me, uncle! I'm not myself at the moment, my head's in a whirl' (iii, p. 380). Ippolit's constant repetition of stock phrases—'It is all over! Good-bye forever!' and 'My eyes will close forever and my heart will cease to beat!'—also suggests that he is playing a role, and even his use of poetry—'Black raven, why dost thou hover over my head!'—comes from a favourite ballad of inn guitarists.[17] Ostrovsky's principal aim here is surely humour. He is parodying the traditional romantic hero, reducing him to the level of farce (the contrast between Ippolit's melodramatic tones and the down-to-earth Feona and Akhov only serves to heighten the comic effect). Yet it is none the less significant that he chooses to make Ippolit use role-play in order to escape the reality of his true character.

A similar role-player is Apollon in *Wolves and Sheep* (again the name is that of a mythical hero—the Greek god Apollo). He practises deception in a futile attempt to mask his drunkenness. In Act One, Scene 4, Pavlin describes how Apollon 'takes his gun, pretending to go hunting, but goes straight to the village tavern' (iv, p. 119); and when Apollon himself enters (Scene 5), he is dressed as if for a hunt,

---

[17] See *PSS* iii, 551.

with Vlas, the houseboy, carrying his gun and hunting bag. Almost his very first words are to say how tired he is after the hunt, and when Pavlin points out that he does not appear to have bagged any game, he goes into a long explanation about the bad luck he experienced, before demanding some vodka, as he is 'feeling unwell' and must have 'caught a cold in the swamp' (iv, p. 121).

In many ways Apollon appears to live in a fantasy world, casting himself as some kind of romantic hero. His dog, Tamerlaine (named after the great Mongol warrior), whom he refers to as 'a lion, not a dog' (iv, p. 189), but whom the other characters refer to as 'a mongrel' and 'the wolf's cutlet' (iv, p. 196), is a reflection of this. Apollon is full of swagger and boasting. He speaks very melodramatically and his conversation is scattered with appalling renditions of French phrases. His favourite words are 'parol donyor'—an attempt at 'parole d'honneur'—yet his actions show that his 'word of honour' leaves much to be desired. In Act One, Scene 7, when Murzavetskaya accuses him of wild antics in the pubs, he protests theatrically that people are spreading rumours about him. When it is clear that Murzavet´skaya does not believe him, he swears he will not touch another drop and boastfully offers to lay a bet with her that he will never drink again. Yet within minutes he is faking acute pains in his chest and claiming that he will die if he does not have just one last little drop. Similarly in Act Two, Scene 4, he is full of claims about how he can make women fall in love with him with just 'ten words', claiming that using more than ten is 'too dangerous' as the women start 'hurling themselves into rivers' (iv, p. 146). Yet when he is left alone with Kupavina, supposedly to seek her hand in marriage, he instead borrows five roubles from her to go and buy a drink. When he returns in Scene 5, he is so drunk that he mistakes Anfussa for Kupavina and continues paying court to her. When disabused of his mistake, he claims that it is he who has been 'terribly deceived' (iv, p. 164).[18]

In his article on 'play-actors' in Ostrovsky's drama, N.Henley suggests that the 'samodur' falls into this category of involuntary role-players. He notes: 'The samodur has much of the play-actor in him, but for him play-acting is not a means for reaching the top, it is

---

[18] M.Hoover notes the comedy of Apollon's character, which 'derives from the emptiness of his heroic mask'. (See Hoover, 99.)

his way of life. He believes in his role, for he himself is his role, all that he has to do is project himself onto society just as he is, whether society wants him or not.'[19] He does not, however, discuss whether such play-acting is a means of avoiding reality.

Avoiding Reality: Drunkenness

In the cases of Ippolit and Apollon discussed above, role-playing is on both occasions connected to drink. Indeed it could be argued that drink was largely responsible for the fantasising of the two characters. Drunkenness itself is frequently used in Ostrovsky's drama as another mechanism for escaping from, or coping with, reality. Thus in *An Old Friend is Better than Two New Ones*, we learn that Gavrilo, Vasyutin's father, has 'quite lost all sense from living a dissolute life' (ii, p. 288). Vasyutin and his friends all drink heavily and Vasyutin even goes so far as to state that he drinks 'so that there is fantasy in the head'.

> **Vasyutin.** Yes, Mama, I know it myself. One shouldn't turn up drunk at one's fiancée's house. It's a squalid thing to do. But the fantasy in the head is necessary. If I don't have fantasy what will I say to them, mama? What will I talk about? If I knew something, if I had read some books or something, then it would be a different business. But without that, I need fantasy.
> **Merchant.** Yes, it's better with fantasy.
> **Vasyutin.** I can never talk to women without fantasy, I approach them so timidly. But with a little fantasy, it's completely different. That's where bravery comes from! (ii, pp. 294/5)

Vasya in *You Can't Live as you Please* uses drink as an escape mechanism, drowning his sorrows over losing Grusha to Petr. When Grusha realises that Petr has been deceiving her, she too turns to alcohol. In *Difficult Days*, Andrei writes to Aleksandra to say that he will 'lose himself' if she does not come to meet him. When she asks what it means to 'lose yourself', he replies: 'It's very simple. You go on such a good drinking bout that you are immersed in it for the rest of your life' (ii, p. 459). Baraboshev in *Truth is Fine, but Luck is Better* declares: 'What wine I drank from grief!' (iv, p. 271), and in *The Poor Bride*, Khorʹkov finally sinks into drunkenness as his

---

[19] Henley, 'Ostrovskij's Play-Actors, Puppets, and Rebels', 319.

means of avoiding reality. When he makes his drunken confession of love for Mar´ya at the end of Act Four, Milashin notes: 'He's been drinking for four days; he went straightaway from you and started at it. He just paces the room, crying and drinking' (i, p. 264).

In *Poverty is No Vice*, Lyubim Tortsov is another character who uses drink as a means of escaping reality and Grisha says of Mitya's circumstances that 'a life like that could drive you to drink!' (i, p. 337). In *The Storm*, Tikhon uses drink to escape from reality. In Act One, Scene 6 he bemoans the difficulties of his life and Varvara declares: 'I can read in your eyes what you want ... to go to Dikoi's and have a drink with him' (ii, p. 220). In Act Two, Scene 2, Varvara, talking of Tikhon's trip, states: 'As soon as he's left he'll start drinking. This very minute he's listening to her and thinking of how quickly he can wrench free' (ii, p. 229). Tikhon himself talks of his trip as 'two weeks with no kind of threat hanging over me and no shackles on my feet' (ii, p. 231). In Act Five, Scene 1, he describes what he did while he was away, noting that 'as soon as I left I went on a spree. I was so glad that I'd torn free. I drank all the way to Moscow, and I drank all the time I was in Moscow ... not once did I remember the family ...' (ii, p. 258). He tells Kuligin: 'I've just called in at Dikoi's, well, to have a drink. I thought it would make things easier' and predicts that he will '... ruin the last of my wits with drink' (ii, p. 258).

As a final example, there is Miron in *The Unfree*. Miron is an alcoholic who harbours delusions of grandeur, fantasising a far more important role for himself than the reality of his position as a lowly servant. He tells the housekeeper Marfa that waiting on guests in the hall 'is not my place. I'm set much higher.' '... I do a really important job for the master! As a matter of fact I don't really know how much it is worth! But it really is very important!' (v, p. 169). As with Ippolit and Apollon before him, drink acts as a catalyst for Miron's fantasising, yet unfortunately for him, it also serves to remove him further from reality; he spends most of his time in drunken oblivion. As he states wryly in Act Three: 'It's my weakness! It's conquered me! Here, you need your eyes, but I have so flooded mine that I can't see this world. I can't even distinguish between day and night' (v, p. 193).

R.Reid has noted that 'the fact that much social activity can be interpreted in terms of role and performance would suggest that drama, uniquely among literary forms, is capable of interpreting and clarifying interpersonal relations rather than just fictionalising them.'[20] And indeed, the deception, role-playing, self-delusion and blindness to reality in Ostrovsky's work are not just examples of his realistic depiction of mid-nineteenth-century Russian society, but involve the study and portrayal of complex human psychological behaviours—behaviours which are universal in nature. As such, they undermine a further often expressed view of Ostrovsky's dramas—that they lack psychological content of any note. V.Terras, in his *History of Russian Literature*, speaks for many when he states that 'Ostrovsky's plays are objective representations of a reality that he knew intimately, without any shade of subjective involvement or any attempt at psychological complexity'[21]; as does A.V.Knowles, who criticizes Ostrovsky for the 'lack of psychological depth of his characters.'[22] Perhaps most famously, Prince Mirsky merely states bluntly that Ostrovsky 'is no psychologist'.[23]

Perhaps unsurprisingly, it is often those critics and scholars who have recognised Ostrovsky's universality who also note the psychological content of his work. L.Hanson, discussing *Talents and Admirers*, asserts that 'psychologically the play is faultless', before going on to praise its 'universal theme'.[24] Similarly D.Magarshack, discussing *Even Wise Men Err*, suggests that it is 'a play in which the characters lose their essentially Russian features and become common, general types of humanity', before noting that the play is 'a brilliant satire on Moscow upper class society, but also a satire on humanity at large'.[25] And P.Kropotkin, discussing *Poverty is No Vice*, states: 'This drama is so typically Russian that one is apt to overlook its broadly human signification. It seems to be typically Muscovite; but, change names and customs, change a few details and rise a bit higher or sink a bit lower in the strata of society; put, instead of the drunken

---

[20] Robert Reid, *Lermontov's 'A Hero of Our Time'* (London: Bristol Classical Press, 1997), 65.

[21] Terras, *History of Russian Literature*, 372.

[22] Knowles, 'Introduction', xii.

[23] Mirsky, 235.

[24] Hanson, xxx/xxxii.

[25] Magarshack, *Easy Money and two other plays*, 291.

Lyubim Tortsov, a poor relation or honest friend who has retained his common sense—and the drama applies to any nation and to any class of society. It is deeply human.'[26]

The critic I.Esam states of Ostrovsky: 'On the surface level, [he] set his plays in the kind of environment familiar to his audience. But if one reads 'Zapiski zamoskvorech´ego zhitelya' ['Notes of a Zamoskvorech´e Inhabitant'], where indirectly Ostrovsky first states his artistic beliefs, it appears that his choice of the merchant setting is not for ideological reasons, but in order to depict the human soul in search of its identity struggling against the stifling oppression of *byt*.'[27]

Here, perhaps, is the key to appreciating fully Ostrovsky's drama. The emphasis should not, as has usually been the case, be placed on the specifics of the social setting, on the specifics of the *byt* (or everyday reality), but rather on the human reaction to it. His plays depict a universal human condition: 'the human soul in search of its identity'.

---

[26] P.Kropotkin, *Ideals and Realities in Russian Literature* (London: Duckworth, 1905), 205. Similarly, Eugene Bristow, who also asserts the universality of Ostrovsky's work, notes: 'The work of social scientists has been used recently as a way to examine drama, and Ostrovsky's plays readily lend themselves to this kind of analysis.' (He too cites Eric Berne's *Games People Play* as a useful study.) See Bristow, *Five Plays of Alexander Ostrovsky*, 24.

[27] I.Esam, 'Folkloric Elements as Communication Devices. Ostrovsky's Plays', *New Zealand Slavonic Journal*, 2 (1968), 67-88 (p. 71).

CHAPTER SIX

The Blurring of Reality and Illusion: What is Reality?

> 'Only Kseniya ... does not
> think about life ... as she is
> not of this world.' *Not of
> this World* (v, p. 438)

S o far, this study has aimed to demonstrate that the exploration
of reality in Ostrovsky's drama goes beyond the social level to
incorporate a considerable psychological content. Yet the theme of
reality in his plays transcends both these levels to raise questions of a
philosophical nature. The web of deceit, conscious and subconscious
role-play, the superficial nature of appearance, the suggestion that
things are not as they initially seem, are not only a realistic depiction
of social mores, nor simply an exploration of universal human behaviour. These elements all serve further to create a sense of uncertain
reality. As an Ostrovsky play unfolds, both the audience and the protagonists are frequently forced to reassess their perceptions of reality:
is that character really who he or she claims to be? Are events and
situations really as they first appear? We are left with a sense of
insecurity about the true nature of the world depicted on the stage: are
events and characters 'real' or are they merely a consciously (or subconsciously) created illusion? Indeed, with the presence of dreams
and fantasy role-players, Ostrovsky goes beyond the depiction of
uncertain reality to question the very nature of reality and to ask
whether such a thing as a comfortably defined 'reality' actually
exists.[1]

---

[1] The difficulty in differentiating between dream and reality has long been a subject of
philosophical debate. The philosopher Bertrand Russell, for example, noted: 'It is
obviously possible that what we call waking life may be only an unusual and persistent
nightmare, ' and went on to state: 'I do not believe that I am now dreaming, but I

The suggestion that Ostrovsky's plays challenge the notion of a comfortably defined reality is reinforced by the frequent blurring of the boundaries between real and fantasy worlds in his drama. This was first encountered in the idealists and blind-to-reality characters who frequently seem to adhere to beliefs which bear little relation to the world around them, and whose ideals are portrayed as little more than self-indulgent delusions. It is reinforced by the presence of fantasy role-players—characters who slip into fantasy worlds, momentarily living out their fantasies, such as Ippolit in *All Good Things Come to an End*, Mar'ya in *The Poor Bride*, Bal'zaminov in *You'll Find what you Seek*. Although such fantasising is a psychological behaviour—a mechanism for escaping an unpleasant reality—it also serves to raise questions about the nature of reality. Is the perceived reality (the 'fantasy') of such characters any less valid than the more generally accepted actuality?

Such a question is posed in *Not of this World*, a play which focuses on the blurring of reality and illusion. As Kseniya moves towards her death she becomes increasingly out of touch with the real world. She starts losing her voice, becomes forgetful, so that at times she does not know where she is, or why. Her dreams appear real to her; she imagines that there are snakes and frogs in her room; and she becomes tormented by seemingly irrational fears. One of these is her sudden terror of Murugov, an acquaintance of Vitalii's. The other characters in the play see Murugov as an amusing, easy-going companion:

> **Kochuev.** Yes, he is the kindest of men.
> **Elokhov.** He's never hurt a fly in his whole life. (v, p. 465)

But for Kseniya he takes on the persona of a terrifying demon who, she believes, has come to take away her soul. This belief reaches its climax as she lies dying:

> **Khoniya.** Your mama's arrived, and some other guests ... She's fallen asleep. (*Loudly*) Kseniya Vasil'evna, Kseniya Vasil'evna!
> **Kseniya** (*waking up*). Ah? What is it?
> **Khoniya.** Your mama's arrived, with some other guests. They're out in the hall. Vitalii Petrovich is there.

---

cannot prove that I am not.' See *The Encylopaedia Britannica*, vol 27, 15th edn (Chicago, 1997), 308.

Kseniya. Who's arrived? Is it him, is it him?
Khoniya. Who?
Kseniya. Murugov ... he's come for my soul ... don't let him come
to me ... call Vitalii Petrovich, he'll stand up for me ... there's a
snake here, a snake. (*Loudly*) Protect me! (*Falls on to the armchair,
unconscious.*) (v, p. 470)

Such behaviour by Kseniya is dismissed by the other characters in the
play as evidence of nervous hysteria, the delusions of a mortally ill
woman. It demonstrates her growing alienation from the 'real world'
until she finally reaches a position where she can no longer distinguish between reality and imagination. The boundaries between the
real world and her illusory world have become blurred. However,
Ostrovsky does not allow us to draw such simple, comfortable conclusions. Murugov's name does, in fact, link him with the devil. The
critic I.Esam has noted that the *mur* stem suggests the word *murin*
which Ostrovsky defined as 'the devil' in his *Material for a Dictionary
of Russian Popular Speech*. (She also notes that this links Murugov
with the 'dark and evil' Murin in Dostoevsky's *A Gentle Creature*).[2]
The connection is made stronger by the fact that Kseniya is the only
character in the play to refer to Murugov by his surname—which she
does throughout the play. The other characters use his first name and
patronymic. Murugov is indeed the person whose philosophy of life
poses the most direct threat to Kseniya and her belief in the overriding sanctity of the family. Whenever Kseniya is making headway
in her attempts to draw Vitalii into her world of piety and morals,
Murugov arrives to tempt him back to worldly pleasures of picnics
and parties. As V.Lakshin puts it: 'Even when [Vitalii] paints idyllic
pictures of family evenings and domestic unity, the rich, fast-living
Murugov springs up behind his back like a demon-tempter sent after
him to return him to the world he has deserted.'[3] Ostrovsky thus
includes enough hints in the play to suggest that Kseniya may not be
unjustified in her perception of Murugov as a threat to her ability to

---

[2] Esam states: 'Just as the sensitive Kseniya of 'Not of this World' cannot distinguish
between the 'reality' around her and the reality of her imagination in which she sees
Murugov as an evil spirit coming to claim her soul, so similarly in 'Khozyaika' the sick
and feverish Ordynov sees Murin as a dark and evil tyrant who craftily cheats the
'innocent little dove' Katerina into subjugation and captivity.' (See Esam, 'An analysis
of Ostrovsky's *Ne ot mira sego*', 70.)
[3] Lakshin, *PSS* v, 489.

live successfully with Vitalii. The question is raised as to whose perception of the 'real' Murugov is the right one.

Such a blurring of reality and illusion is a common feature of Ostrovsky's plays.[4] Krutitsky in *A Change in Fortune*, for example, is an extremely wealthy man who has created for himself and his family a false reality of extreme poverty. He hides his wealth even from his family, forcing them and himself to live in hunger and poverty, and he goes to the lengths of ordering his niece to beg in the streets for money for her dowry. The illusion of poverty is eventually revealed for what it is, but for Krutitsky it is already too late. He becomes increasingly paranoid at the thought of losing his money, so much so that he gradually sinks into madness—thus further removing himself from reality. Eventually he hangs himself over the loss of a few thousand roubles, despite the millions he has hidden away.

An Ardent Heart is a play of much confusion and blurring of reality and illusion. Numerous characters find themselves uncertain as to what is real and what is fantasy or created illusion. One of the main protagonists, Kuroslepov (whose name means 'night blindness') exists in an almost permanent half-awake, half-asleep state, and is constantly confused as to what is dream and what is real. As Silan states in Act One: 'He sleeps nights, he sleeps days. He's slept so much he doesn't understand anything, not a thing. He doesn't even see what's right under his nose. When he's just woken up, then what's real and what he's seen in a dream—he gets it all mixed up ...' (iii, p. 82).

When Kuroslepov first appears on stage he 'sits on the porch and spends a few minutes yawning', and then declares:

> And why was the sky falling? Well, if it falls, it falls. Or did I dream it? Try and guess what's going on in the world—is it morning or evening? And there's no-one about, may they rot! ... Matrena! That's when it's so frightening, when you don't know what's going on in the world ... it's terrifying. Was I dreaming or what? There was a lot of firewood stacked up, and devils. I asked them, 'What's all the wood for?' And they say: 'to roast sinners.' Could I be in hell? Where has everyone vanished to? What a fear I

---

[4] Eugene Bristow is one of the few critics to note this; discussing *It's All in the Family*, *The Poor Bride* and *The Forest*, he states that 'Ostrovsky manipulated the concepts of illusion and reality'. See Bristow, 23.

feel today! Is that the sky falling again? It is, it's falling ... Oh God! And now there are sparks. What if the end of the world is coming, right now! And no wonder! It could all very well happen ... there was a smell of tar somewhere, and somebody singing with a wild voice, and the sound of strings or a trumpet ... I just don't understand it.' (iii, p. 83)

Much deception is taking place under Kuroslepov's nose. His wife is having an affair with one of his assistants, Narkis, and is stealing money and wine from him; and a young neighbour, Vasya, is secretly visiting his daughter, Parasha. When Parasha runs away from home to follow Vasya into exile in the army, dream and reality really do become interwoven for Kuroslepov. In Act Five, Parasha returns to her father's house without his noticing her arrival. When he recalls her disgrace, the other characters in the play claim that Parasha's escapade was merely something Kuroslepov has dreamed, arguing that she has been at home all along (ii, p. 160).

Other characters in the play are taken in by the elaborate theatrical illusions of Khlynov and his entourage. Khlynov, a man who has more money than he knows what to do with, lives for constant amusement which is all connected to a desire to escape from the tedium of his lethargic life. Significantly, his means of amusement all involve play-acting, creating the illusion of different reality (when Vasya first stumbles into Khlynov's world he declares: 'This isn't life... !' (iii, p. 88)). Thus Vasya describes their dramatization of an old Russian folksong: 'They've fashioned this kind of play-boat. It's a proper boat, and it sails on the pond around an island. And on the island they've got wine and snacks laid out all ready. Alistarkh acts the host, all dressed up like a Turk. Three days in a row they played this game, then they got bored with it.' (iii, p. 89).

The other characters in the play fall victim to Khlynov's illusions. In the arrest scene in Act Two, Matrena believes that she is being attacked by pirates, yet the idea that there are pirates in the vicinity is an illusion, stemming from the play-acting of Khlynov. Similarly in Act Four, Khlynov and his retinue dress up as robbers and hide in the woods, capturing unsuspecting passers-by and forcing them to drink. Both Narkis and Parasha are taken captive in this way and both believe that they have really fallen into the hands of robbers. As discussed earlier, drunkenness is once again connected with a removal from reality. Khlynov and his group are constantly drinking, and they often force other people to drink—thereby removing them from reality also. Thus the 'robbers' force their victims to get drunk, ensuring, as with Ippolit and Apollon before them, that role-playing, the acting out of fantasies, is connected with drinking. When Kuroslepov and Gradoboev visit Khlynov in Act Four, he forces them to get drunk also. Kuroslepov connects the drinking with his dreams—another removal from reality: 'You are firm, but I am firmer. You can stab me with a knife, but I won't drink any more. I did you the favour, so let it be. You should see the dreams I've been having. Good God! All kinds of wild animals, with trunks, all grabbing at you and catching you, and the sky falling ...' (iii, p. 133).

Aside from the blurring of reality and illusion discussed above, the play is one of much confusion with wrongful arrests, cases of mistaken identity, and people lost in the woods. There is also a significant use of disguised appearance, notably Khlynov's play-acting, but also by other characters: Parasha disguises herself as a pilgrim in order to visit Vasya in jail: 'They won't recognise me. You can see how I'm dressed; and I'll cover myself with a scarf' (iii, p. 123); and Matrena dresses up as her husband in order to meet secretly with Narkis (iii, p. 155). The overall impression created by the play is one of an insecure world. The characters exist in constant uncertainty as to the true nature of people and events. It is symbolic of this that most of the action takes place in either the dark or half-dark.

Life as Literature

An interesting feature of *An Ardent Heart* is a small, easily over-looked reference to Russian literature. When Narkis is lost in the woods, he comes across a small shack and asks: 'What is this little hut on chicken legs?' (iii, p. 140). His words would be easily recognisable to a Russian audience as a reference to a staple character of Russian folk tales, the witch Baba Yaga. Narkis' comment could easily be dismissed as simply another realistic touch by Ostrovsky. It is, indeed, very much the kind of thing a Russian might say when coming across a mysterious hut in the woods. But the timing of his words gives them a greater significance. It is at this hut that Narkis will be captured by Khlynov's make-believe robbers, and it is surely too great a coincidence that, at this very time, Ostrovsky chooses to have Narkis refer to another world of make-believe, that of the Russian fairy-tale. Such an occurrence might well be dismissed as coincidence, if it were not for the frequency with which references to fiction, novels and literature appear in Ostrovsky's drama, almost always connected with characters and events relating to fantasy or illusion.

The comedy *Incompatibility of Character* is a case in point. This is a play which again focuses on blindness to reality, contrasting the idealistic, blind-to-reality gentry with a more realistic, pragmatic merchant family. Numerous characters in the play are shown to be removed from reality to varying degrees. The old aristocrat, Prezhnev, for example, is almost entirely removed from reality. In the *dramatis personae*, he is described as 'a totally decrepit old man, almost without any kind of movement' (ii, p. 142), and when he appears on stage, in Picture One, he is asleep in a wheelchair. He wakes briefly to ask his son whether he has been to the theatre lately and to enquire as to who plays marquises these days, only to be told that no-one has done so for some time. He is then wheeled out on to the balcony to be read 'old newspapers' by the manservant (ii, pp. 145/6). Ostrovsky's principal aim here is, perhaps, to emphasise the decline of the gentry as a class and their connection to the past, rather than the present day. However, in so doing, he also demonstrates a removal from present-day reality. Prezhnev is senile, he lives in a world of memories and is somehow separate from the reality of life around him.

In many respects, Prezhnev acts as a marker—a signal of the blindness to reality of those around him. His wife, Prezhneva, whilst still relatively young and active, is also removed from reality. We first encounter her at the opening of Picture One, where she is lying on a divan, reading a novel. Thus immediately, as with the hut in *An Ardent Heart*, so Prezhneva is linked with a world of make-believe. If this were too oblique a signal, Prezhneva's opening monologue leaves us in no doubt of her romantic, idealistic character:

> It is cruel! Terrible! I could never act like that! Nous autres femmes ... we ... oh! We believe, we trust blindly, we never analyse. No, I cannot go on reading this novel. A young man of

good birth, handsome, clever, an officer in the army, declares his love to her in such exquisite language; and she—she has the strength to refuse him! No, she is no woman! ...' (ii, p. 142)

Prezhneva's use of the word 'blindly' acts as an immediate warning that she is a character who avoids, or is blind to, the true nature of reality. She goes on to talk about how 'woman is a weak creature of impulse! ... how easy it is to deceive us!' (ii, p. 142) and of how cunning and deceitful men are:

> We women are so loving, so trusting, so ready to believe anything, that it is only after bitter (she sinks into thought), yes, bitter, experience that we realise the immorality of the ones we adore. (*Silence.*) But, no! Even after a betrayal, after several betrayals, we will again give in to impulse and believe once more in the possibility of pure and honourable love. Yes! Such is our fate! And all the more so, when the whole thing takes place in such exquisite surroundings - as in this novel: springtime, flowers, a beautiful park, gurgling streams. He came to her dressed for the hunt, with a rifle, a hound lying at his feet. Ah! ...' (ii, p. 143)

Thus we are faced with the familiar pattern of an idealistic woman who is concerned with appearances and settings rather than with the actuality of events. However, the fact that Prezhneva reads novels is more than simply a signal that she is avoiding reality. As the play progresses, we see that Prezhneva seems more caught up in this fictitious world than in the actuality of her present circumstances. With considerable irony, she dismisses 'material considerations' as 'prose': 'Of course, there are among us women whose sole interest in life consists of vulgar material considerations and household affairs. But that is prose, prose! ...' (ii, p. 143) - it is precisely this disdain for prose which is her downfall.

Prezhneva's romantic and idealised view of the world is emphasised constantly throughout the play. She talks of her son Pol as 'such a sensitive, nervous boy!' (ii, p. 143). Yet when Pol enters, the discrepancy between Prezhneva's description of her son and the actuality of his character quickly becomes apparent. Pol, through force of necessity, is much more aware of the reality of their situation than his mother. Through him, we discover that Prezhneva has indeed failed to learn from the 'bitter experience' of betrayal and deceit by men, and that her disdain for 'prose' has led to the loss of their fortune. When Prezhneva protests: 'What could we do, my dear? People are so wicked, so cunning, and you and I are so trusting, ' Pol responds: 'It is you who are trusting, Maman. If they got into my hands, I would give them what for!' (ii, p. 145) He goes on to bemoan his having to work in an office with people who stand in street doorways eating onion pies, and when Prezhneva attempts to sympathise: 'Yes, yes, I understand ... with your tender heart ... you are so sensitive! ...' he again immediately gives the lie to her statement by declaring: 'If there were a chance, then I really would have no qualms about cheating someone at cards' (ii, p. 145). The discrepancy between Prezhneva's view of her son and reality is further emphasised when she suggests that he should marry. Pol replies that he has no objections but asks who he could marry. Prezhneva declares: 'Yes, that is the question! I know you, Pol. Why are you so well brought up? Why do you have such a tender soul? Because of this you will never be happy. You have no match! A girl would need many, so many, virtues to win your love and make you happy.' Pol's response is, indeed, pure prose: 'You think, perhaps, Maman, that I am attracted by domestic bliss? I'm not a child, I'm twenty-one. That is all too Arcadian! (*He laughs.*) I simply want money' (ii, p. 146). The final lie to his 'sensitive nature' is given when his old nanny, Pereshivkina, enters. He mocks her, calling her an 'old hag', and she recalls one of his childhood 'jokes' when he set her cap on fire from behind and burnt off all her hair (ii, p. 147).

Incidentally, Ostrovsky's concern with blindness to reality in this play does not end with Prezhneva and her husband. In Pictures Two and Three, the blind-to-reality Prezhneva is contrasted with the wealthy widow, Serafima. A merchant's daughter, Serafima is well aware of the status her wealth brings her: 'What would I be if I didn't have money?—I would be nothing' (ii, p. 167) and she is anxious to maintain that wealth. Seeing Pol walk past her window one day, she falls in love with him and determines to marry him. He agrees, realising the benefits her money can bring him, and the two are married. Events come to a head in Picture Three when Serafima, seeing that Pol is squandering her money, decides against following the path of Prezhneva by sacrificing herself to love. Instead she leaves Pol, taking her fortune with her. Such behaviour would seem to suggest Serafima is more realistic than her noblewoman counterpart. Yet, typically, Ostrovsky's message is more complex. Serafima and Pol marry on first sight—she attracted by his looks, he by her money—without ever having got to know one another. It is this reliance on superficial appearance which dooms their marriage to failure. In reality, as E.Kholodov points out, he gets a 'thrifty wife' and she gets a 'frivolous, fast-living' husband.[5] Rather than simply contrasting Prezhneva with a more realistic son and daughter-in-law, Ostrovsky reveals them all as guilty of blindness to reality.

A *Last Sacrifice* is another play which sees literature as both a mechanism and a signal for removal from reality and the creation of a fictitious world. When Pribytkov talks of his good-for-nothing nephew, Lavr Mironych, he notes how Lavr uses novels as a means of avoiding reality:

> He isn't much bothered about jail. You fix him up with some appointment—he's an able fellow—and he lives very well for a year or so. Then suddenly, in one minute, he's fallen into debt. How he manages it, amazes me. And the debts don't bother him at all, he can't even think of paying them, but he doesn't even blink an eyelid. From somewhere or other he gets fifty or so translated French novels and he goes to jail as calmly as if he were visiting friends. He settles down to read his novels, he reads them day and night, and if he had to sit there for ten years, then it would be all the same to him. Well, I buy him out from pity. But when I do so, he just combs his side whiskers, puts his hat on at a jaunty angle, and goes out to play the dandy all over Moscow as if nothing had happened. (iv, p. 345)

Again, as the play progresses, we see that Lavr lives largely in his imagination, believing, with no basis in reality, that Pribytkov will provide a massive dowry for his daughter, and ordering extravagant banquets with no means of paying for them. Significantly, when he hears (falsely) that Pribytkov is to give a million to Irina for her dowry, he declares: 'This is a novel! A novel in real life' (iv, p. 351).

Lavr has passed on his obsession with literature to his daughter, Irina, and she, like him, lives largely in a world of make-believe. When Lavr is planning an extravagant supper, she laughs at his worrying over such a trifling matter: 'No, I live only on poetry, on the most elevated poetry. What is supper? Prose. There is the moon, the

---

[5] E.G.Kholodov, 'A.N.Ostrovskii v 1855-1865 godakh', *PSS* ii, 669.

stars! ...' (iv, p. 369); and later notes: 'I haven't experienced life, but I've read a lot of novels, and I understand everything, everything!' (iv, p. 379). Father and daughter's preoccupation with literature over life is made particularly clear during Irina's first appearance on the stage. She is in love and melancholy:

> **Irina.** Ah, I'm unhappy ... I'm the most unhappy girl possible ... If there is any unhappy girl in the world it is I.
>
> ...
>
> **Lavr Mironych.** My poor Irene is in love.
> **Pribytkov.** I think it is caused more by reading.
> **Lavr.** Yes, dear uncle, we both of us constantly follow European literature. We send for every translated novel that appears, however many there are, absolutely every one.
> **Irina.** It is the only consolation I have in life. Papa reads less than I do—he's occupied with business—but I am simply absorbed in it, absorbed ...
> **Lavr.** The old novels were better. Nowadays they don't write so interestingly. At the moment I'm reading *Monte Cristo* for the fourth time. How real it is! How true to life!
> **Pribytkov.** What truth is there in it? All it is, is the play of imagination.
> **Lavr.** Monte Cristo is very like me, uncle, just as if he'd been based on me. (iv, p. 347)

Thus we see how Lavr and Irina live 'absorbed' in 'the play of imagination', with Lavr even believing that he is a fictional character. (Curiously, M.Hoover, discussing *A Last Sacrifice*, describes Lavr as a 'materialist' in contrast to Irina and Dulchin, whom she describes as the 'Romantic pair'.[6] While Dulchin is undoubtedly playing the role of a Romantic hero—acting the part cast for him by Irina—it is surely he who is the true materialist. Lavr, with his ability to sit happily in prison reading romantic novels, demonstrates a blithe disregard of the material in favour of the romantic.)

Numerous plays use a connection to literature as a signal for delusion or removal from reality. Thus when the dreaming Lipochka in *It's All in the Family* first appears on stage, she is 'sitting by the window, with a book' (i, p. 86), and in *A Lucrative Post*, the idealist Zhadov reads throughout the pivotal Act Three in which he is con-

---

[6] Hoover, 104.

trasted with the more successful, bribe-taking Belogubov. Later in the play, he himself states that he 'must give up tilting at windmills' (ii, p. 96), thus connecting him with the fictional Don Quixote and again suggesting that his ideals are little more than self-delusory illusions.

Similarly, in *A Hangover from Someone Else's Feast*, the idealist Ivan buries himself in his books, removing himself from everyday reality. In the opening sequence, he tries to ignore Agrafena's attempts to make him face up to the reality of his situation by 'sitting at the table and opening a book' (ii, p. 8). When Liza enters, Ivan is described as 'not noticing her, he reads with passion, waving his arm around' (ii, p. 11); and he later admits that he might not have noticed whether she had fallen in love because: 'I am for ever at my books' (ii, p. 12).

A Young Man's Morning, with its focus on the blind-to-reality Nedopekin, is full of references to books and writing. In Scene One, Ivan talks of how they have 'all sorts of books, journals, notes of all kinds ...' (i, p. 155) and is himself described as having spent the morning reading *The Northern Bee* (i, p. 156). In Scene Two, Lisavsky sits reading a journal. In Scene Three, the First Young Man and Lisavsky discuss a letter in verse that Lisavsky has written (i, p. 159). Scene Four sees Nedopekin talking of how he reads late into the night and subscribes to all the latest journals (i, p. 159) and the First Young Man suggests he should be reading his French novels in the original. Nedopekin also states that he writes verse (i, p. 160). In Scene Five, the French novels are again mentioned (i, p. 160) and Nedopekin and Lisavsky read some verse Lisavsky has written (i, p. 163). And in Scene Six, Smurov and Vasya mock Nedopekin's French novels, noting that he has put them out 'just for show' (i, p. 165).

In *Difficult Days*, Mudrov talks of all the terrible novels which are being written nowadays, suggesting: 'People with unfirm minds shouldn't read fashionable books' ... 'I read, but I myself don't believe anything which is written; whatever document they bring to me, I don't believe it. If it was written down that twice two is four, I wouldn't believe it; because I have a firm mind.' When Nastas'ya asks: 'Why do they write books which there's no point reading?' Mudrov replies: 'From delusion. They've gone astray' (ii, pp. 464/5).

An interesting feature of the use of literature and writing in Ostrovsky's plays is the frequency with which it is linked with deception—once more connecting the written word to a sense of illusion, of make-believe. Repetitive use is made of forged or fake documents. Lavr Mironych, for example, forges promissory notes in *A Last Sacrifice*, as do Pertsov in *Difficult Days*, Koprov in *Hard-earned Bread*, and Kisel´nikov in *The Abyss*. Merich fakes letters and a diary in *The Poor Bride* and there is an illegal printing press in *A Change in Fortune*.

Much of the deception in *Even Wise Men Err* is linked to writing. The play opens with Glumova complaining about the anonymous letters Glumov is forcing her to write, which contain 'various slanders and fantastic stories!' (iii, p. 8). Act One, Scene 2 revolves around the slanderous epigrams Glumov is known to write and Golutvin's desire to make easy money out of them. In Act One, Scene 4, when Glumov and Mamaev first meet, Glumov sits at his desk and 'pretends to be busy' (iii, p. 13) with writing. Glumov's ingratiation with Krutitsky and Gorodulin involves writing in both cases—he re-writes Krutitsky's treatise for him and writes a speech and an article for Gorodulin. And in Act Three, Scene 2, Krutitsky warns Turusina of the dangers of taking so-called 'pilgrims' in from the streets, noting that when someone else he knew did so, the 'pilgrims' turned out to be forgers (iii, p. 43). Interestingly, in this play writing is also the vehicle by which the truth is revealed, as Glumov notes at the end of the play: 'The only times I was being honest were when I was writing that diary' (iii, p. 79).

Deception in *Wolves and Sheep* is similarly linked to books and writing. Again, much of the deception is carried out by means of forged letters and documents. Elsewhere, Murzavetskaya puts the money she gains by false means into the Bible (iv, p. 138). Before embarking on her deception of Lynyaev, Glafira is described as reading from a small book (iv, p. 150) and the chief deceiver, Berkutov, tells Lynyaev that he 'doesn't read enough, ' noting that 'a number of new books and pamphlets to your taste have recently been published. I've brought quite a few of them with me. If you wish I'll give them to you...' (iv, p. 177). Berkutov then goes on to tell Murzavetskaya that he 'has brought a few books of a religious nature with me...' and offers to give them to her (iv, p. 193).

Other plays which link deception with literature include: *A Family Picture*—when planning their secret rendezvous with their admirers, Mar´ya tells Dar´ya to ask the men to bring them some books to read (i, p. 67); and *A Lucrative Post*—when Kukushkina, in her efforts to win Zhadov as a suitor for Polina, is falsely pretending to care about love and romance, she declares: 'You can't imagine, Vasilii Nikolaich, how I suffer when I see two loving hearts separated by any kind of obstacle. When I'm reading a novel, and I see how circumstances are preventing the lovers from seeing each other—either the parents don't agree, or financial considerations don't allow it— then I suffer just as at this moment. I cry, I simply cry!' (ii, p. 66). Similarly, in *Not of this World*, the incriminating bills which lead to Kseniya's death are conveyed to her by the deceiving Barbarisov in a book.

Perhaps the most surprising link with literature in Ostrovsky's drama, however, is the presence of easily recognisable literary types. Many of Ostrovsky's fantasy role-players seem to adopt the personas of familiar literary stereotypes. The critic A.Kaspin notes this phenomenon in his essay 'A Superfluous Man and an Underground Man in Ostrovskij's *The Poor Bride*', in which he argues persuasively that the characters Khor´kov and Milashin in *The Poor Bride* are variants of two common types in Russian literature—a superfluous man and an underground man.[7] Kaspin notes that Khor´kov is from humble stock, but has become educated and in so doing has separated himself from the rest of the townspeople. He has become *déclassé*, a 'raznochinets'. Kaspin suggests that evidence of this alienation is found in his name, which derives from 'khorek', a dialect word meaning a small island in a river or lake.[8] (Curiously, this derivation links Khor´kov to Ostrovsky himself—the word 'ostrov' also means island—although no real significance can probably be attached to this). Further evidence of Khor´kov's alienation can be seen in the fact that he appears very rarely in the play. We mainly learn about him through other characters, particularly his mother. Kaspin goes on to note that Khor´kov is probably a civil servant (his mother boasts

---

[7] See Albert Kaspin, 'A Superfluous Man and an Underground Man in Ostrovskij's *The Poor Bride*', *Slavic and East European Journal*, 6 (1962), 312-21.

[8] Alternatively, Khor´kov's surname could be connected to the Russian word 'khorek', meaning 'pole-cat' or 'ferret'.

that he is on the way to becoming a nobleman) yet he does very little work. The references to sloth, dressing-gown and pipe immediately recall Oblomov—the archetypal superfluous man of Goncharov's novel. Kaspin argues that the type of education Khor'kov has received further serves to alienate him from his original social level. He is the product of Moscow University in the 40s, the period of Hegel and German idealism, of Belinsky and Romanticism. Kaspin asserts that it is likely that Khor'kov became imbued with these ideals but on returning to the realities and brutalities of life has retreated into a shell of dreams and inactivity. Thus, he sees Khor'kov as the type of idealist in conflict with reality discussed earlier.

Kaspin notes that the weakness of Khor'kov's character is apparent from his very first speech. He believes that only Mar'ya is capable of inspiring him to act (again, a typical feature of the superfluous man who saw the natural purity of Russian women, unsullied by formal education, as the catalyst to spur them into action) yet is unable to declare his love, leaving the field open to his rivals. Even though he holds proof that Merich is a philanderer, he does not act himself, instead giving his evidence to Milashin to pass on to Mar'ya. When he finally makes his drunken confession of love it is too late. 'Learning has fostered his natural delicacy and gentleness to the stage where it has enervated him. Rather than act, he prefers to retreat into the beautiful world of his dreams and await events with apprehensive immobility.'[9]

Kaspin notes that Milashin, in contrast, is an example of the character type in Russian literature which, following Dostoevsky's novel *Notes from Underground*, came to be known as the 'underground man'.[10] He is a man who has come to rationalise his lack of willpower and inability to act as signs of a superior being—convincing himself of the futility of pursuing any course of action but his own inaction. His feelings of inferiority egg him on to prove his superiority to himself again and again. He fantasises acts of revenge

---

[9] Kaspin, 316.

[10] Although Dostoevsky's *Notes from Underground* was not written until 1864, Kaspin notes that the Underground Man had many precursors in Russian literature, citing: Pushkin's Eugene (*The Bronze Horseman*) and Hermann (*The Queen of Spades*), Gogol's Poprishchin and Akakii Akakievich, and Turgenev's Chulkaturin (*The Diary of a Superfluous Man*). He includes Milashin within this group. (See Kaspin, 317.)

which prove his superiority over those who are successful (his offer to fight a duel with Merich is one example of such fantasising). But 'defeated by the enormity of the chasm which separates the ideal from reality and his inability to bridge the gap he retreats into his moral underground of bitter speculation.'[11] (Again, we see the conflict between the real and the ideal.) Milashin, Kaspin asserts, is the poor clerk in the tradition of Gogol's little man. He has no hope of winning Mar´ya's hand yet he refuses to accept that reality and continues to insist that Mar´ya loves him, even when she has made it clear that she does not. In almost every line he speaks there is a constant preoccupation with himself, constant comparison with others, an embittered argumentative tone and continual attempts to assert his superiority over his rivals. He is, for example, extremely proud of his grammar school education, which he uses to assert his superiority over Merich.

A second critic, V.Lakshin, also takes his example from *The Poor Bride* when he links the third suitor in Mar´ya's circle, Merich, with Lermontov's Pechorin (it is noteworthy that neither critic observed that all three of Mar´ya's suitors were literary stereotypes): 'Merich is the played-out, superficial Lermontov hero Grushnitsky posing as Pechorin. Even his name carries a few literary hints—the root is the Lermontovian 'Mary' (incidentally the name by which Merich refers to Mar´ya) with the common Lermontovian ending 'ich' (Vulich, Zvezdich etc.) ... this element of the play was even more apparent in an earlier draft when Mar´ya is shown holding a Lermontov book and Merich (then Zorich) tells pure Pechorinesque tales of easy conquests over women's hearts.'[12] Lakshin goes on to describe Merich as 'a literature imitator'.[13]

Examples of literary stereotypes besides those noted by Kaspin and Lakshin can also be found in Ostrovsky's plays. Karandyshev in *Without a Dowry* is another example of an underground man. He is the laughing-stock of the town, desperate to prove his superiority to those around him.[14] Vozhevatov describes his treatment at Ogudalova's house and his desperation to prove himself worthy as a suitor for Larisa:

---

[11] *Ibid.*, 317.

[12] Lakshin, *PSS* i, 477.

[13] *Ibid.*, 483. Interestingly, Dobrolyubov does not see the link between Merich and Pechorin. He specifically states: 'He is not Onegin, not Pechorin, not even Grushnitsky.' (See Dobrolyubov, 363.)

[14] Lakshin states that Karandyshev 'like Dostoevsky's heroes ... has a painfully

When a lull set in and there weren't any rich suitors in sight, then they clung to Karandyshev, invited him in so that the house wouldn't be empty. But when, as happened sometimes, some rich man turned up, then it was simply pitiful to look at Karandyshev. They didn't talk to him or look at him. He would sit there, in the corner, playing various roles, throwing out wild looks, pretending to be in despair. Once he wanted to shoot himself, but nothing came of it, he just made everybody laugh. Here's a funny one: when Paratov was there they had a costume party. So Karandyshev dressed up as a highway robber, took an axe in his hands, and threw wild looks at everybody, especially Sergei Sergeich. (v, p. 15/6)

Thus again, we see Karandyshev fantasising acts of revenge over his superiors yet proving unable to act on those fantasies. Karandyshev does eventually succeed in winning Larisa as his fiancée, although largely by default, and rather than increasing his self-esteem, it serves only to further his desperation to prove his superiority over his rivals. As Vozhevatov again notes:

He should marry her as quickly as possible and take her away to his little estate until all the talk dies down—that's what the Ogudalovs want. But he drags Larisa along the boulevard, holding her by the arm, his head held so high he'd crash right into you if you didn't look out. And he's taken to wearing glasses for some reason—he never used to wear them. (v, p. 16)

He thought up the idea of decorating his apartment, and it's really odd. In his study he put a cheap rug on the wall, and hung up daggers and pistols from Tula. It wouldn't be surprising if he hunted, but he's never held a gun in his hands. He drags you to his place to show you it all, and you have to praise it or he takes offence. He's an egotistical man, and envious. He ordered a horse from the country, some nag of all different colours, and he has a little coachman who wears a kaftan handed down from a big coachman. And he takes Larisa Dmitrievna out driving with that camel; he sits there as proudly as if he were driving a thousand trotters. (v, p. 16)

---

inflated sense of self-importance.' (See Lakshin, 'Mudrost′ Ostrovskogo', 10.)

Karandyshev is attempting to hide his sense of inferiority behind a mask; to avoid reality by creating the illusion of a new reality.

Without a Dowry also contains an example of a Pechorin-type romantic hero—Paratov. (V.Lakshin calls him a 'late Pechorinesque copy'[15]). Like Pechorin, Paratov is a callous womaniser, unconcerned by his destruction of Larisa—he asserts that 'it is a woman's lot to cry'. As before, Ostrovsky includes hints at links to Lermontov in the play. When Larisa confronts Paratov with his deception, she looks at him and quotes from the Lermontov poem 'To a Portrait'; and Paratov's name summons up reminders of another famous Lermontov poem, 'The Sail'.

Other literary stereotypes include Oleshunin in *The Handsome Man* and Babaev in *We All Have our Cross to Bear*. Made impotent by a society that values only good looks, Oleshunin has retreated underground. Like the Underground Man, he is very egotistical and has an inflated view of himself. He dreams of 'showing' others what he is 'really like'. He is full of grand plans for action which end in farce. For example, he claims that he will open Zoya's eyes, yet his so-called 'love' scene with her is ridiculous; and his challenge to fight a duel with Okoemov ends in his being chased unceremoniously from the house. In contrast, Babaev, in *We All Have our Cross to Bear*, seems almost to take words out of the mouth of Pechorin in his comments about women, his former exploits and his references to fate.

The presence of such literary figures poses an intriguing question. Why would Ostrovsky, the realist playwright, who brought realistic characters to the Russian stage, also populate his plays with fictional stereotypes? For Lakshin, the presence of the Pechorinesque figure, Merich, in *The Poor Bride*, is further evidence for his 'literary polemic' interpretation of the play. He notes: 'In Merich, Ostrovsky wanted to compromise the artistic pose, to discredit it from the point of view of life.'[16] No doubt Lakshin would apply this analysis to *Without a Dowry* and *We All Have our Cross to Bear* also. Thus, Larisa becomes a victim for her idealistic love for Paratov, while Tat'yana is attracted to the worthless Babaev because he conforms to the Romantic ideal. Indeed, it could be said that this argument holds

[15] Lakshin, *PSS* v, 479.
[16] Lakshin, *PSS* i, 477.

up more strongly in *We All Have our Cross to Bear* and *Without a Dowry* than it does in *The Poor Bride*, where Lakshin has failed to notice that Mar´ya's supposed 'true love', Khor´kov, is also a literary stereotype.[17]

Similarly, such literary types are a form of escape mechanism, a means by which the characters escape the reality of their inadequacies. Thus Khor´kov reconciles his ideals with reality by sinking into a life of inactivity and dreams, and when those dreams are shattered he avoids reality by turning to drink—another escape mechanism. Likewise Milashin and Karandyshev bridge the gulf between the real and the ideal by fantasising about performing heroic deeds. However, as for the other fantasy role-players in Ostrovsky's work, for these characters also the boundaries between their real and imagined worlds have become blurred. Although Ostrovsky lets it slip at the end of *The Poor Bride* that Merich and Milashin are playing roles—he allows Merich one speech which does not conform to his romantic persona (i, p. 272) and we briefly see Milashin practising his desired facial expression (i, p. 273)—these are only momentary lapses, and the other stereotypes discussed above never slip out of their literary personas. For these characters, the illusory worlds into which they have retreated have become reality. Life and fiction have become blurred.

Given this interpretation, the use of the Pechorin character is particularly interesting. A significant feature of Lermontov's Pechorin is his desire to fictionalise life, to live his life as if it were a chapter in a book. A.Barratt and A.D.P.Briggs in their study of *A Hero of our Time* note: 'In the course of our study we shall see example after example of literary values, concepts and expressions impinging on the actual lives of characters, and particularly that of Pechorin ... it is intriguing to follow, as best we can, the twists and

---

[17] It is important to note that there *are* elements of literary parody in Ostrovsky's plays. Ostrovsky himself wrote to the young dramatist N.Solov´ev: 'it is the duty of every honest writer (in the name of eternal truth) to destroy the ideals of the past when they have become outdated, vulgarised and false. So in my memory the ideals of Byron and our Pechorin became outmoded, and now the ideals of the 40s are becoming outmoded...' See A.N.Ostrovskii, *Polnoe sobranie sochinenii*, ed. I.Shiryaev, 16 vols (Moscow: Khudozhestvennaya literatura, 1949-1953), XXII, 154. However, the significance of the literary stereotypes discussed here goes beyond that of literary parody.

turns which mark the movement in and out between 'real life' and literature ... What the narrators do capriciously on the page in 'Bela' Pechorin will imitate with devastating seriousness in real life.'[18] Ostrovsky's Pechorinesque characters also show a desire to fictionalize their lives. Thus Merich creates a fictional past for himself with faked letters and diaries; and Larisa describes Paratov's shooting prowess as if he were Silvio in the Pushkin short story *The Shot*. (This is a reference which again links him to Pechorin—Silvio has frequently been noted as a precursor to Lermontov's hero.) Some of Babaev's very first words refer to both books and intrigue: 'How stupid that we didn't bring any books! Although perhaps we can find a casual affair of some kind for these four days or so' (ii, p. 393) and he talks of his thoughts as if they might form a story or play of some kind: 'What wonderful thoughts come into my head! If they were developed at leisure, in the country perhaps, then they could form a short tale, or a comedy in the manner of Alfred de Musset' (ii, p. 403). After Babaev's first meeting with Tat´yana, he states: 'Well, the novel is beginning, I wonder how it will end?'[19] (ii, p. 406)—words which call to mind Pechorin's statement in 'Knyazhna Meri': 'The stage is set ... we'll see if we can provide a dénouement to this comedy.' It is surely a deliberate twist that Babaev, a character in a play, uses the metaphor of a novel, while Pechorin, a character in a novel, uses a theatrical metaphor to express the same sentiment.[20]

Such literariness is by no means the only similarity in theme between *A Hero of our Time* and the interpretation of Ostrovsky's work put forward in this study. Intriguingly, Barratt and Briggs also find a 'central issue' of Lermontov's novel to be 'the gulf between

---

[18] Andrew Barratt and A.D.P.Briggs, *A Wicked Irony: The Rhetoric of Lermontov's A Hero of Our Time* (Bristol: Bristol Classical Press, 1989), 24-5.

[19] The Russian word *roman* can mean 'love affair'; however, Babaev's previous assertion that his thoughts might form the basis for a short story or play suggests that the meaning 'novel' is also strongly implied.

[20] The literary allusions drawn in *We All Have our Cross to Bear* do not stop at links to Pechorin. The meeting between Tat´yana and Babaev (ii, pp. 404-6) calls to mind the famous meeting between Onegin and another Tat´yana at the end of Pushkin's *Evgenii Onegin*. They both talk about gardens of the past; they are both married women meeting with past loves; and they both admit greater love for their lovers than for their husbands. Yet rather than follow her predecessor's grand sacrificial gesture by swearing to remain true to her unloved husband, Ostrovsky's Tat´yana bathetically agrees to a 'casual affair' with Babaev.

appearance and reality. Appearances can be deceptive.'[21] They go on to point out that 'Deception [is] a constant problem throughout "A Hero of our Time".'[22] Most significant of all, however, is Pechorin's role-playing. Pechorin is a consummate play-actor, playing out a variety of fantasy images of himself to devastating effect. Critics have noted that one of Pechorin's favourite images of himself is as a 'master playwright', the manipulator of other people's lives.[23] He sees himself as 'playwright, director and hero'.[24] This image of himself manifests itself most obviously in his abundant use of theatrical metaphors and terms—a device which, as we shall see below, is common to Ostrovsky's drama also.[25] R.Reid describes 'Knyazhna Meri' as 'a performance scripted in diary form for performance in real life.'[26]

We are left with an intriguing situation whereby Ostrovsky has chosen to make his Pechorinesque fantasy role-players adopt the role of a literary character who is himself fictionalizing life. Pechorin, too, has found literature such an effective means of escape from reality that he has become incapable of distinguishing between fiction and real life. (Ironically, this is compounded further by the fact that all the literary role-players are themselves characters in a work of fiction, be it novel or play.)

Interestingly, such 'bookishness' applies to the Underground Man also. Barratt and Briggs have noted that 'in Pechorin, Lermontov created a character whose unhealthy commitment to inauthentic 'bookish' behaviour makes him a direct forebear of the Underground Man'.[27] And indeed Dostoevsky's Underground Man is a character whose desire to fictionalise life overwhelms even that of Pechorin.[28]

---

[21] Barratt and Briggs, 7.

[22] *Ibid.*, 49.

[23] *Ibid.*, 68.

[24] J.Mersereau, *Mikhail Lermontov* (Carbondale: S.Illinois Press, 1962), 139.

[25] For interesting examples of this, see Barratt and Briggs, 69 and 101.

[26] Robert Reid, *Lermontov's 'A Hero of Our Time'* (London: Bristol Classical Press, 1997), 64.

[27] Barratt and Briggs, 131.

[28] For discussion of the Underground Man's desire to fictionalise life, see R.Anderson, 'Notes from the Underground: The Arrest of Personal Development', *Canadian-American Slavic Studies*, 24 (1990), 413-30; Scott Consigny, 'The Paradox of Textuality: Writing as Entrapment and Deliverance in *Notes from Underground*', Canadian-American Slavic Studies, 12 (1978), 341-52; J.M.Holquist, 'Plot and

Such obvious links between the works of Ostrovsky and Lermontov would suggest that the (extensive) critical discussion of the blurring of life and literature in Lermontov's work might shed light on this similar (but little-noted) aspect of Ostrovsky's plays. *A Hero of our Time* has been seen as a literary polemic which criticises the lack of realism of previous literary traditions.[29] (This is similar to the Lakshin interpretation of Ostrovsky's work, although it is a testament to the complexity of Lermontov's work that Lakshin includes Pechorin as precisely the kind of romantic hero that other critics suggest Lermontov is parodying.) However, the use of literature as a retreat, a means of avoiding reality, has also been attributed to Lermontov's novel. Even more significantly, C.Turner has noted both psychological and philosophical elements in the work. Turner suggests that man in general is 'an inveterate actor, whether as a result of direct social pressures or through the agency of the Freudian superego ... and we no longer know where this role ends and the authentic person begins' and goes on to assert that '... [this] is a pattern of which Pechorin, with his aggression, his divided self and, not least, his role playing, is a patent exemplar.'[30] The challenge to our perception of 'the authentic' has also been noted by M.Gilroy, who discusses 'the undermining of the reader's sense of the distinction between art and reality' in *A Hero of our Time*.[31]

Life as Theatre

Just as references to literature and writing in Ostrovsky's drama act as a signal for other realities—the creation of illusory or make-believe worlds—so do the numerous references to the theatre in his plays. The overwhelming abundance of role-play in Ostrovsky's drama has been discussed throughout this study both as a means of conscious deception and as a subconscious escape mechanism. Yet such role-play again involves the creation of different realities. It

---

counter-plot in Notes from Underground', *Canadian-American Slavic Studies*, 6 (1972), 225-38.

[29] See Herbert Eagle, 'Lermontov's "Play" with Romantic Genre Expectations in *A Hero of Our Time*', *Russian Literature Triquarterly*, 10 (1974), 299-315.

[30] C.J.G.Turner, *Pechorin: An Essay on Lermontov's 'Hero of Our Time'* (Birmingham: Birmingham Slavonic Monographs, 1978), 54.

[31] Marie Gilroy, *The Ironic Vision of Lermontov's 'A Hero of Our Time'* (Birmingham: Birmingham Slavonic Monographs, 1989), 43.

again results in a blurring of reality and illusion and, once more, it leads to a sense of uncertain reality. As E.Bristow states of the role-playing in *The Forest*: 'By the time the actors walk out, their life of illusion has achieved a greater sense of reality than the illusion of life experienced by the landed nobility.'[32]

As with references to novels and books, so references to the theatre—another place of illusory reality—are frequently used as a marker of removal from reality. Thus almost the sole words of the decrepit, removed-from-present-day-reality Prezhnev in *Incompatibility of Character* are to ask his son if he has been to the theatre lately. Khlynov in *An Ardent Heart* stages plays as a means of escape from reality. (Also in this play, Vasya talks of going to the theatre in Moscow to see the play *The Bigamous Wife*. Again, his words suggest a link between real life and that of the theatre: he is talking to Narkis, who is conducting an affair with his master's wife.) In *Poverty is No Vice*, Lyubim Tortsov escapes his position as a poverty-stricken drunkard by playing the role of a buffoon and clown, endlessly quoting from the tragedies he saw in his youth: 'I mostly went to see tragedies, I was a great lover of tragedies, but I saw little and remembered less, seeing as how I was mostly drunk. (*Stands up.*) "A knife in the chest of Prokop Lyapunov!" ...' (i, p. 343). (A.Kaspin states that '... Lyubim Tortsov is an actor, even if only on the lowest scale. Aside from being the *skomorokh* with witty phrases, amusing songs and couplets, and droll dance steps, he acts a role and knows that he is acting, but this acting has already become part of him.'[33]) Similarly Kapiton Titych in *A Hangover from Someone Else's Feast* uses theatre as an escape mechanism both by physically attending performances and by hiding behind dramatic roles. He is constantly quoting lines from well-known tragedies and striking dramatic poses: '(*He walks around the room making tragic gestures*)'; '(*striking a pose*) "Get out of the way! Stand aside! A lion has broken loose from its cage! A bull has escaped from the abattoir! Stand aside!"' (p. 25); '(*tragically*) "I will amaze the world with my tyranny. The corpses lying in their graves will thank God that they are already dead!"' (ii,

---

[32] Bristow, 24.
[33] Albert Kaspin, 'A Re-Examination of Ostrovsky's Character Lyubim Tortsov', in *Studies in Russian Literature in Honor of W.Lednicki*, ed. Z.Folejewski (The Hague: Mouton, 1962), 185-91 (p. 188).

p. 28). Kapiton's parents believe that he has been sent mad by his frequent trips to the theatre—thus again connecting the theatre with a removal from reality (ii, p. 15). Similarly, the opening scenes of *The Abyss*, a play which focuses on the blindness to reality and gradual descent into madness of its central protagonist, Kisel′nikov, depict people leaving a theatre.

The theatre is also linked with deception. In *The Poor Bride*, when Mar′ya wants to pretend to her mother that her decision to marry Benevolensky was made lightly, she says to Milashin: 'Let's laugh, let's talk of something else. Haven't you been to the theatre lately?' (i, p. 260). In *Even Wise Men Err*, the deceived Mamaeva first falls in love with Glumov while at the theatre (iii, p. 11). And in *A Family Picture*, Shiryalov describes one of his deceptions as 'a comedy' (i, p. 79). The deceiving Lisavsky in *A Young Man's Morning* writes vaudevilles and frequently talks about them. He also reminds Nedopekin to go to the theatre and ensures that Nedopekin pays for a second ticket for him. Moreover, the blind-to-reality Nedopekin is described as seeing new styles or walks on people when at the theatre and then rushing home to practise them.

A central feature of the connection between life and theatre, and one which emphasises further the indistinct nature of the boundaries between them, is the frequent use of theatrical language. Characters are constantly referring to events in their lives using theatrical metaphors. Perhaps unsurprisingly, this occurs most frequently in plays which feature considerable elements of role-play. *The Forest*, for example, with its focus on the contrast between noble actors and the ignoble, hypocritical gentry, is a play which makes much use of theatrical metaphor. Thus in Act One, Scene 7, Aksin′ya asks Gurmyzhskaya: '... What's the point of this comedy?' Gurmyzhskaya responds: 'Comedy? How dare you? And even if it were only a comedy, suppose it were only a farce, I feed and clothe you and I force you to play this comedy' (iii, p. 265/6). When Gurmyzhskaya accidentally lets slip to Neschastlivtsev that she owes him a thousand roubles, she berates herself, noting: 'It was a mistake to remind him of that debt. Why did I get so sentimental? You play and play a role, and then you get in too deep' (iii, p. 299). Schastlivtsev, talking of Bulanov, notes: '... it's clear that schoolboy is cleverer than you. He is playing his role here better than you are.' Neschastlivtsev asks: 'What role is that then? ... He's nothing but a boy.' Schastlivtsev responds: 'What role? That of first lover' ... 'He plays the role of a lover, and you ... that of a simpleton' (iii, p. 301). And at the end of the play, Gurmyzhskaya twice refers to her situation as a comedy: 'Well, thank God everything is settled now and I can enjoy my happiness to the full. How much unpleasantness I have had to bear in this stupid comedy with my relatives!' (iii, p. 323). 'This comedy is unnecessary' (iii, p. 326). V.Lakshin has noted that 'even Gurmyzhskaya's vocabulary betrays her as an ... actress, a pretender.' He highlights the phrases: 'I came out of my role', 'this stupid comedy with my relatives', 'I force you to play this comedy'.[34]

Even Wise Men Err also contains theatrical references. In Act One, Scene 2, Golutvin complains of Glumov: 'Look at him play-acting; he's our brother all right, a real Isaac' (iii, p. 10). (The 'Isaac' refers to the Biblical story where Isaac pretended that he was Rebecca's brother rather than her husband, for fear that the men of Gerar might kill him in order to take his wife (Genesis 26: 7-10)). And in Act Two, Scene 6, when Mamaeva tells Gorodulin that she wishes to appear before him as a petitioner, he replies: 'That is, you want to switch roles with me?' (iii, p. 30)

Similarly in *Wolves and Sheep*, Glafira tells Kupavina of the 'foul role' she has been playing and declares: '... Enough of playing this comedy' (iv, p. 151). When Lynyaev and Glafira are play-acting at being in love, he asks her: 'have you entered into your role, or don't you consider me to be a man?' (iv, p. 169), and she later notes: 'It seems that you too are beginning to find your role to your taste' (iv, p. 172).

Such references to life as theatre are common throughout Ostrovsky's drama, not simply in those plays where the focus is on role-play. Thus in *Difficult Days*, Dosuzhev talks of his work as '... not business, but comedy' (ii, p. 451). In *An Old Friend is Better than Two New Ones*, Pul´kheriya notes: 'But at the Chepugovs' yesterday, a story came out—the cook told me today at the market—what a comedy!' (ii, p. 273). In *Incompatibility of Character* Pol and Prezhneva talk of their predicament as a tragedy:

---

[34] See *PSS* iii, 488.

Pol. No, Maman, it is a tragedy.

Prezhneva. A tragedy, mon cher!

Pol. And what a tragedy! Those there, with their murders and their poisonings—all that is rubbish! (ii, p. 146)

In *A Lucrative Post*, Vyshnevsky tells Zhadov: 'Noble poverty is only good in the theatre. Just try it out in real life' (ii, p. 50), and Yusov, laughing at Zhadov's convictions and determination to find a position away from his uncle, states: 'It's really a comedy, honest to God, it's a comedy, ha, ha, ha ...' (ii, p. 51).

The Handsome Man is full of references to theatrical terms. In Act One, Scene 4, Apollinariya, remembering the suffering she was caused by being married off before she had learned to value men by their looks, states: 'No, it's a real drama, gentlemen!' (v, p. 293). In Act Two, Scene 8, Okoemov tells Zoya that her principled view of life is untenable: 'it isn't even a life, it's an eternal tragedy' (v, p. 315). Much theatrical language is centred around the 'infidelity scene'. In Act One, Scene 8, in an attempt to reassure Zoya of the rightness of his plan, Okoemov says: 'You know that everyone will know that it is just a comedy' (v, p. 314). In Act Three, Scene 5, when Okoemov stages the 'accidental' discovery of his wife's 'infidelity', he calls it a 'sad scene' and states that he is 'one of the leading players in this family drama' (v, p. 332). In Act Three, Scene 7, Zoya asks: 'Well, my dear, did I play my role well?' and Okoemov replies: 'Yes, so well that it is possible to doubt whether you were playing a role, or whether you do indeed love Oleshunin' (v, p. 334).

In *A Last Sacrifice*, Lavr notes: 'Yes, I understand my role now and I shall know how to act it' (iv, p. 356). In *A Young Man's Morning*, the Second Young Man talks of 'playing roles' (i, p. 158). And in *Hard-earned Bread* Gruntsov's response to Korpelov's account of events at Potrokhov's is to declare: '(*tragically*) A drama in my soul!' (iv, p. 90), while in a later scene the deceiving Koprov tells Natasha: 'It will be like playing a comedy' (iv, p. 93).

In *Without a Dowry*, when Robinson looks at the way Karandyshev has furnished his house, he asks: 'What's that hung there? Stage properties?' (v, p. 54), and later, watching Paratov getting Karandyshev drunk, he notes: 'Karandyshev is a goner. I started him, and Serge'll finish him off. Now they're pouring, they're striking up a pose, it's a living picture. Just see what a smile Serge has! Just like

Bertram. (*He sings from Meyerbeer's opera* Robert le Diable) 'You are my saviour.' ... 'I am your saviour!' ... 'And protector!' (v, p. 56). Later in the same play, Knurov observes: 'It looks as though the drama's about to start' (v, p. 70). Similarly in *Guilty without Guilt*, the actors in the play again use theatrical terms to describe events in real life. Thus, in Act Three, Scene 1, Nina complains to Milovzorov: 'How can you dare to play such heroic lovers on stage, if you are afraid to sacrifice yourself just once in your life for me? ...' (v, p. 392); Shmaga refers to Milovzorov as 'playing the lover, both on stage and in real life' (v, p. 394). When Nina asks Neznamov to escort her to Dudukin's dinner, Neznamov asks Milovzorov: 'what sort of comedy is this?' (v, p. 398) and later complains to him: 'Can't you slip out of your stupid role for a minute!' (v, p. 400). Both Milovzorov and Nina imply that Kruchinina's goodness is nothing but an act. In Act Three, Scene 1, Nina complains: '... And the most annoying thing of all is her falseness. She affects modesty; behaves like an innocent; pretends to be some kind of recluse ... And everyone believes her—that's what's so irritating' (v, p. 390); and when Neznamov talks of the warmth and sincerity in Kruchinina's voice and manner, Milovzorov declares: 'She's an actress, a good actress' (v, p. 400), prompting Neznamov to muse: 'An actress! An actress! So play on the stage. They pay good money for pretence there. But to play in real life, to play with simple, trusting hearts, which have no need for acting ... that is worthy of extreme punishment ... we don't need deception! We need the truth, the honest truth! An actress! ...' (v, p. 401). In Act Three, Scene 6, Nina, pleased with the way her plan is working, declares: 'This means there will be a good show tonight, ' and Milovzorov adds: 'Yes, with a grand finale; Neznamov always brings things to an effective close' (v, p. 401).

As with the references to literature, the effect of this theatrical language is to blur the boundaries between created, fictional reality and so-called 'real life'. Perhaps Ostrovsky's message is most clearly spelt out in *Guilty without Guilt*, when Neznamov declares: 'I would love to know how today's famous actors behave in ordinary life. Do they go on making-believe as they do on stage?' Korinkina replies: 'Most probably. You need a great deal of experience, you must have lived a long time in this world, before you can distinguish between true and feigned feelings' (v, p. 409). Again Ostrovsky appears to be questioning the nature of reality, posing the question of what is truly real.

Questioning the nature of reality and exploring the relationship between life and art are, of course, common themes in world literature and philosophy. (The brief discussion of Lermontov's *A Hero of our Time* is a testament to this.) The sentiment expressed by Shakespeare: 'All the world's a stage, And all the men and women merely players' (*As You Like It*) has now become so familiar, it has almost been reduced to the level of cliché. This in itself makes it doubly surprising that such a considerable element of Ostrovsky's drama has been so neglected in established critical analysis—all the more so, given that Ostrovsky was a man so imbued with the make-believe world of the theatre. Time and again, in his constant references to literature and theatre, his ubiquitous deceivers, role-players and fantasists, Ostrovsky 'the realist', the man who 'put real Russian life on the stage', is also reversing the process. In creating his illusion of reality on the stage, he is suggesting that reality is equally illusory. Similarly, in his frequent blurring of the boundaries between the real and the imagined, Ostrovsky questions our assumptions about the nature of reality. His plays question what is truly real, leaving us with a sense that perhaps there is no such thing as a comfortably defined reality. As ever, such questions are not limited to time or place, but resound with universality.

CHAPTER SEVEN

Through the Looking-Glass: Symbols of Illusion

'I can see into her as if
into a mirror.' *Wolves
and Sheep* (iv, p. 202)

It seems clear that the exploration of reality in Ostrovsky's drama extends far beyond the limits set down by traditional critical interpretation of his plays. His work does not end with the recreation of contemporary social realities, but goes on to consider reality on psychological and philosophical levels. His plays explore a number of universal questions relating to the nature of reality itself; the existence of different realities; the relationship between real and illusory worlds; the means of reconciling the ideal with the real.

A striking manifestation of Ostrovsky's concern with these themes (and one which, to the best of this author's knowledge, has been entirely overlooked in critical analysis) is the repeated use of mirrors in his plays. As Appendix G illustrates, mirrors are looked into, discussed, or specifically mentioned as forming part of the scenery in at least twenty-six of the forty-one original works analysed in detail in this study, often occurring more than once within a given play. The incidence of use listed in Appendix G is probably not comprehensive, yet even as it stands it represents a preoccupation amounting to a minor obsession. No fewer than fifty-seven references to mirrors are listed.

Using mirrors is, of course, an ordinary, everyday human activity, and its occurrence in his plays can be seen as simply another touch of realistic detail on Ostrovsky's part: the young girl checking her appearance in anticipation of a visit from an admirer; the employee straightening his clothes before reporting to his boss. Certainly, the repeated use of a particular item of stage property is not in itself necessarily surprising, nor is it a unique phenomenon among playwrights. Chekhov had a similar preoccupation with clocks—thirteen timepieces appear in *Three Sisters* alone. But, as Chekhov's obsession with clocks reflected his preoccupation with the passage of time, so Ostrovsky's use of mirrors takes on greater significance if one takes as one's starting-point a concern with the nature of reality and the relationship between reality and illusion. As in the adventures of Lewis Carroll's 'Alice', mirrors often symbolise a bridge between actual and fantasy worlds. They represent an inversion of reality and a concern with superficial appearances. We stand before a mirror when donning a mask or disguise, or when practising a deliberate facial expression. When we look into a mirror we are reducing our field of vision, focusing inwards on the self and ignoring the world around us.[1]

The image of the mirror is a well-established literary device. It spans many countries and centuries, encompassing fairy-tales ('Mirror, mirror on the wall, Who is the fairest of them all?'), gothic horror, psychological tales and classical narcissism. The critic T.Ziolkowski provides a comprehensive analysis of the significance of mirrors in European literature in his book *Disenchanted Images: A literary iconology*, which includes a whole chapter on 'The Magic Mirror'.[2] He divides mirror usage into three principal categories—'the catoptromantic mirror', which the viewer consults for information; the 'doubling' mirror, where the viewer confronts his own

---

[1] I.Esam, discussing the symbolic use of names in *Not of this World*, is one of the few critics to notice the paradox inherent in reconciling Ostrovsky's realism with his use of symbols. She notes: 'Although a realistic painter of manners and morals, Ostrovsky resorted to symbolism and the language of symbolism on numerous occasions.' (She does not, however, see mirrors as an important symbol in Ostrovsky's work.) See Esam, 'An Analysis of Ostrovsky's *Ne ot mira sego*', 73. Further discussion of symbols in Ostrovsky's work is found in N.P.Kashin, 'Simvolika Ostrovskogo', *Zhizn'*, 3 (1922), 5-26, and in S.S.Danilov, *Ocherki po istorii russkogo dramaticheskogo teatra* (Moscow: Iskusstvo, 1948), 344, who notes: 'Objects in Ostrovsky's plays are not decorative accessories, but also a means of scenic expression, actively taking part in the development of the action.' He too fails to mention mirrors.

[2] Theodore Ziolkowski, *Disenchanted Images: A literary iconology* (Princeton: Princeton University Press, 1977), 149-227. For further examination of mirrors and mirror worlds in literature, see: M.H.Abrams, 'Imitation and the mirror' in *The Mirror and the Lamp: Romantic theory and the critical tradition*, by M.H.Abrams (New York: O.U.P, 1953), 30-47; and Beverly Lyon Clark, *Reflections of Fantasy: The Mirror-Worlds of Carroll, Nabokov and Pynchon* (New York: Peter Lang, 1986).

double (usually signifying the viewer's soul or psyche); and the 'penetrable' mirror, through which the viewer can enter another world. He also draws attention to the traditional metaphorical image of literature holding up a mirror to life, and the Christian Platonic image of the mirror as a metaphor for the world of superficial appearances, distracting men from the divine truth. He cites James 1: 23-24: 'For if any be a hearer of the word and not a doer, he is like unto a man beholding his natural face in a glass: For he beholdeth himself, and goeth his way, and straightway forgetteth what manner of man he was.'[3]

All the uses of the mirror symbol discussed by Ziolkowski are well documented in Russian (and Western European) literature and Ostrovsky must surely have been familiar with many of them. Certainly, he would have been aware of the sudden explosion of works in the 1840s involving doubles (and their psychological implications)—Dostoevsky's *The Double*, for example, which makes frequent mention of mirrors. Similarly, he would have been aware of the popular Russian practice of divination using mirrors (the 'catoptromantic' mirror) which is well-described in Russian literature (notably stanzas IX and X in Chapter Five of Pushkin's *Evgenii Onegin*); and the famous epigraph to Gogol's *The Government Inspector*: 'There is no point grumbling at the mirror, if your own mug is crooked, ' with its implications about the duty of literature to hold up a mirror to life, whatever is reflected within.

Examination of the use Ostrovsky makes of mirrors in his plays clearly suggests a significance far beyond simple background detail. The characters who use mirrors are almost always those who are distorting or avoiding reality in some way. In *A Young Man's Morning*, for example, the mirror user is the blind-to-reality Nedopekin, a young landowner obsessed with appearing fashionable. He is connected with mirrors on no fewer than six occasions, and each one emphasises his concern with appearance at the expense of reality. Thus he is shown parading before the mirror, trying on new clothes and practising the latest fashionable walk, all the while blithely ignoring the reality of his mounting debts and the confidence tricks of his acquaintances, who are exploiting him for every penny they can. In *The Unfree* the mirror-user is Miron, an alcoholic with delusions of

[3] Ziolkowski, 152.

grandeur, who spends much of his time in drunken oblivion, unaware of what is happening around him. He employs a mirror when trying to disguise the fact that he has a hangover by tying a handkerchief around his face and pretending he has toothache (iv, p. 181).

Often the sole mirror user in a play is a character who is practising some kind of deception. Glumov in *Even Wise Men Err* is twice connected to mirrors, once when Mamaev tells him to practise 'making eyes' in the mirror—thus mirrors are connected to Glumov's role-playing (iii, p. 34), and once just before he discovers the loss of his diary (the means by which his deception is revealed) (iii, p. 66). Vikhorev in *Don't Get Above Yourself* checks his appearance in the mirror before going to meet Avdot'ya, whom he hopes to cheat out of her dowry (i, p. 292). Evgeniya in *At a Lively Spot* primps before the mirror after pretending that she does not like to flirt with the customers (ii, p. 546). Belesova in *Rich Brides* looks in the mirror after agreeing to deceive Tsyplunov into marriage (iv, p. 238). Antrygina in *Don't Poke your Nose into Others' Squabbles* smartens herself in front of a mirror before pretending to be in love with Bal'-zaminov (ii, p. 333). Gradoboev in *An Ardent Heart* keeps the promissory notes he collects behind a mirror (iii, p. 118).

Elsewhere, the mirror-user is a character who avoids or is blind to reality, such as the day-dreaming Bal'zaminov in *A Holiday Dream before Dinner*, who checks his appearance in the mirror in Picture One, Scene 2, or the other-worldly Kseniya in *Not of this World*, who twice looks in a mirror during her conversation with Elokhov in Act One, Scene 9. (Kseniya's use of the mirror reflects the dichotomy between the real and the ideal at the basis of the play. She looks in the mirror to check her appearance, expressing her fear that Vitalii might no longer find her attractive—a worldly concern. Yet the timing of her two glances is telling: the first glance occurs immediately after she has sought reassurance from Elokhov that Vitalii still loves her, and the second immediately after Elokhov has told her of Vitalii's plans to buy an estate in the country, prompting her to declare: 'Really? And I have dreamed so often about just that. It's as if he has read my mind' (v, p. 443). Thus the mirror is also linked to her fantasy 'ideal'.)

The precise point in a play at which Ostrovsky chooses to make his characters look into mirrors is of crucial significance. Although the characters are performing everyday, realistic tasks, such as grooming their hair or tying on a scarf in preparation for going out, it is striking how frequently such action takes place in the middle of discussion relating to dreams and fantasies, or when characters are adopting a role of some kind. On other occasions when grooming hair or putting on a scarf would seem to be equally appropriate, mirrors do not appear. A character's distortion or avoidance of reality is often made clear at the point at which he or she looks into a mirror. The mirror serves to demonstrate to the audience that a character is ignoring (or is blind to) the true nature of reality; such people are concerning themselves with outward appearances or inner fantasies. In *Talents and Admirers*, for example, the only point at which a mirror is used is in Act Three, Scene 2, when Velikatov describes his country estate to Domna Pantelevna. To her, his estate sounds 'like paradise'. She immediately goes to the mirror to try on a shawl he has bought her and stands there, imagining herself as a lady on such an estate. The mirror serves as a link to her fantasy world. In *The Handsome Man*, Susanna, a woman who believes that beautiful men can do no wrong, and who is therefore constantly deceived by them, breaks off in the middle of discussing her latest love to go and check her own appearance in the mirror (v, p. 318)—thereby demonstrating the narrowness of her focus and her concern with appearance at the expense of reality. Similarly, it must surely be significant that the one point in *The Storm* where a mirror is used occurs when Varvara, covering her head with a scarf, explains to Katya the arrangements for a secret meeting with their lovers (ii, p. 234). Again, a mirror is employed at a point when a momentary escape from reality, a possible fufilment of fantasy, is being discussed. Significantly, a recent production of *The Storm* in Moscow, produced by Genrietta Yanovskaya, had mirror doors forming part of the set. It is from behind these doors that people with dogs' heads appear before Feklusha. Varvara and Kudryash elope by running through them, and Katerina's dead body is brought out on stage from behind these same mirror doors. Thus not only does Yanovskaya physically represent on stage a barrier between the real world and some kind of other, fantasy world (a reviewer of the production refers to the area behind the doors as a 'fantastic' or 'otherworldly' space, noting: 'Yanovskaya's productions in general are very frequently built on the juxtaposition of real and fantastic, otherworldly worlds'[4]) but she chooses to use mirrors to create this barrier. In stark contrast, recent UK productions of *The Storm* and *It's all in the Family* both omitted mirrors from their productions altogther, failing even to have a mirror as part of the background scenery.[5]

One of the most striking scenes in which a mirror appears is Scene 10 in Part Two of *All Good Things Come to an End*. Faced with either losing his fiancée or confronting his boss and requesting a pay-rise, the cowardly Ippolit first gets drunk, then looks in a mirror, and only then, completely transformed, and speaking in the elevated language and melodramatic tones of a romantic hero, does he go and confront his boss. As noted earlier in the section on the Psychological Level, alcohol undoubtedly plays a large part in effecting his transformation, but it is notable that Ostrovsky chooses to make Ippolit look in a mirror at the exact moment at which he adopts the role of a romantic hero.

Mirrors even seem to have significance in those plays where they are simply mentioned as forming part the scenery. It is surely deliberate that in *Incompatibility of Character* it is the drawing-room of the idealistic, self-deceiving Prezhneva which is described as containing two long narrow mirrors with gilt frames. In *Poverty is No Vice*, there are mirrors on every wall in the drawing-room of the obsessed-with-appearance Gordei Tortsov, yet none are mentioned in Mitya's or Arina's rooms. The reception room of the deceiving Vyshnevsky in *A Lucrative Post* has a mirror on each side wall. And in *Wolves and Sheep*, it is the scheming, role-playing Murzavetskaya who has two long, narrow mirrors in her drawing-room—there are no mirrors mentioned in the Acts which take place in Kupavina's home. The deceiving Murzavetskaya is connected with mirrors on a further occasion. Talking to Kupavina in Act Five, Scene 9, she claims: 'I can see into her as if into a mirror' (iv, p. 202). Again, the mirror is mentioned when deception is taking place—Murzavetskaya is pre-

---

[4] Marina Davydova, 'Za zerkal´noi dver´yu: "Groza" v Moskovskom TYUZe, postanovka Genrietty Yanovskoi' in *Elektronnaya versiya 'Nezavisimoi gazety'*, no. 048 (1373), 18 March 1997.

[5] The two productions were: *A Family Affair*, The Drayton Court Theatre Company, London, March 1997 and *The Storm*, The Rosemary Branch Theatre, London, May 1997. (In the former case, the production used the Nick Dear adaptation of Ostrovsky's play, which itself does not contain any references to mirrors.)

tending to be acting on her own initiative when in fact she is acting at the behest of Berkutov. This mirror reference has again been overlooked in English translation. D.Magarshack translates it as: 'I can read her like a book.'[6]

This complex symbolic role of mirrors as a link between real and fantasy worlds, or as an indicator of blindness to reality, or a signal of deception, is perhaps best illustrated in two plays which make multiple use of mirrors: *It's All in the Family* and *The Poor Bride*. In the first of these plays, it is Lipochka who most frequently looks into mirrors. Since she is a young woman seeking a husband, this is perhaps not surprising, but it is important to note that she is a character who is unhappy with the reality of her situation as the daughter of a coarse Moscow merchant. She wishes to escape from that reality by adopting a new role, that of the wife of a fashionable nobleman or officer, and she constantly fantasises about such a life. Lipochka glances into a mirror on three occasions and each is linked to discussion about her fantasy world.

Thus, in Act One, Scene 6, she describes to her mother and the matchmaker how her nobleman should look, and then glances in the mirror to check her own appearance:

> **Lipochka.** It doesn't matter if he's fat, so long as he's not short. Of course, it would be better if he was tall, rather than some kind of runt. But most of all, Ustin'ya Naumovna, he mustn't be snub-nosed, and he absolutely must be dark-haired. Well, of course, it's understood that he will dress like the men in magazines. (*Looks in the mirror.*) Agh, heavens! But I'm all dishevelled myself today, my hair looks like a broom! (i, p. 94)

In Act Three, Scene 3, she again checks her own appearance in the mirror and then declares that she would like to marry a soldier—again the mirror is linked with her fantasy world:

> **Lipochka.** Well, I'll stay then, mama. (*Goes and looks in the mirror, then approaches her father.*) Daddy!
> **Bol'shov.** What do you want?
> **Lipochka.** I'm ashamed to say it, daddy!
> **Agrafena.** What's there to be ashamed of, you little fool! Speak, if you need something.

---

[6] See Magarshack, *Easy Money and Two Other Plays*, 284.

Ustin´ya. Shame isn't smoke, it won't sting your eyes.

Bol´shov. Well, go and hide yourself, if you're ashamed.

Agrafena. You want a new hat, is that it?

Lipochka. There, you haven't guessed right at all, it's definitely not a hat.

Bol´shov. Well, what do you want then?

Lipochka. To marry a soldier! (i, p. 129)

(It is noteworthy that the link here between bridegrooms and mirrors has connotations with the divination practices—the catoptromantic mirror—mentioned above.)

In Act Three, Scene 5, Lipochka learns that her actual husband is going to be her father's assistant, Podkhalyuzin. At first she is disgusted by the idea, but when he tells her that he has control of her father's wealth, and he describes how they will live in luxury, and dress in the latest fashions, it seems that her fantasy world is about to become reality, and she again goes and primps in the mirror:

Lipochka. So look here, Lazar Elizarych, we'll live by ourselves, and they'll live by themselves. We'll do everything according to fashion, and they can do what they want.

Podkhalyuzin. That's exactly how it will be.

Lipochka. Well then, call daddy now. (*She stands and primps in front of the mirror.*) (i, p. 136)

The final use of a mirror in the play is in Act Four, Scene 1, which shows Lipochka and Podkhalyuzin in their luxurious new apartment. Podkhalyuzin is standing before a mirror in a stylish frock-coat, and declaring that he looks just like a Frenchman. It appears that Lipochka and Podkhalyuzin have succesfully realized their fantasy:

Olimpiada Samsonovna sits by the window, luxuriating; she is wearing a silk blouse and the latest style of bonnet. Podkhalyuzin, wearing a fashionable frock-coat, stands in front of the mirror. Tishka stands behind him arranging and adjusting his clothes.

Tishka. Look at you, how well it fits. It's just right!

Podkhalyuzin. Well, Tishka, do I look like a Frenchman? Eh? Stand a bit further away and look!

Tishka. Two peas in a pod.

Podkhalyuzin. That's enough, you fool! Well, now, look at us! (*Walks around the room.*) So, Alimpiada Samsonovna! You

wanted to marry an officer. Don't I come up to scratch? Here, I just
grabbed the frock-coat and put it on. (i, p. 139)

It is here also that a second significance of the use of mirrors in the
play becomes apparent: the concentration on outward appearances.
As noted earlier in the section on the Psychological Level, dreams of
rising in rank are almost always couched in terms of appearance.[7]
Lipochka is no exception to this rule and throughout the play she
couches her dreams of a different life in terms of appearances: the
clothes she will wear, the carriages she will ride in and so forth.
Similarly, her constant grooming in the mirror emphasises how much
her attention is focused on appearance. As Act Four makes clear,
however, outward appearance is often superficial, for despite their
grand appearances Lipochka and her husband remain in essence the
uncouth merchants they have always been. Their new life is little
more than illusory.

The other character to use a mirror in the play is Tishka,
Bol´shov's downtrodden houseboy. He pulls faces in a mirror and his
accompanying words imply that he is imitating Bol´shov:

> **Tishka** (*with a broom at the front of the stage.*) Oh, what a life,
> what a life! Sweep the floors before it's light! What business is it
> of mine to sweep floors? ... But if you wanted to tear yourself away
> from the house, to play cards or stick-to-the-wall with your mates,
> maybe—well it's better not even to think of it! Yes, and there's
> something not right with my head! (*Kneels on the stool and looks
> in the mirror.*) Hello, Tikhon Savost´yanych! How are you? Well
> enough to praise God? ... But you, Tishka, play a little trick. (*Pulls
> a face.*) That's it! (*Pulls another.*) Just like ... (*Bursts out
> laughing.*) (i, p. 107)

Thus he too takes momentary respite from the harshness of his life to
indulge in fantasy—and a mirror is again the link. On this occasion,
however, the implication drawn from the play is that the role he
adopts is likely to become reality, as Bol´shov himself started out
from similarly humble beginnings. (In an early draft of the play,
Ostrovsky planned to open the play with this scene of Tishka before
the mirror—perhaps, again, emphasising the importance of mirrors in
the work.)

---

[7] See pp. 115-17.

In *The Poor Bride* it is another young woman, Mar´ya, who makes most use of mirrors. In Act One, Scene 5, she twice looks in the mirror when she sees Merich approaching the house. This, again, is an ordinary, everyday action—a young woman preparing to meet the man she loves—which takes on greater significance given that, at this point in the play, she views Merich as the subject of her fantasy world, her means of escape from her position as a dowerless young woman, while being unaware of his true nature. The link between mirrors and fantasy is made even more explicit in Act Five, Scene 3, when Mar´ya talks of her hopes to improve Benevolensky, the coarse, ill-educated civil servant she is eventually forced to marry. She asks Dobrotvorsky whether her hopes to change her husband are mere childish dreams, before sinking down in thought on to a stool. The stool is situated in front of a pier-glass:

> **Mar´ya.** Listen, Platon Markych, I got this idea in my head. Perhaps you'll think it's funny. I thought and thought, and do you know what I came up with?
> *Dobrotvorsky looks at her.*
> Only don't laugh at me ... It seemed to me that I was marrying him in order to improve him, to turn him into a decent person. Is that stupid, Platon Markych? It's probably silly, an impossible thing to do, hm? Isn't that so, Platon Markych? Just childish dreams?
> **Dobrotvorsky.** Animals are wild, but they can be tamed ...
> **Mar´ya.** Without this thought, Platon Markych, it would be so difficult for me. It's the only thing keeping me alive now. Help me through it, Platon Markych.
> **Dobrotvorsky.** You know what, young lady, I'll tell you a Russian proverb: 'What will be, will be, and it will be as God wills it.' But there's another one: 'You can't overtake a bridegroom, even on horseback.'
> *Mar´ya sits on a stool near the pier-glass and sinks into thought.* (i, p. 269)

Benevolensky himself looks into mirrors twice and on both occasions the accompanying discussion makes clear his concern with appearance and the falsity of his image of himself as a good catch for Mar´ya. In Act Two, Scene 10, for example, he talks of how he must have a good-looking bride to show off in society, then: '(*takes a comb and combs his hair before the mirror*)', asking: 'Well, my friend, so you say the young lady is pretty?' (i, p. 222)—emphasising his concern with appearance. And in Act Five, Scene 8, shortly before he is to marry Mar'ya, he notes: 'I tell you, sir, I shan't be ashamed to appear in society with such a woman' (again demonstrating his concern with appearance), before looking in a mirror and remarking to Dobrotvorsky: 'Well, what do you think, will we make a good match?' (i, p. 273). He cannot understand why Dobrotvorsky laughs in reply, highlighting his inflated opinion of himself.

The other character in the play to use a mirror is Milashin, a man who, as noted earlier, bases his whole life on a refusal to accept reality, and who has instead constructed a fantasy image for himself.[8] He is shown looking in a mirror in Act Five, Scene 7, practising the facial expression he wishes to adopt when attending Mar'ya's wedding:

> **Milashin** (*alone.*) ... I hope my face shows how deep my hurt is. (*Looks in the mirror.*) God, what a stupid expression, it actually looks ridiculous! No, let her notice the evil irony in my eyes. (*Looks in the mirror.*) ... (i, p. 273)

The examples discussed above are, as Appendix G illustrates, simply a fraction of the instances where mirrors appear in Ostrovsky's plays, and it is the repetitive nature of their use—constantly appearing at moments relating to discussion of dreams and fantasies and involving characters who are in some way distanced from reality—which strongly suggests that their significance goes beyond mere realistic detail to encompass a symbolic importance. As such, the presence of mirrors in his work is a further indication that, in their exploration of reality, Ostrovsky's plays go beyond social levels to consider more complex questions of the nature of reality.

Pictures in Ostrovsky's Drama

Whilst occurring much more infrequently than mirrors, references to pictures, both in dialogue and as stage properties, are of similar interest. Once more, it is possible to argue that a picture on a wall or a phrase such as 'pretty as a picture' are simply further examples of Ostrovsky's realism: to decorate a room with paintings is a common, realistic touch, and analogies with pictures are common figures of

---

speech. Yet again, given the context of a concern with the nature of reality, the use of pictures, both physically and metaphorically, is imbued with far greater significance. A picture is an image, a representation of reality; a picture is an illusion of reality; and as such it once more acts as a signal that the reality presented on stage may be equally insubstantial.

As with mirrors, it is the timing of the references to pictures which gives them their significance. They frequently occur in conjunction with characters who are themselves little more than images, either unduly obsessed with appearance at the expense of reality, or projecting a false representation of reality. Strikingly, where pictures are specifically mentioned as forming part of the scenery, it is often in association with mirrors. Thus in *At a Lively Spot*, the room at the inn which, as has been noted earlier, is a den of deception (or false representations of reality) has 'a mirror hanging in the space between two windows' on both sides of which hang 'crude portraits' (ii, p. 544). Similarly in the description of scenery in Act One of *Late Love*, there is 'an ancient mirror, on both sides of which hang two faded pictures in paper frames' (iv, p. 8). And the blind-to-reality Nedopekin in *A Young Man's Morning* not only has a pier-glass on the wall, but also 'etchings' (i, p. 154).

Pictures which appear on their own in the descriptions of scenery are just as significant. In the Puzatovs' house in *A Family Picture*— again a place of much deception—there are 'portraits above the divan' (i, p. 66). And Act Two of *Jokers*, an Act which contains numerous instances of deceit, takes place 'near the city gates, where pictures are traded' (ii, p. 509).

Equally significant are the references to pictures in speech. Again, almost without exception, these occur in relation to characters who are either unduly concerned with appearance at the expense of reality, or are presenting a false image, distorting reality in some way. Most frequently perhaps, references to pictures occur in association with false lovers: men who are acting the part of a devoted lover in order to deceive their unwitting (blind-to-reality) victims and gain their fortunes. Thus in *A Last Sacrifice*, Dulchin is described as '... so young and handsome ... and dressed up like a picture ...' (iv, p. 322). In *The Forest*, Bulanov is described as '... a picture, not a mere man'. (iii, p. 315); while in *Don't Get Above Yourself*, Avdot´ya exclaims to

Vikhorev: 'How handsome you are! I've never seen the like ... just as if you'd been painted!' (i, p. 313). In *Hard-earned Bread*, Natasha, having learned of the cheating and deception practised by Koprov, takes out a portrait of him and talks to it, thereby emphasising most forcefully the suggestion that his role of lover had been little more than an image: she can even substitute talking to a portrait for talking to the 'real' man. Similarly, in *Guilty without Guilt*, Lyubov learns of Murov's deception by being shown a picture of him.

On other occasions, references to pictures are used to emphasise a character's concern with appearance. In *It's All in the Family*, Lipoch-ka, dreaming of dancing with officers, notes that she would be 'dressed all in flowers, like a doll or a picture in a magazine' (i, p. 86) (a doll is another false representation of reality). Later, she declares that she wants her husband to 'dress like the men in magazines' (i, p. 94). When she herself is all dressed up in expectation of meeting a prospective husband, Bol´shov notes: 'We don't have to put her in a picture frame!' (i, p. 125). In the Bal´zaminov trilogy, the dreaming Bal´zaminov, who is obsessed with appearance, is frequently referred to in terms of images. Krasavina's very first words to him in *You'll Find what you Seek* are: 'Here's a picture of beauty, what a painting!' (ii, p. 345).

Elsewhere pictures are used to highlight a character's blindness to reality. In *A Last Sacrifice*, shortly after Irina and Lavr discuss their obsession with literature, Irina asks: 'Uncle dear, isn't that a new picture hanging in your ballroom?' and suggests to Lavr that they '... go and look at it more closely ...' (iv, p. 349). Thus they exchange one representation of reality—literature—for another. In *The Abyss*, a reference to pictures is used ironically. When his university friends point out to the blind-to-reality Kisel´nikov the very real dangers of giving up his university education to marry a merchant's daughter, he dismisses their concerns with the words: 'What gloomy pictures!' (ii, p. 594)—thus the real is dismissed as false. In contrast, shortly after-wards, the pompous Pogulyaev, eulogising on the beauty of the scene around him, begins his eulogy with the statement: 'What a picture!' (ii, p. 594), thereby emphasising the falseness of his words.

Further examples of significant allusions to pictures occur in *The Storm*, where Katya's dreams of escape include visions of a paradise where the temples, gardens, hills and trees are 'not at all like ordinary ones, but like those painted on icons' (ii, p. 222); and in *A Lucrative Post*, where Yusov, a chief representative of the bribe-taking civil service, likens his situation to a picture (namely a cheap popular print of 1820-21, significantly entitled 'Vanity of Vanities') (ii, p. 103).

As with mirrors, the frequency with which references to pictures occur in conjunction with characters who are in some way distorting or avoiding reality suggests that they have a symbolic meaning above and beyond the faithful depiction of social realities. And again, such references add further weight to the assertion that the exploration of reality in Ostrovsky's plays goes beyond the limits traditionally set down in critical analysis of his work.

CHAPTER EIGHT

Supernatural Reality

'The people here boil as if in hell: there is noise, up-roar, devilish songs!' *You Can't Live as you Please* (i, p. 381)

In the exploration of reality in his plays Ostrovsky largely overlooks consideration of the existence of a supernatural reality. Indeed, D.Magarshack, discussing the 'microcosm ... of ... heaven and hell' that is *The Storm*, notes specifically that 'the stature of Ostrovsky as a creative artist can perhaps best be judged from the fact that to create this world he does not resort to any symbolism and supernatural machinery, but bases it firmly on the solid facts of human nature.'[1] Overt suggestions of some kind of 'other', super-natural reality occur in depth in only two of the Ostrovsky plays con-sidered in detail in this study: one is *Not of this World*, which, as was discussed earlier, contains elements that hint at a link between Murugov and the Devil[2]; the other is *You Can't Live as you Please*. This latter play falls into the category of Ostrovsky plays commonly described as the 'Slavophile' plays, which are generally viewed as an attempt by Ostrovsky to move away from the satirical flavour of his earliest plays and instead portray traditional Russian characters and customs in a positive light. Ostrovsky himself wrote in a letter to Pogodin at this time: '... My direction is beginning to change ... the view of life in my first play seems to me juvenile and too harsh; ... it is better to let the Russian people rejoice, seeing themselves on stage,

---

[1] David Magarshack, 'He Created Russia's National Theatre', *Anglo-Soviet Journal*, 9 (1948), 6-10 (p. 8).
[2] See p. 129.

rather than be sad ... to have the right to improve the people you must not insult them, you must show them that you know that there is good in them ...'[3] *You Can't Live as you Please*, however, differs from the other 'Slavophile' plays in its explicit resemblance to the traditional morality play. Here, more than in any other play, Ostrovsky depicts a traditional battle between good and evil, with Christian virtue triumphing over Diabolic vice.

The slightly surreal atmosphere of the play is set right from the beginning, as a note from the author explains that the contents of the play 'have been taken from fairy-tales' (i, p. 379). The plot follows the fortunes of Petr, a merchant's son who has fallen into a path of drunken debauchery and is deceiving his wife, chasing after other women. The play charts his descent into ever-escalating vice until, on the point of certain death—he almost falls into an ice-hole whilst in a drunken stupor—he is saved by the sound of church bells. Fully redeemed, he returns to a life of virtue.[4]

The moral tone of the play is set in the opening pages. Il´ya, Petr's father and the chief representative of Christian virtue in the play, warns against the temptations of the Devil, referring to Moscow as if it were some kind of hell: 'I've seen enough of everything, only I've seen more evil than good ... I live like an old hermit in his cell. But here, I leave my monastery for a little while; I come to Moscow, to see you, and what vileness do I witness! The people here boil as if in hell: there is noise, uproar, devilish songs!' (i, p. 381). In a prescient warning of Petr's near death, he notes: 'Yesterday, they say, they picked up two dead bodies in the street, and someone drowned in an ice-hole. Is that a Christian death! Where will they end up?' (i, p. 381), before going on to warn of the dangers of temptation: 'He who sinks into revelry and debauchery falls from grace, and the

[3] See A.N.Ostrovskii, *Polnoe sobranie sochinenii*, ed. I.Shiryaev, 16 vols (Moscow: Khudozhestvennaya literatura, 1949-53) XIV, 39. It is important to note that this interpretation of Ostrovsky's 'Slavophile' plays is not universally accepted. Dobrolyubov, for example, sees nothing in the three plays which glorifies the old way of Russian life. (See N.A.Dobrolyubov, 'Temnoe tsarstvo' and 'Luch sveta v temnom tsarstve', in *Russkie klassiki*, ed. Yu.Oksman (Moscow: Nauka, 1970), 70-188.)

[4] In this tale of Christian redemption, a number of critics have noted links between *You Can't Live as you Please* and Tolstoy's *The Power of Darkness*. See, for example, David Matual, 'Ostrovskij in the Background of Tolstoj's "Vlast´ t´my"', *Russian Language Journal*, 121-2 (1981), 125-31.

Enemies of humankind rejoice that their will has been done. They set to business, teaching evil, wrath, sorcery and every kind of intrigue ... terrible days are coming, come to your senses!' (i, p. 383)

Elements of witchcraft are also hinted at early in the play. Petr, regretting ever having married his wife, notes gloomily: 'She bewitched me with something ... probably a potion of some kind' (i, p. 382); and later he accuses Grusha, the young girl he hopes to make his mistress, of bewitching him also (i, p. 393). Yet it is with the entrance of Eremka, the blacksmith, in Act Three, that suggestions of some evil supernatural power at work really come to the fore. Eremka is constantly associated with the Devil: Grusha refers to his having a 'cursed soul' (i, p. 393), Afim´ya, noting that Petr has got himself into bad company, suggests that he has 'probably thrust himself on some kind of werewolf' (i, p. 409), and even Petr refers to him as 'the devil!' (i, p. 407). It is Eremka who encourages Petr in his belief that his wife has somehow bewitched him and, stating that he himself is a 'magician', he tells Petr that he can take him to a sorcerer who will solve all his problems. Events come to a head in Act Three, Part 1, Scene 2. Petr returns home, full of threats against his wife: 'I'd better not lay eyes on her! I'll kill her! I'll strangle her with my own hands! She is my enemy, not my wife! Today a man told me all about her, told me everything. He knows everything, he's a sorcerer ...' (i, p. 410). In an atmospheric scene with a snowstorm raging and dogs howling outside, he suddenly sees Eremka at the window:

> **Petr.** Ah, good friend! What are you looking at me like that for? You yourself taught me how to destroy my wife! ... What are you saying, eh? Well, yes! And I say so too, you strange fellow! Let's go together. Quickly, quickly. (*He stops.*) Ha, ha, ha! You funny fellow! Here's the knife. (*He exits*). (i, p. 412)

The significance of this scene lies in the fact that Petr is the only person in the room to see Eremka. His aunt, Afim´ya, who is also in the room, sees nothing, and clearly believes that Petr is talking to the devil (a suggestion reinforced by Petr's description of Eremka as a 'strange fellow'—the Russian word *chudak* contains the suggestion of some kind of alien being):

> **Afim´ya.** Who's he talking to—there's no-one here. Ours is a holy place! Keep away from me! Keep away from me! (i, p. 412)

The implication is that Il´ya's prediction is coming true: Petr is being led to his doom by the Devil. Petr returns, saved by the sound of church bells, but his account of events clearly suggests that he was being led by devils; he again talks of '... strange and unfamiliar people ...':

> ... Here's what revelry leads to. I even wanted to kill my wife, to kill an innocent ... I took a knife as if to go after her. I imagined strange and unfamiliar people. I followed them, followed them ... I asked them 'Where is my wife?' They laughed and pointed somewhere. I walked and walked ... suddenly, somewhere, I heard bells ... I raised my arm, I saw that I was standing on a very high, exposed place on the Moscow River, on the edge of an ice-hole ... Even now it gives me the creeps! My past, dissolute life was all there, as if on the palm of my hand in front of me! ... I recalled my father's words: that I was walking in evil, on the edge of a fall. They were truthful words ...' (i, p. 414)

Despite the obvious undertones in the play of some kind of supernatural reality, they remain simply that: undertones. Just as Kseniya's fears about Murugov in *Not of this World* can be dismissed as the nervous hysteria of a dying woman, so Ostrovsky provides a rational explanation for Petr's supposed encounter with the Devil. Here Ostrovsky provides the rationale employed before him by Pushkin in *The Queen of Spades* and Gogol in *Christmas Eve*: that of drunkenness. Throughout the play there is a constant emphasis on widespread drunkenness. Spiridonova notes that 'it's Shrovetide, the people are all spinning' (i, p. 398); and Vasya and Grusha are both shown drinking heavily. Yet it is Petr who is most frequently connected with drink. Afim´ya notes in the opening words of the play: 'The whole of Shrovetide, he's been gadding about, spinning like a madman' (i, p. 380), and Petr himself often refers to his drunkenness: 'I'm quite dizzy' (i, p. 386), 'My head's going round in circles, just as if a fog has been let loose in me' (i, p. 393). Most significantly, shortly before he 'sees' Eremka at the window and sets out into the snowstorm to kill his wife, it is made clear that he has just returned from a drinking spree with Eremka (who is again the instrument of temptation). The option remains of rationalizing the 'supernatural' elements in the play as simply the hallucinations of a drunken man.

The only other concession Ostrovsky makes to the possibility of a supernatural reality is the widespread practice of fortune-telling and the concern with superstition depicted in his plays. This, however, is generally turned to comic effect by Ostrovsky, and those who express superstitious beliefs or make recourse to fortune-telling are often the subject of ridicule. Thus Dosuzhev in *Difficult Days* notes gloomily that he has fallen into 'those parts where the days are divided between lucky and unlucky; and where the people strongly believe that the world stands on three fishes and the latest news is that one of these fishes has started to move ...' (ii, p. 450/1); and Shablova in *Late Love* notes that Lebedkina '... even sends for me to tell her fortune from the cards. I spin her some nonsense or other, and she cries and laughs like a little baby' (iv, p. 11). References to such practices are, of course, further evidence of Ostrovsky's realism: fortune-telling was a popular pastime in nineteenth-century Russia and its depiction in his plays can be seen as yet another example of his attention to realistic detail. As so often, however, its use appears to take on further interest as, almost without exception, it is the most naive, blind-to-reality characters who indulge in its practice. It has already been noted how Glumov turns the blind-to-reality Turusina's obsession with fortune-tellers to the advantage of his schemes in *Even Wise Men Err*, and time and again, it is the blind-to-reality characters who seem most eager to turn to fortune-tellers. Thus in *A Last Sacrifice* it is Yuliya, the victim of the role-playing Dulchin, who considers resorting to fortune-tellers in an attempt to 'attach' Dulchin to her. In *An Old Friend is Better than Two New Ones*, it is Olin´ka, soon to be deceived by Vasyutin, who talks of a recent visit to a fortune-teller. In *Don't Poke your Nose into Others' Squabbles*, it is Antrygina, who mistakenly believes that Ustrashimov is deceiving her, who reads her fortune in the cards. In *Don't Get Above Yourself*, Avdot´ya and Arina, both victims of the deceiving Vikhorev, frequently turn to reading the cards in order to learn their fate. In *A Lucrative Post*, it is the naive Polina who indulges in reading the cards. (In her case reading the cards is also a means of avoiding reality; she tells her fortune in order to stave off what she considers to be the tedium of her life of poverty.) And in *The Unfree*, it is the blind-to-reality Miron who contemplates visiting a fortune-teller. One of the most telling instances of fortune-telling in Ostrovsky's drama occurs in *The Poor Bride* . Here, the initially realistic Mar´ya at first dismisses the possibility of knowing the future: 'If it were possible to know the future, then how I would wish to find out how our love will end ... but what will be will be' (i, p. 230/1). Then, as she becomes increasingly desperate in her attempts to avoid the reality of marrying Benevolensky and begins to sink into a fantasy world, she goes on to ask Dar´ya to read her fortune in the cards (i, p. 249). Even at this point, however, remnants of her realism remain and she tempers her request with the question: 'Well, Dasha, do you get any result? It's all nonsense, I suppose' (i, p. 249).

The suggestion of some kind of supernatural reality is not something Ostrovsky explores in any great detail in his plays. Hints at the existence of a supernatural world remain just that: hints. For the purposes of this study, the interest of such suggestions lies in the fact that they once again allude to the uncertainty of the 'reality' depicted in his plays. Like *Not of this World*, *You Can't Live as you Please* provides yet further examples of the blurring between the real and the illusory. Is Petr's sighting of Eremka at the window real or imagined? Are his visions of demons leading him across the ice real or drunken hallucinations? If such visions are imagined, then are they any less 'real' than the actuality of events as perceived by the other characters in the play?

Perhaps of greater interest is the use of fortune-telling in his plays. While not exhibiting anything close to the level of significance enjoyed by the references to mirrors and pictures discussed earlier, instances of fortune-telling do appear to act as yet another signal that the character involved is avoiding or blind to the true nature of reality, and as such, they are yet another testament to Ostrovsky's interest in this theme.

CHAPTER NINE

The Final Picture: An Analysis of *Easy Money*

'Pretending costs nothing.'
Easy Money (iii, p. 197)

Thus far, this study has examined the exploration of reality in Ostrovsky's drama thematically. It has attempted to demonstrate how a series of elements relating to the theme of reality—deception, the superficiality of appearances, blindness to reality, references to literature, theatre, mirrors, pictures, and so forth—appear with an obsessive regularity throughout Ostrovsky's work; and to prove that these elements are indicative of an interest in the theme of reality which goes beyond the realistic depiction of social mores to encompass universal questions of a psychological and philosophical nature. In this final chapter, the elements discussed in the course of the study will each be examined in relation to a single play: *Easy Money*. This play is particularly suited to detailed analysis, not only because it incorporates nearly all the elements discussed above, but also because it is one of Ostrovsky's most well-received plays, both critically and by popular acclaim. D.Magarshack, for example, notes that *Easy Money* is 'one of the finest masterpieces in the world repertory of plays'[1], and I.Beasley states that it is 'undoubtedly among Ostrovsky's best plays'.[2] While this particular study has not the space to explore in any detail the relative stageworthiness of Ostrovsky's plays, a case could be made that those plays which deal in most detail with the themes explored in this study are also among his most successful works. (A brief glance at Appendix H reveals that *It's All in the Family*, *The Poor Bride*, *A Lucrative Post*, *Easy Money*, *Even Wise Men Err*, *Wolves and Sheep*, *The Forest*, and *Without a Dowry*—

---

[1] Magarshack, *Easy Money and Two Other Plays*, 292.
[2] Beasley, unpublished doctoral thesis, 176.

all plays generally considered to be among Ostrovsky's best—each contain at least nine of the thirteen elements discussed.)

Easy Money is a play in which deception, the superficiality of appearances and blindness to reality are all closely interwoven. The plot centres on Cheboksarova and her daughter Lidiya: two society women who are accustomed to living in luxury, yet have squandered all their money. They are determined to maintain an illusion of wealth and continue with their luxurious lifestyle, whilst desperately searching for a rich husband for Lidiya to marry. Ironically, they fail to realise that all the people they turn to for help (with the exception of Vasil'kov) are themselves poverty-stricken, yet equally adept at maintaining the illusion of wealth. (They even turn to Vasil'kov under false pretences: believing the false rumour spread by Glumov, that Vasil'kov is the owner of rich goldmines.) Once more, the play works both on a specific level—Ostrovsky is exposing the hypocrisy of contemporary Moscow high society—and a universal one—he is yet again presenting a world of uncertain reality. The reality presented in *Easy Money* is constructed from a tissue of lies, deception and illusion, in which the deceivers become the deceived and confusion reigns.

Deception, Concern with Appearance, Blindness to Reality

Lidiya's and Cheboksarova's concern with appearance is emphasised right from the start of the play. When Cheboksarova is first introduced to Vasil'kov, and told (falsely) that he is the owner of rich goldmines, she is described as 'looking at Vasil'kov', and declaring: 'You don't say! You would never have guessed it from his appearance' (iii, p. 176). As Vasil'kov's supposed wealth is further embellished, she begins 'gazing at Vasil'kov very tenderly' and reverses her earlier opinion: 'You know, he's not all that bad-looking' (iii, p. 176). Later in the play, at a further meeting between the two characters, Cheboksarova tries to explain away Vasil'kov's provincial appearance, by noting: 'Yes, yes, I remember ... it's all the rage now ... even among rich people ... getting closer to the people ... Well, of course, you wear a red silk shirt ... a velvet kaftan. Last winter, on the train, I saw a millionaire in one of those simple skin things ...' (iii, p. 187). (In contrast Vasil´kov responds by stating that he does not change his clothes according to fashion.)

The two women's concern with clothes and the trappings of wealth is frequently emphasised. Soon after Vasil´kov has expressed a wish that Lidiya would 'change her way of looking at people; pay more attention to their inner qualities' (iii, p. 188), she herself enters the stage and grumbles about how boring Vasil´kov is, with his talk of economic laws. She complains to her mother: 'I hope that the only laws to concern you and me are the laws of fashion and good taste. If everyone is wearing a certain kind of dress then I will wear it or die' (iii, p. 189).

Their concern with appearance is most evident, however, when they are discussing their poverty. We first learn that their lifestyle is illusory in Act Two, Scene 3, when Cheboksarova, first emphasising that 'As far as the others are concerned, we've got to remain wealthy people', admits to Kuchumov that they have no money (iii, p. 184). When, two scenes later, she admits the truth of their position to Lidiya and suggests that they should cut down on their expenses a little, Lidiya's reaction is emphatic: 'Agh, no, no, God forbid! That's impossible, impossible! The whole of Moscow would know that we are ruined; they would come to us with long faces, with feigned concern and stupid advice. They would shake their heads and sigh, and it would all be so artificial and insincere—so humiliating! Believe me, they won't even pretend to conceal their delight. (*She covers her face with her hands*). No! No!' (iii, p. 191). Lidiya's solution to their plight is to maintain their dignity: 'We'll have the flat done up again, we'll buy a new carriage and order new livery, we'll choose new furniture, and the more expensive the better' (iii, p. 191). She determines to marry a rich husband who will support them, and it is here that she begins to embark on a course of deception; first attempting (unsuccessfully) to court Telyatev into marriage, and then reluctantly agreeing to marry Vasil´kov. Her acceptance of Vasil´kov's marriage proposal is one of the few times in the play when she appears to talk honestly. She tells him that she does not love him, saying: 'Don't be angry, but rather thank me for being so open with you. Pretending costs nothing, but I don't want to do it. All brides say that they love their fiancés, but don't believe them—love comes later. Throw aside your ego and agree. Why should I love you? You're not very good-looking, your first name is unheard of, and your surname is vulgar. These are all details, it's possible to get used to them, but not immediately. Why should you be angry? You love me, I thank you. Earn my love and we will be happy' (iii, p. 197).

Lidiya's path of deception continues in Act Three when she pretends to be in love with Vasil´kov in order to persuade him to pay her bills. The blind-to-reality Vasil´kov is taken in by her performance: 'All I looked for in you was a beautiful exterior, but now I've found a kind, loving heart' (iii, p. 212). Lidiya repeats her performance at the end of Act Three, when, realising that she has little choice, she agrees to Vasil´kov's demands that they move to a cheaper apartment and live a less luxurious lifestyle. She promises out loud that she will try to reform, while whispering to her mother: 'I'll lead him by the nose' (iii, p. 215).

It is in Act Three that Cheboksarova and Lidiya discover the lie regarding Vasil´kov's goldmines. They angrily accuse him of deceiving them, when in fact it is Glumov who is the true deceiver, and they themselves are far more guilty of deceit than Vasil´kov. It is in this Act also that we learn the extent of deception which Cheboksarova is prepared to condone in order to maintain Lidiya's luxurious lifestyle: she tries to persuade Vasil´kov to embezzle money, as her 'dear husband' had done: '... he loved me and our daughter so much, that when a large sum of money was needed to maintain our social standing or even to satisfy one of our whims, he ... well, he found himself unable to distinguish between his own money and the government's. You understand me? He sacrificed himself for the sacred feeling of family love. He had to stand trial in the end and was obliged to leave Moscow' (iii, p. 215).

In Act Four, we see that Lidiya's idea of 'leading Vasil´kov by the nose' involves being prepared to become Kuchumov's mistress in anticipation of his extravagant promises of money:

Kuchumov... . You are our gossamer-winged fairy, have you forgotten your powers? You just have to make one gesture and this hovel will be transformed into a palace.
Lidiya (*flinging herself around his neck.*) This sort of gesture, dear papa?
Kuchumov. Yes, that, that ... (*He screws up his eyes, and sinks into a chair.*) Will forty thousand do you to begin with? (iii, p. 219)

Again, Cheboksarova's main objection to this arrangement is that of maintaining appearances: 'Let's go into my room, we must consider this from all angles. The main thing is that propriety must be preserved' (iii, p. 221). And this too is her main concern when, on discovering Lidiya and Kuchumov at their tryst, Vasil´kov throws Lidiya out of his home: 'What's all this noise!' '... It happens that people split up, but they do it quietly, with decorum' (iii, p. 229).

Act Five sees Cheboksarova and Lidiya back in their luxurious apartment and back in debt, living in anticipation of financial help from Kuchumov. They remain concerned with appearance—in Scene 1 Cheboksarova declares: 'I'll go and ask if the carriage has arrived. I managed to trick a coachmaker into giving us one on credit, and I got him to put our coat of arms on it. We can always hire horses from a cabbie, but we simply must have our own carriage. A hired one can be spotted so easily' (iii, p. 232).

When Kuchumov again fails to deliver on his promises of money, Lidiya begins to doubt his sincerity and is finally set straight on the true nature of Kuchumov's supposed wealth by Telyatev. Telyatev tells her that the real money is to be found with Vasil´kov who, through honest work, will make a fortune one day. At first Lidiya does not believe him, but on seeing a luxurious carriage outside her husband's house ('Agh! I'm going to faint! That's not a carriage, it's a dream!' (iii, p. 239)), she embarks on a final act of deception: pretending that she is fatally ill, and demanding that Vasil´kov be sent for. Vasil´kov sees through her charade, but agrees to take her back providing that she work as his housekeeper. Lidiya, with no other option, eventually agrees, although, with typical ambivalence, Ostrovsky fails to make clear the sincerity of her capitulation.[3] Once more, one of the central messages of the play is a warning of how a concern with appearance results in blindness to reality. Lidiya cannot see beyond Vasil´kov's provincial appearance, manners, and simple way of life to his seemingly honest love for her and his potential for future wealth. Instead she is taken in by the superficial appearance of wealth in the fine clothes and polished manners of Telyatev and Kuchumov.

---

[3] The critic E.G.Kholodov suggests that Lidiya will deceive Vasil´kov again. E.G.Kholodov, *Masterstvo Ostrovskogo* (Moscow: Iskusstvo, 1966) 316.

Like Lidiya and Cheboksarova, Telyatev and Kuchumov are also maintaining illusions of wealth. Kuchumov boasts of extravagant meals, is constantly making extravagant promises of money to Lidiya and Cheboksarova, yet always 'forgets to bring his wallet' or has his money 'stolen by some valet'. He is not, however, a conscious deceiver, but a prime example of a fantasy role-player. He lives in a fantasy world, so wrapped up in playing the role of a wealthy nobleman that he himself appears to believe it is the truth. As Telyatev states, when setting Lidiya straight as to the true state of Kuchumov's financial affairs: 'We all love him, only he's very forgetful. He actually did have a large fortune, but he often forgets that he spent it all. It's easy for him to forget, he still has great dinners, and balls, and suppers, he rides in magnificent carriages, only the money's all his wife's and it's been put in trust for her nieces. All he's allowed is ten roubles a day to go to the club ...' (iii, p. 236). Kuchumov is escaping the reality of his squandered fortune by living out the fantasy of a wealthy man.[4]

Telyatev is no conscious deceiver either. For him, living a luxurious life on credit is simply a normal way of life and he is quite open about it. (Lidiya's belief in his wealth seems more a result of her own blindness to reality than any conscious deception on his part.) Telyatev's whole nature is light-hearted and irresponsible and he is quite unconcerned about the consequences. He tells Lidiya quite cheerfully that he is due to go to the debtors' prison: 'I found out yesterday that I'm some three hundred thousand in debt. Everything of mine you've ever seen, it all belonged to somebody else: horses, carriages, apartments, clothes. No money was ever paid for it ... And tomorrow more creditors will be calling on me: it will be a remarkable picture. Furniture, carpets, mirrors, pictures, they were all hired, and they will all be taken back.' (iii, p. 237).

Glumov however, is, like Lidiya, a conscious deceiver. It is he who sets the entire plot in motion with his false claims to Cheboksarova regarding Vasil'kov's ownership of goldmines. And it is he who

---

[4] Such subconscious deception is generally unrecognised. V.Lakshin sees Kuchumov as a deliberate but unconcerned deceiver: 'Kuchumov lies crudely, he lies despairingly, he lies dangerously, unafraid of being exposed. Tomorrow they may not ask, but if they ask, then he will get out of it somehow. The important thing is to deceive now, to seduce at this moment ...' See *PSS* iii, 478.

deliberately tries to set up Vasil´kov, Telyatev and Kuchumov as rivals for Lidiya's affections. He ends the play having found a job as a 'private secretary' to a very wealthy, but very elderly woman—and thus his fortune is assured.

In contrast, Vasil´kov is set up as the foil to the deception and hypocrisy depicted in society. He is repeatedly emphasised as being an outsider and his name, clothes and manners all reflect this. (Lidiya refers to him as 'an alien' (iii, p. 189).) He is depicted as an honest, hardworking, and down-to-earth businessman, in contrast to the polished but superficial members of 'high society', who are concerned with living an easy life of luxury at another's expense. Yet as so often in Ostrovsky's plays, his role is not entirely unambiguous: there is a question mark over the sincerity of his love for Lidiya since he frequently notes that he needs a beautiful society wife to further his business concerns, leaving open the suggestion that he is exploiting her as much as she is him.[5]

Links with Literature

Although connections to literature are not as apparent as in some of Ostrovsky's other plays—there are no 'literary role-players', for example—those references to literature which do appear in *Easy Money* are, once again, closely linked to deception and illusion. Lidiya, the chief deceiver, is most frequently linked with literature. Cheboksarova describes her as having 'the highest level of education', remarking: 'We have an extensive library of French literature. Just ask her something from mythology, just ask her! Believe me, she is so up on French literature, she knows things other young women wouldn't even dream of. The most cunning scandalmonger couldn't say anything that would surprise her' (iii, pp. 187/8); and immediately after feigning love for Vasil´kov in order to get him to pay her bills Lidiya is described as 'lying down on the divan and picking up a book' (iii, p. 213). Similarly, when she is attempting to court Telya-

---

[5] V.Lakshin notes: 'Ostrovsky vacillates in his relationship with his hero.' He points out that Vasil´kov is often a figure of fun, but decides that Ostrovsky 'prefers the decent, business-like efficiency, the European methods, of the new smart operators to the Asiatic, dissolute deceit, the grasping and swindling of people like Kit Kitych that were so well known to him ... not for nothing did Ostrovsky emphasise the nobility of [Vasil´kov's] nature ...' See *PSS* iii, 479.

tev into marriage, he describes her in terms of mythical, literary (and thus false, illusory) figures: 'I can't believe my ears. Am I dreaming? What a lucky day! ... You were a Diana, despising the male sex, with the moon in your hair, and a quiver of arrows on your shoulder. But now you have transformed into a simple, warm-hearted, and even naive, peasant girl, like one of those you see at the ballet, dancing around and flapping their aprons. Like this. (*He demonstrates common peasant dance movements.*)' (iii, p. 193/4).

Telyatev also applies literary allusions to himself—at one stage he states that he is 'not "The Bronze Horseman", nor "The Stone Guest"' (iii, p. 194) and on a later occasion he threatens to surprise Lidiya and Kuchumov at their tryst like 'the statue of the Commendatore' (iii, p. 224)—thereby indicating the illusory nature of his own lifestyle.

Links with Theatre

Perhaps unsurprisingly, given the extensive role-playing in *Easy Money*, references to the theatre and the use of theatrical metaphors are particularly numerous. Again, most references appear in connection with the chief deceiver, Lidiya: in Act Two, Scene 8, when accepting Vasil´kov's proposal, she declares: 'Let's play this comedy. Let's try and earn each other's love.' Vasil´kov responds: 'I don't want any comedy, just a bright and happy life', but Lidiya replies: 'No, it's a comedy you want. You've made me a proposal and I have expressed my agreement. What more do you want?' (iii, p. 193). In Act Four, Scene 11, when, having discovered Lidiya with Kuchumov, Vasil´kov expresses a desire to kill himself, she laughs and declares: 'What a tragedy!' (iii, p. 229). She goes on to state: 'You were playing out a comedy, and we were playing out a comedy. We have more money than you, but we are women, we don't like to have to pay ... What did you think of my acting ability? With talent like that, a woman will never be ruined' (iii, p. 230) (the irony in her words is worthy of note: she is telling the truth by admitting that she was playing out a comedy, yet is continuing to play a part by insisting that she has more money than Vasil´kov). In Act Five, Scene 3, when Lidiya discovers that neither Kuchumov nor Telyatev can help her financially, she declares that she 'will become an actress' (iii, p. 238); and in Act Five, Scene 6, when Lidiya is pretending to be ill, Telyatev agrees to stay, but notes: 'Only, grant me a non-speaking part in this comedy' (iii, p. 243).

However, Lidiya is not the only character in the play to be connected with the theatre. Throughout the play, Kuchumov is constantly singing fragments of opera, a device which links him to another illusory reality and signals that his words and actions may themselves be nothing but a performance. In Act One, Scene 2, when Glumov first thinks up his plan to tell Cheboksarova that Vasil´kov owns goldmines, his language is full of theatrical metaphor: he talks of a need 'to play a comedy' and when Telyatev warns him: 'We might end up playing the comic roles in this comedy of yours', Glumov responds: 'No, we'll play the villains, or at least I will' (iii, p. 171). After setting events in motion he declares: 'Well, the comedy has begun' (iii, p. 176). Thus the theatre is once again connected to deception—a connection which is repeated in Act Four, Scene 5: here Glumov, while orchestrating a confrontation between Vasil´kov, Telyatev and Kuchumov, declares: 'That will be a scene!' (iii, p. 222). (This significant theatrical metaphor has once again been overlooked in English translation: Mulrine translates it as 'That'll be fun'.[6])

In Act One, Scene 4, when first meeting Vasil´kov, Cheboksarova orders the servant to 'have the carriage wait by the theatre' (iii, p. 175)—thus her illusion of wealth, maintained by outward trappings such as the carriage, is once again placed in association with the theatre, a place of illusion.

In Act Two, Scene 5, Vasil´kov, talking of his hopes of marrying Lidiya, notes: 'I was going to give up, I don't want to play a pitiful role' (iii, p. 188). And in Act Four, Scene 8, Vasil´kov, again preparing for a confrontation with Lidiya and Kuchumov, declares: 'What will I do then? How shall I behave? No, no, it's shameful to prepare for something like this; shameful to act out a role ...' (iii, p. 225).

Mirror Usage

References to mirrors are also frequent. Most significant, perhaps, is the reference in Act Five, Scene 3, when Telyatev informs Lidiya that

---

[6] Stephen Mulrine, *Four Plays by Alexander Ostrovsky*, tr. Stephen Mulrine (London: Oberon Books, 1997), 232.

she has a wrinkle, thus indicating the concern with appearance in the play:

> **Telyatev.** What are you so serious for? Oh no, oh dear! (*He looks at her intently.*)
> **Lidiya.** What is it? What's the matter with you?
> **Telyatev.** You've got a wrinkle, right there, on your forehead; it's a small one, but it's a wrinkle.
> **Lidiya** (*in alarm*). It can't be.
> **Telyatev.** Look in the mirror! Oh dear, oh dear! At your age. How embarrassing!
> **Lidiya** (*in front of the mirror*). Can't you say anything better! You're boring me.
> **Telyatev.** You shouldn't think, Lidiya Yur'evna. Most of all you should guard against thinking. God preserve you! That's how our women keep their beauty, they never think about anything. (iii, pp. 234/5)

In Act Five, Scene 3, Telyatev is again connected to mirrors: when talking of the furniture his creditors will be taking away, he specifically mentions mirrors (iii, p. 237), thus emphasising the illusory nature of his fine lifestyle.

On two further occasions Lidiya is specifically connected to 'plate glass'—the Russian term for which translates literally as 'mirror window'. On both occasions the 'mirror windows' are referred to in connection with her luxurious apartment (iii, p. 230 and p. 231)—an apartment which is rented on credit and is therefore part of an illusion of wealth.

Picture Usage

References to pictures in the play are equally significant. In Act Three, Scene 11, when Lidiya is pretending to Vasil'kov that she is in love with him, he demands her 'marvellous hand' and taking it, declares: 'How beautiful your hand is! What a pity I'm not an artist' (iii, p. 212). Thus once again, a connection with art (and therefore image) is made at a point when deception is taking place. (It is presumably also significant that it is the honest, straightforward Vasil'kov who is 'not an artist'.)

In Act Two, Lidiya and Vasil'kov's apartment, luxuriously decorated by Lidiya (again on credit), is described as having pictures on the walls (iii, p. 182). In Act Five, when Telyatev describes how his creditors will be removing all his (hired) belongings, he notes that it will be 'a remarkable picture' (iii, p. 237) and, as with mirrors, specifically mentions pictures as being among the things which will be taken away. Again, the reference to pictures acts as a signal that Telyatev's lifestyle has been nothing but a carefully created image.

Even in this brief analysis of one play, themes and symbols of a concern with the nature of reality occur in abundance. Similarly, the various levels of reality dealt with in Ostrovsky's work are clearly apparent. There is the depiction of specific contemporary Russian society, yet also a portrayal of universal human psychology—the desire to escape an unpleasant reality through the creation of a different one, either consciously or subconsciously. Likewise, there is the creation of an uncertain reality and references to the illusory realities of art, literature and theatre which raise questions as to the true nature of reality and the validity of conflicting 'other' realities. *Easy Money* does not contain all the elements of the exploration of reality apparent in Ostrovsky's work, but the fact that the same (and more) themes and symbols occur time and again throughout his entire body of drama must surely indicate the overwhelming importance of this subject to the playwright.

CONCLUSION

In its exploration of the theme of reality in Ostrovsky's drama, this study has in no way intended to deny or belittle the realism of his plays. Ostrovsky undoubtedly played a major role in developing the realist movement in Russian drama. His plays did indeed depict everyday life to a far greater extent than had ever been seen on the Russian stage before, particularly the everyday life of the middle classes. His plays aside, Ostrovsky argued vociferously for greater realism in acting technique, insisting that actors should perform by drawing on their real-life experience. (In this he was an early exponent of the 'method acting' later developed by Stanislavsky. D.Magarshack has noted that 'when one compares Ostrovsky's and Stanislavsky's system of stage presentation there is very little to distinguish them from each other ... Ostrovsky's views on scenery, gesture, and stage diction are in all essentials identical with those of Stanislavsky.'[1]) Those who, like I.Beasley, claim that Ostrovsky 'was to drama what Tolstoy and Turgenev were to the novel' have good reason to do so.[2]

What this study has attempted to demonstrate, however, is that Ostrovsky was more than just a realist, more than simply a painter of contemporary Russian life. Social and literary criticism undoubtedly form a part of his work, but by removing his plays from their immediate social and historical context you get a far more complete picture of their complexity. The facets of Ostrovsky's drama discussed in this study—realism and idealism, the web of deception, a concern with the superficiality of outward appearance, blindness to reality, the psychological and philosophical elements, the mirror and

---

[1] David Magarshack, 'Alexander Ostrovsky: The Founder of the Russian Theatrical Tradition', in *The Storm*, tr. David Magarshack (Ann Arbor: Ardis, 1988), 5-13 (pp. 8 and 12).

[2] Beasley, unpublished doctoral thesis, 350.

picture symbolism—all point, layer after layer, to a preoccupation with reality which transcends the specifics of time and place to take on universal dimensions. A degree of repetition in the above materials has the justification of inevitability; these elements appear with such overwhelming abundance that it scarcely seems credible that this universal aspect of Ostrovsky's drama has been overlooked.

'It is all deception, all a dream, all is not what it seems.'
(N.V.Gogol, *Nevsky Prospect*)

One of the greatest ironies in the neglect of Ostrovsky's interest in the theme of reality is that this notion is so universal in world literature. The existence of different realities, the greater validity of one reality over another, the relationship between art and life, have been constant themes in literary works regardless of time and place. Examples range in scope from Plato to Voltaire, from the *Arabian Nights* to Shakespeare, from Calderón to Kafka. In more modern times, a recent novel by the Norwegian writer, Jostein Gaarder—*Sophie's World*—which constantly turns perceived reality on its head, was a bestseller in more than forty countries.

In nineteenth-century Russian literature, one of the chief exponents of the theme of reality was Nikolai Vasil'evich Gogol. His works teem with hints of different realities, deceptions, dreams, mistaken identities, apparent inversions of the real and the unreal. Intriguingly, Gogol is also someone who was initially perceived as a purely 'realist' writer. Much has been said of Gogol's position as a precursor to Ostrovsky. R.Peace, writing about Gogol's play *Marriage*, notes that 'in recognizing the comic potential of the merchant milieu, and putting it on the stage, [Gogol] laid the foundations for the later plays of Ostrovsky.'[3] And C.English, also discussing *Marriage*, states that the play 'foreshadows the work of Ostrovsky, with his comedy of mores ...'[4] M.Hoover describes the Bal´zaminov trilogy as a parody of Gogol's work, noting that the trilogy 'harks back to Gogol and mocks his work'[5], and much has been made of the greatly vaunted legend that, on hearing a reading of *It's All in the Family* at Pogodin's

---

[3] R.A.Peace, 'Introduction' in *Plays and Petersburg Tales* by Nikolai Gogol, tr. Christopher English (Oxford: O.U.P., 1995), xxv.

[4] Christopher English, 'Explanatory Notes' in *Plays and Petersburg Tales*, 352.

[5] Hoover, 42.

house, Gogol passed Ostrovsky a note which declared him as his successor.

Perhaps unsurprisingly, given the widespread critical view that Ostrovsky was a strictly realist writer, examination of the links between Gogol and Ostrovsky has largely (if not completely) ignored discussion of the two men's treatment of the theme of different realities. If, however, you take as a basis the central arguments of this study, then the two men's exploration of reality shows a number of striking similarities. Indeed, a simple list of selected critical comment on Gogol's work is noticeable for the frequency with which the epithets used seem to apply equally well to Ostrovsky's drama:

'Two characteristics (which may be oversimplified as 'imagination revealing other realities' and 'art becoming life') are a prominent feature of Gogol's writing.'[6]
'The story ['St John's Eve'] may be seen as a series of deceptive appearances with Gogol focusing upon the treacherous surface of reality.'[7]
'Here [*Diary of a Madman*], we find expressed the essential absurdity and tragedy of life, where dream and reality merge so that we have no means of distinguishing what is true from the illusory.[8]
'"The Nose" is a masterpiece of narrative comic art, with dream and reality intermingling to such an extent that it is hard to tell where the two divide.'[9]
'All this relates to the general Gogolian theme of deceptive appearance ... The effect of this device is to call our attention to a deceptively multiple reality ... we are left with a lingering suspicion that far more of our world is deceptive.'[10]

Most of the above quotations come from a study by W.Woodin Rowe (interestingly entitled *Through Gogol's Looking Glass: Reverse Vision, False Focus and Precarious Logic*) which comprehensively charts what he calls the 'multiple realities' of Gogol's work. He

---

[6] William Woodin Rowe, *Through Gogol's Looking Glass: Reverse Vision, False Focus, and Precarious Logic* (New York: New York University Press, 1976), 1.
[7] *Ibid.*, 10.
[8] Ronald Wilks, 'Introduction' in *Diary of a Madman and other stories* by Nikolai Gogol, tr. Ronald Wilks (London: Penguin, 1972), 7-15 (p. 10).
[9] *Ibid.*, 10.
[10] Woodin Rowe, 190.

concludes his study by declaring: 'Gogol's writing gently but persistently promotes the suspicion that our consciousness—our awareness of reality—is an insidiously soothing deception'[11]—a statement which, perhaps most accurately of all, applies equally well to Ostrovsky's work.

A thorough examination of the similarities between Gogol's and Ostrovsky's exploration of reality is a subject perhaps worthy of a monograph in itself. Certainly there is not space to include it here. But even a cursory glance at Gogol's works demonstrates a startling number of similarities with the themes and features of Ostrovsky's work discussed in this study. Take, for example, Gogol's short story *Nevsky Prospect*. Here, as in Ostrovsky's *The Handsome Man*, we are presented with a work which has as its basis the discrepancy between external and internal beauty—the confusion of appearance with reality. The two central protagonists, Pirogov and Piskarev, are each attracted (on the basis on their external appearances) to different women, whom they see walking along the Nevsky Prospect. Both follow their respective beauties and both are confronted with a rude awakening to reality. Thus, immediately, the tale shares two of the prominent themes in Ostrovsky's plays—the destruction of idealism in the face of reality, and the deceptive nature of superficial appearance.

The superficiality of appearance is emphasised over and again in the Gogol tale. R.Peace notes that the people who promenade along the Nevsky are 'reduced to mere external features: to hats, dresses, scarves, moustaches, swords', adding that 'reducing human beings to the status of objects ... is ... dehumanising: it suggests that they are empty people, 'dead souls', whose vanity (and in essence their personality) centres on some fashionable feature of their external appearance.'[12] It is, he notes, a concern with outward appearance which leads Piskarev to dismiss the idea that his object of beauty could be a prostitute, simply because 'her cloak alone must have cost eighty roubles'.[13]

---

[11] *Ibid.*, 194.

[12] Peace, *Plays and Petersburg Tales*, viii.

[13] Unless otherwise noted, all quotations from Gogol's works are taken from the World's Classics edition: *Plays and Petersburg Tales*.

Fantasizing wildly about the ideal nature of his beauty (as in Ostrovsky's works, Piskarev, a painter, links his woman to paintings and icons—created illusions of real life), Piskarev follows her, not, we learn, for any 'lewd reasons', but simply 'to discover the abode of this divine creature'. The shock, then, on finding himself in a brothel, is great indeed. His confrontation with reality does not, however, end here. Piskarev returns home, where, as Peace notes, 'he manages, through dream and the use of opium, to sustain his idealized view of the woman.' (Thus we have dream—and, on this occasion, drugs— used as a means of escape from reality.) Finally, 'drunk on his own idealist illusion'[14], he returns to the brothel to offer marriage to the prostitute. Finding himself mocked in response, Piskarev goes home and kills himself.

In the parallel story, the 'smug and self-assured' Pirogov meets with a far more prosaic fate. He follows the 'very stupid', but faithful wife of a German locksmith. Certain of his success, despite her lack of encouragement, he pursues her for a fortnight, and is eventually caught 'smothering her in kisses', by the drunken craftsman and his friends. They proceed to give Pirogov 'a very painful thrashing'. Peace notes that the confrontation with reality is far more damaging for the idealistic Piskarev than it is for the 'philistine', Pirogov, whose pursuit of beauty leads to nothing more than a few bruises inflicted by an outraged husband. 'Both have been deceived by the surface of reality, but the blows of disillusionment are far more deadly for the idealist, than for the smug, self-satisfied philistine.'[15]

The above is little more than a plot summary of the tale, but even here we find a surprising similarity of theme with the work of Ostrovsky: destruction of idealism; a blindness to reality based on a narrow concern with outward appearance; dreams and fantasies as a means of escape from reality. There is even a mirror—having formulated his plan (or, more accurately, fantasy) of marrying the prostitute, Piskarev is described as stepping 'up to the mirror' to check his own appearance. Thus a mirror is linked with his fantasy world.

Gogol's *The Government Inspector*, whatever motivation you ascribe to it—social satire, a parody of classical forms, Gogol's own

---

[14] Peace, *Plays and Petersburg Tales*, ix.
[15] *Ibid.*, ix.

explanation of an allegory of the moral battle raging in man's soul—
is a play based entirely on the existence of different realities: the
reality of Khlestakov as a fundless, largely insignificant civil servant;
the reality, created by the guilt-stricken townspeople, of Khlestakov
as an important government official; and even the suggestions in the
play of a supernatural, diabolic reality. Here, again, there are many
features in common with Ostrovsky's plays. Most noticeably,
perhaps, the blindness to reality of the mayor and his entourage, who
persist in their misconception of Khlestakov's identity despite overwhelming evidence to the contrary. There are similarities also in the
wild fantasies and dreams of self-aggrandizement, largely perpetrated
by Khlestakov—a character for whom, as V.Gippius remarks, 'the
boundaries between the real and the imaginary are easily obliter-
ated'[16]—but also the mayor, who reaches the rank of general in his
fantasies. (The desire to better yourself, to escape reality by 'crossing
class boundaries', seems as much a central feature of Gogol's work
as it is of Ostrovsky's: thus Poprishchin in *Diary of a Madman*
elevates himself to King of Spain, and Kovalev in *The Nose* refers to
himself as 'major'.) There is even the use of drunkenness as a
facilitator in escaping from reality—again a feature present in
Ostrovsky.

Significantly, when so much attention is paid to the presence of
noses in Gogol's work, here (as with Ostrovsky), in a play devoted to
blindness to reality, references to eyes crop up with extraordinary
frequency. Anna Andreevna seems almost obsessed with Khlestakov's eyes: before she has even met him, she sends Avdot´ya to find
out about him, instructing her: 'Have a peep through the keyhole and
see what colour his eyes are, ' and she later asks Osip: 'What sort of
eyes does your master like best, Osip?' Dobchinsky and Bobchinsky
both refer to the 'hawk-like' quality of Khlestakov's eyes, and
Khlestakov himself states that 'there is something in my eyes that
strikes fear into people's hearts'. Other examples include the mayor
rubbing his eyes in initial disbelief that Khlestakov and his daughter
are kissing; Anna Andreevna, fantasizing about her house in the
capital, stating that 'when you come into my room there'll be such an

---

[16] Vasily Gippius, 'The Inspector General: Structure and Problems', in *Gogol from the Twentieth Century*, ed. Robert A.Maguire (Princeton: Princeton University Press, 1974), 216-65 (p. 231.)

exquisite aroma you'll have to shut your eyes tight' and 'screwing up her eyes'; Korobka, during the reading of Khlestakov's letter, declaring: 'My eyes are better than yours'; and of course, the famous first meeting between Khlestakov and the mayor, when they both stare 'goggle-eyed' at each other for several minutes (yet still fail actually to see each other for what they really are—they remain blind to reality). Interestingly, there has been some critical comment on the presence of eyes in Gogol's work. W.Woodin Rowe talks of 'Gogol's favored word *vid*'[17], and discusses the use of 'seeing' language in *The Carriage* and the emphasis on eyes in *Rome*. L.Stilman, also, has observed that 'eyes, or vision, are a basic image in nearly everything Gogol wrote.'[18] He notes the emphasis on eyes in *Viy* and *The Portrait*.[19]

This brief discussion of *Nevsky Prospect* and *The Government Inspector* demonstrates many of the common features in Gogol's and Ostrovsky's exploration of reality, but there are numerous others. W.Woodin Rowe talks of 'Gogol's favored notion that "clothes make the man"', noting the importance of clothes as a status symbol, and suggesting that the obsession with clothing in his works 'may be seen as part of his general fascination for deceptive appearances.'[20] Clothing is, of course, an essential feature of Ostrovsky's plays, acting both as an indicator of concern with superficial appearance and forming the central feature of his characters' dreams of bettering themselves—escaping reality by crossing class boundaries.

Mirrors (as was noted above) also form a central feature of the works of both men. The famous epigraph to *The Government Inspector*—'There is no use grumbling at the mirror if your own mug is crooked'—with its multiplicity of interpretations, is an obvious example.[21]

---

[17] Woodin Rowe, 128.

[18] Robert A.Maguire, 'Introduction', in *Gogol from the Twentieth Century*, 3-54 (p. 50.)

[19] See Leon Stilman's article, 'The "All-Seeing Eye" in Gogol', in *Gogol from the Twentieth Century*, 376-89.

[20] Woodin Rowe, 147.

[21] Robert Maguire, for example, sees the epigraph as aphorizing Gogol's view of 'the workings of his own mind: he saw the characters in his stories as projections, or mirrors, of bad qualities of his own, and his better self as a reflection of something outside and beyond him' (see *Gogol from the Twentieth Century*, 19); whereas Woodin Rowe argues that the epigraph means both 'Don't blame your own faults on others' and

R.Peace notes: 'In the earlier Ukrainian stories the bright reflecting surfaces of rivers, lakes and mirrors had often distracted the reader's vision from darker depths beneath.'[22] And W.Woodin Rowe discusses how, in *Sorochintsy Fair* , the personified river is described as a mirror which 'turns everything upside down'.[23] Later in the story, with behaviour redolent of Lipochka in Ostrovsky's *It's All in the Family*, Parashka, the heroine, dreams of marriage (and in particular the appearance of her suitor) and gazes into a mirror:

> Parashka mused, sitting alone in the hut with her pretty chin propped on her hand. Many dreams hovered about her little head ... 'How handsome he is! How wonderfully his black eyes glow! ... How his white jacket suits him! But his belt ought to be a bit brighter! ... I will weave him one when we settle in a new hut. I can't help being pleased when I think, ' she went on, taking from her bosom a little red-paper-framed mirror bought at the fair and gazing into it, 'how I shall meet her [her stepmother] one day somewhere and she may burst before I bow to her ... But I was forgetting ... let me try on a cap, even if it has to be my stepmother's, and see how it suits me to look like a wife?' Then she got up, holding the mirror in her hand and bending her head down to it, walked in excitement about the room ...[24]

Significant mirrors also occur in *The Nose*, when, on awakening into what many critics have termed a dream or nightmare world, the first thing Kovalev does is call for a mirror, to check a pimple on his nose—only to discover that his nose itself has vanished; and in *The Overcoat*—where the 'important personage' rehearses his tone of voice in a locked room in front of a mirror.[25]

Other similarities in the two men's work include the use of both conscious and subconscious role-play as a means of escape from

---

'What you see should not be blamed if you expect the wrong thing'; thus the mug (Khlestakov) should not be blamed if the mirror (the image imposed on him by the townsfolk) is crooked. (See Woodin Rowe, 140.)

[22] Peace, *Plays and Petersburg Tales*, xi.

[23] Woodin Rowe, 14.

[24] Translation taken from: *The Complete Tales of Nikolai Gogol*, ed. Leonard J.Kent, 2 vols (Chicago: University of Chicago Press, 1985), I, 30-31

[25] See Peace's discussion of *The Nose* in *Plays and Petersburg Tales* and Woodin Rowe, 100-104. A.Remizov, also, has described Gogol's work as 'a series of wakeless dreams with an awakening in sleep'. [A.M.Remizov, *Ogon´ veshchei* (Paris: YMCA-Press, 1954), 28.]

reality. Characters such as Poprishchin, Chichikov and Khlestakov all create their own reality as a means of escape from the actuality of their situations. Even one of Gogol's most famous escape mechanisms—the troika—reappears in Ostrovsky. Like Poprishchin, who, locked in a lunatic asylum, wishes for a troika with bells to fly him away from this world; Khlestakov, whose dreams of arriving home in a carriage materialise at the end of *The Government Inspector*; and of course, the famous winged troika at the end of *Dead Souls*, which whisks Chichikov away from retribution; so too Katya in *The Storm*, dreaming of escape from the grim reality of her life, longs to 'go racing along in a troika ...' (ii, p. 233).

It is important not to read too much significance into the similarities between the works of Gogol and Ostrovsky touched on in the above discussion. There are undoubtedly equally many differences in the two men's treatment of reality. Certainly Gogol's 'multiple realities' are far more absurd and extreme than anything found in Ostrovsky's plays. Ostrovsky makes very little use of the 'other reality' of madness—a repeated feature in Gogol's work. Nor (as discussed earlier) does Ostrovsky make much reference to the diabolic and supernatural world which underpins Gogol's entire body of work.[26] What significance there is, however, surely lies in the fact that, although he was 'initially misunderstood as a realist'[27], critical acceptance of the different levels of reality in Gogol's work is now commonplace. Ostrovsky, whose exploration of reality contains so many common features, and whose work serves also to challenge our comfortable perceptions of reality, remains labelled as a realist in the narrowest possible sense of the word.

The Historical Plays and *The Snow Maiden*

In the Introduction, it was noted that owing to pressures of time and space, the historical plays and *The Snow Maiden* would not be included in the detailed analysis of Ostrovsky's drama, and that this exclusion was made on the grounds that they did not strictly fall under the mantle of Ostrovsky's 'realist' works. Yet even a cursory reading of these plays reveals that they too contain many of the

---

[26] See, for example, Dmitry Merezhkovsky's article 'Gogol and the Devil' in *Gogol from the Twentieth Century*, 57-102.
[27] Woodin Rowe, 27.

elements relating to the theme of reality found in Ostrovsky's other plays. The play *The False Dmitry and Vasily Shuisky*, for example, involves much deception and intrigue. Indeed, the entire plot of the play is based around false appearances and pretence—that of Dmitry the Pretender, the false Tsar. This play has a particularly high incidence of language connected with 'seeing' and 'blindness'. There is much emphasis on blindness: 'The people are blind' (vii, p. 18); 'They've clouded our eyes' (vii, p. 27); 'A fog in my eyes' (p. 55); 'The people are blind, but we are sighted' (vii, p. 89).

A Seventeenth-Century Comic and *Tushino* also contain examples of deception and false appearances: *Tushino*, like *The False Dmitry and Vasily Shuisky*, has a false Tsar and traitors pretending loyalty to the true Tsar, while *A Seventeenth-Century Comic*, a play about the birth of theatre in Russia, sees the timid Yakov trying to hide from his father the fact that he has been made a member of Grigory's acting troupe. *One-armed Minin* and *The Voevoda* both make extensive use of dreams, and even *The Snow Maiden* has an intriguing use of mirrors: in Act Four, Scene 2, the Snow Maiden, asking Spring to give her the ability to love, remarks: 'Today when washing in the cold stream, I glanced into the mirror jets and saw in them my face in tears, haggard with the anguish of sleepness nights' (vii, p. 448/9). Thus even here a reference to mirrors occurs at a point when the fufilment of fantasy is being discussed.

Of this group of plays, *The Snow Maiden* is perhaps the most interesting. Contemporary critics expressed surprise that Ostrovsky should suddenly break from the mould of realism and write a fairy-tale fantasy: In 1873 V.Burenin wrote: '... his realistic pen, which has described so many living forms of the 'Dark Kingdom', has produced the illusory, meaningless images of the Snow Maiden, Lel, Mizgir and similar characters who inhabit the bright kingdom of the Berendei, a people as stupid as they are fantastic.'[28] Their surprise has been echoed by the critics who followed them. M.Hoover comments: 'It seems strange that the realist Ostrovsky, famous for his depictions of contemporary life, should in mid-career write a fairy-tale drama in verse.'[29] C.Manning describes it as 'a charming study of the imagination' that 'stands quite apart in the entire list of

---

[28] See *PSS* vii, 590.
[29] Hoover, 68.

Ostrovsky's works.'[30] And B.Varneke notes that *The Snow Maiden* 'constitutes Ostrovsky's only abandonment of the world of reality for the realm of creative fancy.'[31] (He is mistaken in this. Ostrovsky did embark on another fairy-tale play, *Tsarevich Ivan*, but it was never completed.) Yet given (as this study argues) that Ostrovsky was interested in the exploration of different realities, the blurring of real and fantasy worlds, then his decision to write a fantasy 'fairy-tale' drama no longer seems so surprising. (Indeed the frequent references to fairy-tales which appear throughout his dramatic works—the reference to Baba Yaga discussed earlier is but one—would be enough to suggest that the surprise expressed by his critics is somewhat misplaced.[32])

Perhaps unsurprisingly, even in this fantasy play, critics have tended to emphasise the realistic aspects of the play. They have noted the realism of the setting and the faithfulness of the songs, dances and ceremonies to Russian peasant custom. (L.Lotman notes that 'while working on *The Snow Maiden*, Ostrovsky consulted with historians, archeologists, experts on the everyday life of the olden times'.[33]) Thus, intriguingly, it could be argued that in *The Snow Maiden* Ostrovsky is reversing the pattern of his other plays. Normally, he takes 'reality' and shows how closely it is linked with fantasy and illusion. Here, he is using 'fantasy' and linking it closely to reality. Overall, however, the net effect (and thus the central message) is the same. The play serves to challenge our perceptions of the nature of reality, and to demonstrate how closely various levels of reality are intertwined.

Strikingly, it is with this play, where the trappings of 'realism' have been removed, that critics seem able to comment more easily on universal issues, noting both psychological and philosophical content. Thus M.Hoover comments: 'In this play a universal and personal mystery comes alive: the return of the light and spring after the darkness of winter, the mystery of life and death; and in its individual psychological meaning the play also deals with the gain and loss

---

[30] Manning, 32.
[31] B.V.Varneke, *History of the Russian Theatre* (New York: Macmillan, 1951), 333.
[32] See p. 132.
[33] See *PSS* vii, 589.

inherent in love.'[34] I.Esam on the other hand suggests that in *The Snow Maiden* 'Ostrovsky's philosophy, his conception of good and evil, seems reminiscent of that of Goethe and Bulgakov in "The Master and Margarita".'[35] Such comments, perhaps more than any other, reveal the need to liberate Ostrovsky's other works from the confines of their historical context. It is, however, with a sense of inevitability that Esam goes on to discuss how *The Snow Maiden* 'was only a partial success at first performance as critics considered that it did not sufficiently "clarify the social and moral phenomena" of the times.'[36]

The features of *The Snow Maiden* and some of the historical plays noted above are only those which are immediately apparent on an initial reading of the plays. A more comprehensive analysis would no doubt produce many more similarities with the theme of reality found in Ostrovsky's other plays. It would be interesting to know whether such features also appear in his collaborative works and his extensive translations of plays by European playwrights. Certainly one of his earliest collaborative works, the historical play *Vasilisa Melent'eva*, written largely by Ostrovsky himself, but based on an original draft by S.Gedeonov, contains many of the features discussed above. The play contains much trickery and deception as the young widow, Vasilisa, tricks an admirer into helping her poison the Tsarina and marry the Tsar herself. There is a blurring of reality and fantasy when, having successfully fulfilled her plan, Vasilisa suffers from night terrors, believing that the murdered Tsarina is haunting her. And there is a significant use of a mirror: in Act Four, Part 1, Scene 1, Vasilisa expresses her determination to become Tsarina and talks of how her life will be when she does so. She decides to dress in her richest, most beautiful clothes, abandoning her widow's clothing. She changes, looks in the mirror and declares she will become Tsarina, and then goes on to plot to poison the present Tsarina, using the beauty of her appearance to ensnare the aid of her young admirer. Thus the mirror is linked to her fantasy world, the superficial nature of appearances, and to deception.

---

[34] Hoover, 69.

[35] I.Esam, 'Folkloric Elements as Communication Devices', *New Zealand Slavonic Journal*, 2 (1968), 67-88 (p. 76).

[36] *Ibid.*, 81.

An analysis of Ostrovsky's translations of other European plays would be especially intriguing. What were the criteria by which Ostrovsky chose to translate one particular play over another? Could it be that the plays he selected shared a similar interest in exploring the nature of reality and the relationship between reality and illusion?[37] A.Boyle's introduction to Seneca's *Phaedra*, a play which Ostrovsky began translating in the 1850s but never finished, argues: 'The focus on delusion is emphatic. The movement of Phaedra and the nurse from realism to fantasy has already been noted; Theseus' delusion too—about his marriage to Phaedra, about the relationship of his behaviour and the values he professes ... is dramatically evident. But it is the dramatisation of Hippolytus' self-deception which is perhaps most intriguing ...'[38]

The Lasting Legacy

This study has sought to challenge the prevailing view of Ostrovsky's drama as too 'real' and thus somehow too 'Russian' to be of value to Western audiences. It has sought to counter Mirsky's assessment that 'had he been universal ... Ostrovsky's place would have been among the greatest'[39] with the assertion that Ostrovsky was indeed far more universal in his outlook than he has generally been given credit for. But perhaps the greatest challenge to the traditional interpretation of Ostrovsky as a narrowly realist writer lies in his enduring popularity. If he was indeed concerned solely with the depiction of the lives of Moscow merchants in the mid-nineteenth-century, then surely, as Yu.Aikhenval'd claimed as early as 1909, he would have 'lost meaning as the conditions he describes disappear from Russian life'.[40] (Even during Ostrovsky's own lifetime, the critic N.Shelgu-

---

[37] In a short note 'from the translator', Ostrovsky stated that 'not dwelling on plays rich in outward effects, and with the sole aim of supplying our talented artists with a useful exercise, I chose to translate only those plays in which the roles were written wisely, and which offered some kind of artistic difficulty.' See *Russkie pisateli o perevode XVIII-XX vv.*, ed. Yu.D.Levin and A.V.Fedorov (Leningrad: Sovetskii pisatel', 1960), 349. Further extracts of Ostrovsky's comments on translation are on pp. 350-53.

[38] A.S.Boyle, *Seneca's Phaedra: Introduction, Text, Translation and Notes* (Liverpool: Francis Cairns Ltd, 1987), 25.

[39] Mirsky, 235.

[40] Aikhenval'd, p. 172.

nov wrote: '... the time of Ostrovsky has finished. He is insufficient in the new world, he is not familiar with the new world and he does not depict it.'[41]) In Russia too, Ostrovsky's plays would contain little of significance to modern audiences. Yet this is clearly not the case. Ostrovsky's popularity with Russian audiences has remained as strong in the hundred and more years after his death as it was during his lifetime. In the years following his death until the 1917 Revolution, Ostrovsky's plays were performed on average 1, 358 times a year. After 1917, his popularity increased even further—in 1939 over 11, 000 performances of his plays appeared on the Russian stage.[42] Even today, after perestroika, Ostrovsky remains as popular as ever, and his plays dominate the Russian repertoire. A cursory glance at the Moscow newspapers reveals that in the two-week period between 29 April and 13 May 1997, no fewer than ten different productions of Ostrovsky plays were being staged in seven different theatres.[43] Given such popularity, his plays must surely be offering something of value and relevance to today's audience.

Notably, this has always been the case. As early as 1916, Meyerhold was staging radically unconventional interpretations of Ostrovsky's plays. M.Hoover, discussing the 1917 Meyerhold production of *A Lucrative Post*, describes how he 'gave the play a revolutionary thrust by emphasising the tyranny of the unenlightened elders over the idealistic youngsters. He made a symbol of bourgeois luxury out of the hat which Yulinka hands down to Polina ...', before going on to note in passing that 'the possible variance of reading demonstrates the play's richness of material.'[44] With even greater resonance, K.Rudnitsky, discussing the conflicting responses of the public and the critics to Meyerhold's 1916 production of *The Storm* (which enjoyed wide popular acclaim, but was received harshly by the critics as it did

---

[41] His comments appeared in *Delo*, 2 (1875). See *PSS* iv, 466.
[42] See Magarshack, 'The Founder of the Russian Theatrical Tradition', 5.
[43] See *Kul'tura*, no. 16 (7127), 29 April - 13 May 1998. The productions were as follows: at the Maly: 1, 8 May, *It's All in the Family*; 3, 9 May, *A Change in Fortune*; 5, 10 May, *The Forest*; 13 May, *Wolves and Sheep*; at the Stanislavsky Theatre: 3 May, *Talents and Admirers*; at the Mayakovsky Theatre: 1, 10 May: *Truth is Fine, but Luck is Better*; at the Moskovsky Theatre: 8 May, *Wolves and Sheep*; at the Teatr na Perovskoi: 7 May, *It's All in the Family*; at the Teatr na Pokrovke, 7 May, *Talents and Admirers*; at the Aleksandra Kalyagina Theatre: 13 May, *An Old Friend is Better than Two New Ones*.
[44] Hoover, 52-3.

not depict Kalinov as the traditional 'Kingdom of Darkness'), states: 'By avoiding fidelity to life, rejecting the idea of a direct depiction of the 'Kingdom of Darkness' and by transforming the prosaic and wild Kalinov into a fairy-city Kitezh, Meyerhold removed the dramatic situation of 'The Storm' from the specific historical environment of mid-nineteenth-century Russia. This made obvious the significance for the early twentieth century. Poeticized, it gained the significance of universality. Instead of the specific merchant's dark kingdom and dark life, there stepped forth the power of dark spiritual forces ... what was essentially Russian stepped forth in a generalized and threatening form.'[45]

Such recognition of the universality of Ostrovsky's drama is needed in the West today. Some attempts are being made. A recent production of *The Storm* on the London Fringe claimed, perhaps somewhat enthusiastically: '*The Storm* reflects the climate of fear and loneliness in today's society: fear of losing your job, fear of debt, loneliness and violence. It is set during a period of great change in rural Russian life in the mid nineteenth century ... The community is savage and violent. The 1860s serf uprisings were responsible for the murders of over 600 merchants. The same violent undercurrent pervades today's society. The play touches upon opposite approaches to change—peacefully through intervention, or violently by force.' It goes on to note: 'The characters have powerful modern resonances. The individual search for freedom, fear of intimacy, and a person's sense of isolation. Fear stops people from progressing—stifling personal growth. *The Storm* provokes the question of whether change is possible.'[46] More widely recognised, the RSC production of *Talents and Admirers* in October 1992 received largely welcoming and positive reviews. I.Dodd in *The Tribune* wrote: 'For years Alexander Ostrovsky's plays have been overlooked in the British theatre owing to a misconception that they are too Russian and therefore too inaccessible ... [*Artists and Admirers*] centres on the universal nineteenth-century problem of the vulnerability of actresses ...' P.Taylor in *The Independent* asserts: 'Alexander Ostrovsky was nine-teenth-century Russia's answer to Alan Ayckbourn ...' And I.Wardle

---

[45] Konstantin Rudnitsky, *Meyerhold the Director* (Ann Arbor: Ardis, 1981), 222-3.
[46] See the programme for the May 1997 production of *The Storm* at The Rosemary Branch Theatre, Islington, London.

in the *Independent on Sunday* claims: 'It is like Dickens without the villains.' J.Peter in the *Sunday Times* was perhaps closest to the mark with his suggestion that 'the main lesson of the evening is to see how rewarding it can be to dig up obscure plays from the foreign repertory. Those who have heard of Ostrovsky usually think of him as the author of 'The Storm'. But perhaps there is more to him than that. Someone should examine those early comedies which so upset Tsar Nicholas, where Ostrovsky exhibited the dreadful nineteenth-century equivalents of our yuppies and overpaid executive tycoons. Dostoevsky thought that three-quarters of Ostrovsky's work would be incomprehensible to Western audiences; but then he was a slavophile, with his own preconceptions and prejudices about Western Europe. So: any takers?'[47]

'Takers' are indeed needed if Ostrovsky is to gain the true recognition in the West that he deserves. But perhaps the final words should come from the playwright himself. In his *Notes on the Present State of Russian Drama*, written in 1881, Ostrovsky states: 'Only literary works which have had truly popular appeal in their own country have stood the test of time. Such works in the course of time become intelligible and valuable to other nations also, and finally to the whole world.'[48]

---

[47] All the above quotations are in *Theatre Record* 21, 1992, 1218-1222, and *Theatre Record* 22, 1992, 1316. The comments by Dostoevsky which John Peter alludes to appeared in an article Dostoevsky wrote for the weekly journal *Grazhdanin* in 1873. See *Grazhdanin* 13 (26 March 1873), 423.

[48] See A.N.Ostrovskii, *Polnoe sobranie sochinenii*, 16 vols, XII, 123.

APPENDICES

Each Appendix lists the works in which the particular element appears and provides examples, with the aim of demonstrating the overwhelming frequency with which these elements appear in Ostrovsky's drama. None of the lists pretend to be complete and numerous minor examples have not been included, both intentionally, and, no doubt, through oversight. As discussed earlier, the allocation of certain elements to certain plays is, by necessity, somewhat arbitrary, and only those examples which the author considers to be central to the message of the play have been noted.

Appendix H provides an overview of all the elements discussed in the study and indicates each play in which they appear (with the exception of 'seeing' language which, of course, appears in all the plays, but with greater significance in some than others). Again this table is most probably incomplete, yet even as it stands it is clear that no play contains fewer than five elements, over two-thirds of the plays contain more than seven, and thirteen of the plays contain nine or more. Similarly, no element appears in fewer than thirteen of the forty-one plays examined in detail, and seven of the elements appear in at least twenty-six of the plays—well over half.

APPENDIX A

Ostrovsky's Plays

The list below includes all Ostrovsky's original, completed plays, excluding those written in collaboration.[1] The first date is the initial publication date, the second is that of the first stage production as it is given in *PSS*. The plays in bold are those not included in the detailed analysis of plays for this study.

1. *A Family Picture (Semeinaya kartina).* 1847, 1857.
2. *It's All in the Family (Svoi lyudi— sochtemsya).* 1850, 1861.
3. *A Young Man's Morning (Utro molodogo cheloveka).* 1850, 1853.
4. *An Unexpected Event (Neozhidannyi sluchai).* 1851, 1902.
5. *The Poor Bride (Bednaya nevesta).* 1852, 1853.
6. *Don't Get Above Yourself (Ne v svoi sani ne sadis´).* 1853, 1853.
7. *Poverty is No Vice (Bednost´ ne porok).* 1854, 1854.
8. *You Can't Live as you Please (Ne tak zhivi, kak khochetsya).* 1855, 1854.
9. *A Hangover from Someone Else's Feast (V chuzhom piru pokhmel´e).* 1856, 1856.
10. *A Lucrative Post (Dokhodnoe mesto).* 1857, 1863.
11. *A Holiday Dream before Dinner (Prazdnichnyi son— do obeda).* 1857, 1857.
12. *Incompatibility of Character (Ne soshlis´ kharakterami!).* 1858, 1858.
13. *The Ward (Vospitannitsa).* 1859, 1863.
14. *The Storm (Groza).* 1860, 1859.
15. *An Old Friend is Better than Two New Ones (Staryi drug luchshe novykh dvukh).* 1860, 1860.
16. *Don't Poke your Nose into Others' Squabbles (Svoi sobaki gryzutsya, chuzhaya ne pristavai!.* 1861, 1861.
17. *You'll Find What You Seek (Za chem poidesh´, to i naidesh´)* or *Bal´zaminov's Wedding (Zhenit´ba Bal´zaminova).* 1861, 1863.
18. **One-armed Minin** *(Koz´ma Zakhar´ich Minin—Sukhoruk).* The first version of this play was published in 1862 but was never

---

[1] A similar list of Ostrovsky's plays, including those written in collaboration, appears in *Without A Dowry*, 267/8.

performed. The second version was first performed in 1866 and published in 1904.

19. *We All Have our Cross to Bear* (*Grekh da beda na kogo ne zhivet*). 1863, 1863.

20. *Difficult Days* (*Tyazhelye dni*). 1863, 1863.

21. *Jokers* (*Shutniki*). 1864, 1864.

22. **The Voevoda** (*Voevoda*) or **Dream on the Volga** (*Son na Volge*) . First version: 1865, 1865. Second version: 1890, 1886.

23. *At a Lively Spot* (*Na boikom meste*). 1865, 1865.

24. *The Abyss* (*Puchina*). 1866, 1866.

25. **The False Dmitry and Vasily Shuisky** (*Dmitrii Samozvanets i Vasilii Shuisky*). 1867, 1876.

26. **Tushino** (*Tushino*). 1867, 1867.

27. *Even Wise Men Err* (*Na vsyakogo mudretsa dovol´no prostoty*). 1868, 1868.

28. *An Ardent Heart* (*Goryachee serdtse*). 1869, 1869.

29. *Easy Money* (*Beshenye den´gi*). 1870, 1870.

30. *The Forest* (*Les*). 1871, 1871.

31. *All Good Things Come to an End* (*Ne vse kotu maslenitsa*). 1871, 1871.

32. *A Change in Fortune* (*Ne bylo ni grosha, da vdrug altyn*). 1872, 1872.

33. **A Seventeenth-Century Comic** (*Komik XVII stoletiya*). 1873, 1872.

34. **The Snow Maiden** (*Snegurochka*). 1873, 1873.

35. *Late Love* (*Pozdnyaya lyubov´*). 1874, 1873.

36. *Hard-earned Bread* (*Trudovoi khleb*). 1874, 1874.

37. *Wolves and Sheep* (*Volki i ovtsy*). 1875, 1875.

38. *Rich Brides* (*Bogatye nevesty*). 1876, 1875.

39. *Truth is Fine, but Luck is Better* (*Pravda— khorosho, a schast´e luchshe*. 1877, 1876.

40. *A Last Sacrifice* (*Poslednyaya zhertva*). 1878, 1877.

41. *Without a Dowry* (*Bespridannitsa*). 1879, 1878.

42. *The Heart is not Stone* (*Serdtse ne kamen´*). 1880, 1879.

43. *The Unfree* (*Nevol´nitsy*). 1881, 1880.

44. *Talents and Admirers* (*Talanty i poklonniki*). 1882, 1881.

45. *The Handsome Man* (*Krasavets-muzhchina*). 1883, 1882.

46. *Guilty Without Guilt* (*Bez viny vinovatye*). 1884, 1884.

47. *Not of This World* (*Ne ot mira sego*). 1885, 1885.

APPENDIX B

Principal Productions of Ostrovsky's Plays in England

The Storm, Everyman Theatre Guild, London, December 1929.

The Diary of a Scoundrel (adaptation of *Na vsyakogo mudretsa dovol'no prostoty* by Rodney Ackland), The Birmingham Repertory Theatre, Birmingham, 1949.

The Diary of a Scoundrel (Rodney Ackland adaptation), The Arts Theatre, London, October 1949.

The Storm, The National Theatre of Great Britain, London, November 1966.

The Diary of a Scoundrel (Rodney Ackland adaptation), Bristol Old Vic Theatre School, Bristol, May 1971.

The Forest, The Royal Shakespeare Company, The Barbican Theatre, London, 1981.

The Diary of A Scoundrel (Rodney Ackland adaptation), The Orange Tree Theatre, Richmond, 1985.

The Storm, The Royal Shakespeare Company, The Pit, London, 1987.

It's All in the Family (Nick Dear adaptation of *Svoi lyudi—sochtemsya*), Cheek by Jowl Theatre Company, Donmar Warehouse Theatre, London, April 1988.

Too Clever by Half (*Na vsyakogo mudretsa dovol'no prostoty*), The Old Vic, London, 1988.

Artists and Admirers, The Royal Shakespeare Company, The Barbican Theatre, London, October 1992.

APPENDIX C

Idealism in Ostrovsky's Plays

The list below notes briefly those plays in which idealism in conflict with reality is a significant feature.

It's All in the Family: Lipochka's dreams of refinement and marriage to a cultured nobleman are in conflict with the reality of her position as the poorly-educated daughter of a boorish 'samodur' merchant.

An Unexpected Event: the idealistic Rozovy contrasted with the pragmatic, realistic Druzhnin.

The Poor Bride: Mar´ya's desire to marry for love in conflict with her position as a dowerless, poverty-stricken young woman; her idealistic view of Merich as a Romantic hero in conflict with the reality of his true nature; her dreams of educating and 'making a human' of the uncouth Benevolensky. The conflict between Merich's and Milashin's fantasy self-images and reality. The conflict between Khor´kov's idealism and the reality of the world around him.

Don't Get Above Yourself: Avdot´ya's idealistic view of Vikhorev and her belief in his professed love for her in conflict with the reality of his true nature and motives.

A Hangover from Someone Else's Feast: Liza's and Ivan's idealism—their interest in books and learning at the expense of their material well-being—is contrasted with the more practical, pragmatic, Agrafena.

A Lucrative Post: Zhadov's dreams of earning a principled, honest living in conflict with the necessity of providing an adequate standard of living for his wife.

Incompatibility of Character: Prezhneva's desire to live life as if it were a romantic novel in conflict with the reality of her situation; her and Serafima's idealisation of Pol in conflict with the reality of his true nature.

The Ward: Nadya's dreams of making a good marriage in conflict with the reality of her position as a powerless ward subject to the whims of her 'samodur' mistress.

The Storm: Katya's and Kuligin's dreams in conflict with the reality of life.

You'll Find what you Seek: Anfisa's idealistic view of Chebakov in conflict with his true nature.

We All Have our Cross to Bear: Krasnov's idealisation of Tat´yana in conflict with the reality of her true nature. Tat´yana's and Luker´ya's idealisation of Babaev in conflict with the reality of his true nature.

Jokers: Vera's idealism in contrast with Annushka's pragmatism.

At a Lively Spot: Anna's idealism in contrast with Evgeniya's pragmatism.

The Abyss: Kisel´nikov's idealistic refusal to take bribes in conflict with the need to provide for his family.

An Ardent Heart: Parasha's idealisation of Vasya in contrast with the shallowness of his true nature.

Easy Money: Vasil´kov's idealisation of Lidiya in contrast with the reality of her true, deceitful, nature.

The Forest: the ideal of Art in conflict with reality.

Hard-earned Bread: Natasha's idealisation of Koprov in contrast with the reality of his true nature.

Rich Brides: Tsyplunov's idealisation of Belesova in conflict with the reality of her position as her guardian's mistress.

Truth is Fine, but Luck is Better: Platon's ideal of living honestly and always speaking the truth in conflict with the need to secure his and his family's material well-being.

A Last Sacrifice: Yulia's idealisation of Dulchin in conflict with the shallowness of his true nature.

Without a Dowry: Larisa's idealisation of Paratov in conflict with the reality of his true nature.

The Heart is not Stone: the honesty and compassion of Vera in contrast with the deception and greed of those around her.

The Unfree: Evlaliya's idealisation of Mulin in conflict with the reality of his true nature.

Talents and Admirers: Negina's idealistic refusal to take part in the patronage system in conflict with the reality of her position as a poverty-stricken actress. Melusov's idealism in contrast to the dishonesty and greed of Bakin and Dulebov and the pragmatism of Domna and Velikatov. Narokov's idealism in contrast with the pragmatism of Gavrilo.

The Handsome Man: Zoya's, Susanna's, and Apollinariya's idealisation of the unworthy Okoemov.

Guilty without Guilt: Lyubov's idealism in conflict with the pragmatic and deceiving Murov.

Not of this World: the idealistic 'other-worldly' Kseniya in conflict with the worldly Vitaly and the deceiving, pragmatic Barbarisov.

APPENDIX D

Deception in Ostrovsky's Plays

The list below notes briefly those plays in which deception is a significant feature.

A Family Picture: Mar'ya's and Matrena's secret rendezvous; Antip's and Shiryalov's discussion of the deception and cheating that takes place in the business world.

It's All in the Family: Bol'shov's scheme to declare himself bankrupt in order to avoid paying his creditors; Podkhalyuzin's double-cross of Bol'shov and deception of Ustin'ya and Rispolozhensky; widespread deception practised in business.

A Young Man's Morning: Lisavsky and the two Young Men deceive Nedopekin out of goods and money.

An Unexpected Event: Rozovy attempts to deceive Druzhnin as to his true relations with Sof'ya.

The Poor Bride: Merich's pretended love for Mar'ya; Benevolensky's acceptance of bribes; Mar'ya's pretence that she is entering into the marriage with Benevolensky willingly.

Don't Get Above Yourself: Vikhorev's feigned love for Avdot'ya.

Poverty is No Vice: Afrikan has cheated Lyubim out of his fortune and pretends friendship with Gordei in order to marry Lyubov.

You Can't Live as you Please: Petr is deceiving Grusha by chasing Dasha and is simultaneously deceiving Dasha by pretending to be a bachelor.

A Hangover from Someone Else's Feast: Agrafena cheats money out of Tit Titych using the note signed by Andrei.

A Lucrative Post: dishonest dealings of Vyshnevsky, Yusov and Belogubov; Vyshnevskaya's love affair; hypocrisy of Kukushkina. Polina notes that 'everything in our house is deception, everything, absolutely everything. Mama says she loves us, but she doesn't at all, she just wants rid of us as soon as possible. She flatters the suitors to their faces and then laughs at them behind their backs. She makes us pretend' (ii, p. 68).

Incompatibility of Character: deception of Prezhneva by her former lover.

The Ward: hypocrisy of Ulanbekova and Vasilisa; Nadya's secret meeting with Leonid; Grisha's escape to the fair.

The Storm: cheating and deception among the merchants; hypocrisy of Kabanova; Katya's secret meetings with Boris; Varvara's secret meetings and eventual elopement with Kudryash. Varvara: 'Our whole household is built on deceit' (ii, p. 228).

An Old Friend is Better than Two New Ones: Vasyutin's abandonment of Olin´ka, after promising to marry her.

Don't Poke your Nose into Others' Squabbles: Antrygina's pretended love for Bal´zaminov in order to provoke jealousy in Ustrashimov.

You'll Find what you Seek: Chebakov exploits Bal´zaminov in order to obtain Anfisa; he is also deceiving Anfisa—pretending to be in love with her when in reality he is concerned only with her money; Raisa and Anfisa are deceiving their brothers by conducting secret affairs; Raisa pretends interest in Bal´zaminov in order to relieve her boredom; Bal´zaminov disguises himself as a cobbler in order to gain access to the Pezhenovs' home.

We All Have our Cross to Bear: Babaev's pretended love for Tat´yana; Tat´yana's pretended love for Krasnov; Tat´yana's secret meetings with Babaev.

Difficult Days: whole society based on deception and cheating; Pertsov is a forger who also passes himself off as a 'Lord', provokes a fight with Bruskov and then demands money for dishonour; Mudrov is employed by Bruskov to write slanderous letters about his rival merchants; Andrei meets secretly with Aleksandra.

Jokers: various tricks played on Gol´tsov and Obroshenov by their rich neighbours.

At a Lively Spot: Bessudny robs his clients; Evgeniya is deceiving Bessudny with Milovidov and is deceiving Milovidov as to Anna's true nature.

The Abyss: Kisel´nikov is cheated out of his fortune by his father-in-law, who is in turn swindled by his friends; Kisel´nikov falsifies a court document.

Even Wise Men Err: widespread deception by Glumov, but all the other characters involved in hypocrisy or deception of some kind.

An Ardent Heart: Matrena is deceiving Kuroslepov by having an affair with Narkis and stealing money and wine for him; much trickery practised by Khlynov and his entourage; Gradoboev exploits his position of power for financial gain.

Easy Money: widespread deception, most notably Glumov's deception of Cheboksarova, and Lidiya's deception of Vasil´kov.

The Forest: Gurmyzhskaya's hypocrisy and her secret love for Bulanov; Vos´mibratov's attempt to deceive Gurmyzhskaya out of 1,000 roubles; Neschastlivtsev's and Schastlivtsev's role-playing; Ulita's eavesdropping.

All Good Things Come to an End: Ippolit's deception of Akhov.

A Change in Fortune: Krutitsky's feigned poverty; Petrovich prints false passports and documents.

Late Love: Lebedkina attempts to deceive Nikolai, but is tricked in return; much emphasis on the ubiquitous nature of deception, such as the tale of Margaritov's ruin.

Hard-earned Bread: Koprov's pretended love for Natasha.

Wolves and Sheep: Murzavetskaya's deception of Kupavina; Glafira's capture of Lynyaev as a husband; Berkutov's deception of Murzavetskaya.

Rich Brides: Gnevyshov describes Belesova as his ward, when in reality she is his mistress.

Truth is Fine, but Luck is Better: Gleb's theft of apples; various tricks played on Platon; Baraboshev and Mukhoyarov fiddle the accounts in order to hide their spending from Mavra; Platon's and Poliksena's secret meetings.

A Last Sacrifice: Dulchin's deception of Yulia; Glafira's manipulation of Lavr and Irina—making them believe that Pribytkov will give Irina a large dowry; Yuliya's fake death.

Without a Dowry: Ogudalova uses cunning and trickery in order to exploit Larisa's suitors; she also forces Larisa to encourage her suitors; tricks played on Karandyshev; emphasis on the normality of deception in society—Karandyshev's aunt buys cheap wine with expensive labels stuck on the bottles; Paratov's deception of Larisa.

The Heart is not Stone: Ol′ga's affair with Erast; Potap's false will; Erast's attempts to seduce Vera; Konstantin's attempts first to cheat Vera out of her inheritance and then to steal it from her.

The Unfree: Sof′ya's affair with Mulin; Styrov's surveillance of Evlaliya; various deceptions by Marfa—suggesting that Evlaliya will poison Styrov and that Miron is stealing, she also blackmails Evlaliya into giving her money.

Talents and Admirers: Dulebov's and Bakin's attempts to destroy Negina's career and reputation.

The Handsome Man: Okoemov's deception of both Zoya and Susanna; the false 'infidelity' scene; Susanna's pretence to be Oboldueva.

Guilty without Guilt: Murov's betrayal of Lyubov and his subsequent pretence that Grisha had died; Nina's plan to provoke Neznamov into insulting Kruchinina and her false flirtation with Neznamov.

Not of this World: Barbarisov's flattery of Snafidina and his attempts to break up Kseniya and Vitaly, finally causing Kseniya's death by sending her evidence of Vitaly's previous infidelity; some ambiguity about the honesty of Vitaly's motives—the suggestion that he too may solely be interested in Snafidina's money.

APPENDIX E

Concern with Appearance in Ostrovsky's Plays

The list below notes briefly those plays in which a concern with appearance is a significant feature.

A Family Picture: For Stepanida and Antip, deception and cheating are acceptable as long as they are hidden behind a veneer of respectability and piety; the superficiality of appearances is emphasised.

It's All in the Family: Lipochka is obsessed by appearance, all her dreams of life married to a nobleman are couched in terms of appearance—the clothes she will wear, the carriages she will own. Podkhalyuzin persuades her to marry him by concentrating on the clothes he will buy her, the apartment they will have and so on. Yet despite the trappings of wealth, they remain the same underneath—again emphasising the superficiality of appearances.

A Young Man's Morning: the entire plot of the play is based on the fact that Nedopekin's obsession with appearances leaves him open to exploitation by friends and acquaintances and has led to his financial ruin. His apparent wealth is itself only an appearance—he is living on credit secured on his mother's fortune.

The Poor Bride: Benevolensky's proposal of marriage to Mar'ya is based entirely on his need to have a good-looking wife in order to maintain his position in society. Mar'ya is attracted to Merich because of his appearance, rather than the reality of his true nature.

Don't Get Above Yourself: Avdot'ya and Arina are attracted to the unworthy Vikhorev because of his appearance. In contrast, Arina dismisses the honest Borodkin, who genuinely loves Avdot'ya, as 'bearded rubbish'—emphasising the superficiality of appearance.

Poverty is No Vice: again the entire plot of the play is based on Gordei Tortsov's obsession with appearances and his resulting cruelty towards his family and employees. The superficiality of appearances is also emphasised. Gordei is taken in by Afrikan's fashionable appearance which masks his cruel, deceiving nature. In

The Storm: again, much emphasis on the cruelty and deception that take place in the town hidden behind the appearance of virtue and piety. Kuligin talks of the '... tears that flow behind these locked gates, unseen and unheard! ... And the dark debauchery and drunkenness that goes on behind these bars! And all kept dark ... the master says "You can watch me in the company of others or out in the street, but what I do at home is no business of yours ..."' (ii, p. 241).

An Old Friend is Better than Two New Ones: Again, dreams of a change in status are associated with external trappings: carriages and clothes, indicating that little has changed underneath. Pul´kheriya, who has succeeded in marrying out of her class, is particularly obsessed with appearances.

Don't Poke your Nose into Others' Squabbles: see *A Holiday Dream before Dinner*, above.

You'll Find what you Seek: as above.

We All Have our Cross to Bear: Tat´yana and Luker´ya are particularly concerned with appearances. Luker´ya engineers the meetings between Tat´yana and Babaev because she wants to show the town the kind of acquaintances she has. Tat´yana is attracted to the superficial charms of Babaev and overlooks the genuine love of Krasnov. She cannot see beyond his rough peasant exterior.

Difficult Days: much emphasis on society's concern with appearances. Nastas´ya notes that 'if we have a lot of money then it means that we have to live exactly like all the other rich people, otherwise they'll all judge us. I can't allow myself the smallest pleasure, but must simply watch, right down to the tiniest trifle, how things are done at other people's houses, so that I can do things exactly the same ... if I don't do it exactly right they'll laugh at me' (ii, p. 464).

Even Wise Men Err: the blind-to-reality fools deceived by Glumov are only concerned with outward appearances. They do not look beyond the image presented to them. Thus Mamaeva notes that Glumov will always be successful in society because he is so handsome.

An Ardent Heart: again much emphasis on the superficial nature of appearances. Parasha is attracted to the superficial charms of Vasya and fails to notice the honest love and concern of Gavrilo. When Gavrilo asks for the secret to success with girls, Vasya replies: 'The fellow has to look impressive, be handsome.' The deceiver Narkis is also greatly concerned with appearance—he dresses well, and is shown combing his hair and so on—yet behind the façade he has no real substance.

Easy Money: throughout the play, there is constant emphasis on Lidiya's and Cheboksarova's determination to maintain an appearance of wealth. It has led to the exile of Cheboksarova's husband, and leads Lidiya to deceive Vasil´kov and agree to become Kuchumov's mistress. Yet again, appearances are deceptive. Telyatev's and Kuchumov's appearance of wealth is illusory, and it is the rough, provincial Vasil´kov who has the true wealth.

The Forest: Gurmyzhskaya hides her greed and her love for Bulanov behind an appearance of piety and propriety. Neschastlivtsev is concerned to maintain an appearance of high status in order to spare his aunt's feelings.

All Good Things Come to an End: Akhov is deeply concerned with appearances. Again, he is happy to cheat and deceive as long as it is hidden behind a veneer of respectability. Even when he is outwitted by Ippolit and Agniya he is determined to maintain the appearance of control.

A Change in Fortune: Anna Petrovna talks of the superficiality of society's concern with appearance. She tells of how she needed a new winter coat, but when Krutitsky came home with an old army overcoat she was at first too ashamed to wear it. Eventually, however, she became so cold that she had to wear it, and she realised that warmth was what was important, not the fact that people laughed at her. 'I saw that the human body needs only warmth, it can be happy with warmth, and that a mantilla or a certain cut or pattern is only our fantasy' (iii, p. 408). Ironically, she does not realise that their appearance of poverty is itself superficial, Krutitsky is in fact extremely wealthy. His concern with maintaining an appearance of poverty has led to great hardship for his family.

Late Love: Lebedkina's and Nikolai's concern with maintaining appearances has led him to financial ruin and her into dishonesty and deception. Ironically, her attempts to deceive fail because she does not look beyond outward appearance.

Hard-earned Bread: Natasha's concern with appearances at the expense of reality leads her to fall in love with the deceiving Koprov.

Wolves and Sheep: Murzavetskaya and Glafira both hide their true natures behind pious appearances.

Rich Brides: Tsyplunov's concern with appearances at the expense of reality leads him to associate beauty with virtue.

Truth is Fine, but Luck is Better: the Baraboshevs' concern with appearance means that in choosing a husband for Poliksena, their main concern is with not being out-ranked by their neighbours.

A Last Sacrifice: Yuliya's concern with appearance at the expense of reality leads her to fall in love with the deceiving Dulchin.

The Heart is not Stone: frequent emphasis on concern with appearances at the expense of substance. Thus Apollinariya goes to church in order to look at people and show herself off, in contrast to the truly pious Vera.

The Handsome Man: the superficiality of appearance is the central theme of the play. Thus Apollinariya, Zoya and Susanna all believe that handsome men must, by virtue of their beauty, necessarily be honest and noble; yet the central 'handsome man' is a shallow deceiver. Similarly, Oleshunin is deceived by the appearance of Zoya's love for him, and Okoemov is deceived by the appearance of 'Oboldueva'.

APPENDIX F

Blindness to Reality in Ostrovsky's Plays

The list below notes briefly those plays in which blindness to reality is a significant feature.

A Family Picture: Antip's and Stepanida's blindness to Mar'ya's and Matrena's secret rendezvous.

It's All in the Family: Bol'shov's, Ustin'ya's and Rispolozhensky's blindness to Podkhalyuzin's true intentions.

A Young Man's Morning: Nedopekin's blindness to his acquaintances' exploitation of him.

The Poor Bride: Mar'ya's blindness to Merich's true nature; her belief that she will be able to re-educate Benevolensky.

Don't Get Above Yourself: Avdot'ya's, Anna's and Arina's blindness to Vikhorev's true nature.

Poverty is No Vice: Gordei's blindness to Afrikan's true opinion of him.

You Can't Live as you Please: Grusha's blindness to Petr's deception.

A Hangover from Someone Else's Feast: Ivan's idealism makes him blind to the need to provide for his family.

A Lucrative Post: Zhadov's initial idealism makes him blind to the difficulty of living honestly and still providing for his wife.

Incompatibility of Character: Prezhneva's extensive blindness to the reality of her situation. Pol's and Serafima's blindness to each other's true nature.

The Ward: Nadya's initial idealism makes her blind to the reality of her position as the powerless ward of a 'samodur' landowner.

Don't Poke your Nose into Others' Squabbles: Antrygina's false belief in Ustrashimov's infidelity. Bal'zaminov's belief in Antrygina's feigned love for him.

contrast, the honest and kindly Lyubim and Mitya appear poor and worthless.

A Hangover from Someone Else's Feast: Andrei emphasises the importance placed on appearance over substance in the society in which he lives: 'If you know French and have the right walk, then you can dare ... it means that whatever you see—the hawk in the sky, the pike in the sea—they are all yours.' (ii, p. 16).

A Lucrative Post: throughout the play there is much emphasis on the importance placed on appearance over substance. Thus the deceivers, Yusov, Belogubov, Kukushkina and Yulin´ka, are all shown to be deeply concerned with appearance. Belogubov emphasises the importance of being neatly dressed as a means of attracting his superior's attention. Yusov praises neat penmanship over spelling and content. It is the trappings of appearance—a fashionable hat—that Yulin´ka uses to persuade Polina to leave Zhadov.

A Holiday Dream before Dinner: Bal´zaminov is obsessed by appearances and throughout the Bal´zaminov trilogy he couches his dreams of marriage to a rich bride in terms of the fine clothes he will wear and so on. Again the emphasis is on the superficiality of appearance, as underneath he remains the same. Kapochka is also concerned with appearance—she falls in love with Bal´zaminov because of his fine appearance, and when they meet she is concerned that her uncle will embarrass her with his 'Russian ways'. Her uncle, however, sees beyond Bal´zaminov's appearance to his lack of intelligence and thus his unsuitability as a guardian of Kapochka's wealth.

Incompatibility of Character: Prezhneva's concern with appearances has led to the loss of her wealth. Pol and Serafima enter into an unsuitable marriage on the basis of superficial appearances.

The Ward: the play emphasises the cruelty and tyranny hidden behind the appearance of piety and kindness. Ulanbekova is concerned with maintaining appearances: her disgust at Negligentov's drunkenness is not that he is a drunkard, but that he appeared in her house when drunk.

You'll Find what you Seek: Bal'zaminov is blind to Chebakov's and Raisa's exploitation of him. Anfisa is blind to Chebakov's true motives for his courtship of her.

We All Have our Cross to Bear: widespread blindness to reality. Tat'yana is blind to the true worth of Krasnov and the insincerity of Babaev. Krasnov is blind to Tat'yana's true nature; he believes in her false love for him.

Difficult Days: Bruskov's blindness to the true nature and status of Pertsov.

Jokers: Gol'tsov's and Obroshenov's blindness to the tricks played on them by their neighbours.

At a Lively Spot: Bessudny is blind to Evgeniya's affair with Milovidov.

The Abyss: Kisel'nikov's blindness to the true nature of his wife and father-in-law.

Even Wise Men Err: widespread blindness to the true nature and aims of Glumov. Much self-deception. Turusina's belief in the false oracle Manefa.

An Ardent Heart: Kuroslepov's blindness to Matrena's affair with Narkis. Parasha's blindness to the honest love of Gavrilo, instead attracted by the superficial charms of Vasya.

Easy Money: Lidiya's blindness to the true nature and potential of Vasil'kov; and her blindness to the true financial positions of Kuchumov and Telyatev. Cheboksarova's belief in Glumov's false rumours. Vasil'kov's belief in Lidiya's love for him.

The Forest: Neschastlivtsev's blindness to Gurmyzhskaya's true nature. Everyone's initial belief in the role-playing of Neschastlivtsev and Schastlivtsev.

All Good Things Come to an End: Akhov's blindness to the possibility of Agniya's refusal of him.

A Change in Fortune: All the other characters are blind to Krutitsky's great wealth.

Late Love: Lebedkina's failure to see that the promissory note is only a copy.

Hard-earned Bread: Natasha's blindness to Koprov's deceptions.

Wolves and Sheep: Kupavina's belief in Murzavetskaya's honesty. Lynyaev's failure to notice the threat posed by Glafira.

Rich Brides: Tsyplunov's blindness to the true nature of Belesova's relationship with Gnevyshov.

A Last Sacrifice: Yuliya's blindness to Dulchin's deceiving nature. Lavr's belief that Pribytkov will provide Irina with a large dowry.

Without a Dowry: Larisa's blindness to Paratov's true nature.

The Heart is not Stone: Konstantin's blindness to Ol´ga's affair with Erast.

The Unfree: Evlaliya's blindness to the worth of Styrov and her blindness to Sof´ya's affair with Mulin.

Talents and Admirers: Negina's initial idealism.

The Handsome Man: Zoya's and Susanna's blindness to the true nature of Okoemov. Okoemov's belief in Susanna's deception. Oleshunin's belief in Zoya's love for him and his inflated sense of self-importance.

Guilty without Guilt: Lyubov's blindness to Murov's deceptions.

APPENDIX G

Mirror Use in Ostrovsky's Plays

It's All in the Family

ACT ONE, SCENE 6: Lipa, describing how her suitor should look, breaks off to check her own appearance in the mirror. [Thus the mirror acts as a link with her fantasy world and demonstrates her concern with (superficial) appearances.]

ACT TWO, SCENE 1: Tishka pulls faces in a mirror. [The mirror provides a momentary escape from reality and also acts as a link with the creation of a new reality—Tishka is role-playing, imitating Bol´shov.]

ACT THREE, SCENE 3: Lipa inspects herself in the mirror, then states she wants to marry a soldier. [Again, link with fantasy world; concern with appearances.]

ACT THREE, SCENE 5: Lipa primps in front of the mirror after Podkha-lyuzin has described how fashionably they will live after their marriage. [Link with fantasy world; concern with appearances.]

ACT FOUR, SCENE 1: Podkhalyuzin tries on a frock-coat in front of mirror. [The mirror acts as a link with his fantasy world, and demonstrates his concern with appearances. The scene also makes clear the superficial nature of appearances—underneath his fine clothing, Podkhalyuzin remains a merchant.]

A Young Man's Morning

Pier-glass on wall throughout—Nedopekin is concerned with appearance and is blind to reality.

SCENE 5: Nedopekin tries on new clothes and practises a new walk in front of the mirror, while he and Lisavsky discuss what a beauty he is. [Thus the mirror demonstrates his concern with appearances; his habit of focusing inwards on himself, while remaining blind to the confidence tricks of his acquaintances.]

SCENE 6: Smurov disparages the fact that Nedopekin has hung a pier-glass in his room [again emphasising Nedopekin's concern with appearance].

An Unexpected Event

PART 2, SCENE 2: Sof´ya expresses a wish to buy a mirror.

The Poor Bride

ACT ONE, SCENE 5: Mar´ya twice looks in mirror when she sees Merich walking past the window. [He is the object of her fantasy world, her means of escape from reality; she is unaware of his true nature.]

ACT TWO, SCENE 10: Benevolensky, immediately after he has talked of how he must have a good-looking bride to show off in society, combs his hair before the mirror. [The mirror emphasises his concern with appearances.]

ACT FIVE: pier-glass on wall throughout. [In this Act, the links between fantasy and reality are most apparent—Mar´ya slips into a fantasy world, and the fantasy worlds of Merich and Milashin are made clear.]

ACT FIVE, SCENE 3: Mar´ya tells Dobrotvorsky of her hopes to change Benevolensky, then sits down on stool in front of the pier-glass. [The mirror is linked to her dreams and fantasies.]

ACT FIVE, SCENE 7: Milashin practises adopting the correct facial expression in the mirror. [Milashin is a fantasy role-player, he has created a fantasy image of himself.]

ACT FIVE, SCENE 8: Benevolensky looks in mirror and states that he and Mar´ya are a good match; he cannot understand why Dobrotvorsky laughs. [Again, the mirror emphasises his concern with appearance and also demonstrates the falsity of his self-image.]

Don't Get Above Yourself

ACT ONE, SCENE 6: Vikhorev prepares to meet Avdot´ya by smartening his appearance in front a mirror. [He is the deceiver, the role-player. At this point he is preparing to play the role of a loving nobleman, portraying the right image in order to get money.]

Poverty is No Vice

ACT TWO: Mirrors are described as hanging on each wall in the guest room used by Gordei Tortsov. [He is the character most concerned with appearances.]

A Lucrative Post

ACT ONE: A mirror is described as hanging on each wall in a room in Vishnevsky's house. [Vishnevsky is the chief deceiver in the play.]

ACT ONE, SCENE 3: Yusov primps in front of a mirror. [He is a character greatly concerned with appearances.]

ACT ONE, SCENE 3: Belogubov stands beside a mirror. [Again, Belogubov is a character concerned with appearance over reality; he is also a deceiver.]

ACT TWO, SCENE 1: Yulin´ka and Polina stand in front of the mirror, preparing for their suitors' arrival. [Again, they are characters concerned with superficial appearances and the veneer of respectability. At this point in the play, the mirror is also linked with their desire to escape from their present reality (i. e. their mother), by finding husbands. They are also adopting roles, acting the parts of dutiful fiancées according to rules prescribed by their mother.]

ACT FOUR: A mirror hangs on the wall throughout.

ACT FOUR, SCENE 6: Polina, about to leave Zhadov, tries on a hat in front of a mirror and talks of how beautiful she is. [Again, the mirror emphasises her concern with appearances (in contrast to the principled Zhadov). At this point she is also acting a part, preparing to leave Zhadov.]

ACT FOUR, SCENE 8: Polina again checks her appearance in the mirror. [As above.]

A Holiday Dream before Dinner

PICTURE ONE: A toilette mirror hangs on the wall in Bal´zaminov's house. [Bal´zaminov is obsessed with appearance; he dreams of escaping reality by marrying a rich wife.]

PICTURE ONE, SCENE 2: Bal´zaminov looks in the mirror to examine his burnt hair. [Thus the mirror demonstrates his concern with appearances, but is also linked with his fantasy world—his dreams of escaping reality by finding a rich bride. He has attempted to change reality—by changing his appearance—and to create a new one in its place.]

Incompatibility of Character

PICTURE ONE: Two long narrow mirrors with gilt frames are described as hanging on the wall in the drawing-room of the self-deceiving, blind-to-reality Prezhneva.

The Storm

ACT TWO, SCENE 9: Varvara ties on scarf in front of the mirror, while explaining to Katya the means by which she can secretly meet Boris.

[Thus the mirror is linked with fantasy and discussion of momentary escape from reality.]

Don't Poke your Nose into Others' Squabbles

PICTURE TWO, SCENE 2: Antrygina smartens herself in front of a mirror. [She is a deceiver and is also blind to reality—she believes that Ustrashimov is being unfaithful to her.]

We All Have our Cross to Bear

ACT TWO: small mirror on wall.

ACT TWO, SCENE 1: Tat´yana, dressing up in anticipation of a visit from Babaev, puts on a scarf in front of the mirror. [Tat´yana is a character concerned with superficial appearances. She ignores her husband's love and generosity, blinded by his rough, peasant exterior. In contrast, she believes in the gentlemanly appearance of the deceiving nobleman Babaev.]

At a Lively Spot

ACT ONE: A mirror hangs on the wall in a room at the inn. [The inn is a place where much deception is practised.]

ACT ONE, SCENE 2: Evgeniya, having been told to 'take off her mask', primps in front of the mirror. She protests her inability to flirt but clearly relishes the task. [Thus a mirror is used during discussion of role-playing. Evgeniya is the role-player. She is also a deceiver—deceiving both her husband and sister-in-law in the course of the play.]

Even Wise Men Err

ACT ONE: A mirror hangs on the wall in Glumov's house. [Glumov is the principal deceiver and role-player.]

ACT TWO, SCENE 8: Mamaev asks Glumov to pretend to flirt with his wife and tells him to practise 'making eyes' in the mirror. [Thus mirrors are again linked with deception and role-play.]

ACT FOUR, SCENE 5: Glumov looks in a mirror just before he discovers the loss of his diary. [The mirror is again connected to deception.]

An Ardent Heart

ACT THREE, SCENE 2: Gradoboev talks of keeping his promissory notes behind a mirror. [Gradoboev is a deceiver. Also, promissory notes often prove illusory—the promised money is rarely forthcoming.]

Easy Money

ACT FOUR, SCENE 11: Lidiya declares that they will return to their previous, luxurious apartment, stating: '... and through its mirrored windows we will try not even to glance at this pitiful shack' (iv, p. 230). [The luxury is illusory, the flat is rented on credit.]

ACT FIVE, SCENE 3: Lidiya checks her appearance in the mirror after Telyatev tells her she has a wrinkle. She then learns that Kuchumov, whom she has been relying on to rescue her from her impoverished state, has, like her, been maintaining the illusion of wealth. In reality, he has no money. [Thus the mirror demonstrates Lidiya's concern with appearance and desire to maintain illusion over reality. Her concern with appearance has also blinded her to the true nature of reality. The deceiver is deceived.]

ACT FIVE, SCENE 3: When talking of the furniture his creditors will be taking away, Telyatev specifically mentions mirrors. [Again a mirror is connected to the illusory nature of appearances.]

All Good Things Come to an End

PART ONE: mirror on wall.

PART TWO, SCENE 10: Ippolit looks in the mirror, then adopts the role of a romantic hero. [Thus the mirror is linked to his fantasy role-playing.]

Late Love

THROUGHOUT THE PLAY: An 'ancient mirror' hangs on the wall. [The superficial nature of appearances is one of the central themes of the play.]

ACT ONE, SCENE 1: Shablova, describing the fine men who court Lebedkina, states: '... one of these colonels drives up to the porch ... lets his spurs or sabre fall in the entrance hall; one passing glance over his shoulder at the mirror, a shake of his head and then straight to her in the drawing room. And she, you know, is only a woman, a weak creature ... just one sudden look into his eyes and it's all boiling passion' (iv, p. 11). [Again the mirror is linked to Lebedkina's concern with appearance. She is also a deceiver.]

Hard-earned Bread

ACT ONE, SCENE 6: After Chepurin has talked of his dream of marrying Natalya and how the two of them will trade in his shop together, Korpelov asks Chepurin if he has ever looked into a mirror. [The mirror is thus linked to Natalya's concern with appearance, and to Chepurin's dreams for the future.]

ACT FOUR, SCENE 3: The young merchant, Chepurin, describing the extravagance of the nobleman, Koprov, to his young love, Natalya, states that Koprov has a huge mirror with a silver frame in his bedroom. [Koprov is the deceiver, trying to cheat Natalya out of her dowry—thus the mirror is linked to deception and to Natasha's blindness to reality.]

Wolves and Sheep

ACT ONE: A mirror is described as hanging on the wall in the drawing-room of the deceiving, hypocritical Murzavetskaya.

ACT FIVE, SCENE 9: When Murzavetskaya, at the secret behest of Berkutov, suggests to Kupavina and Berkutov that they should marry, she states: 'I know better than both of you what is good for you ... I know her soul, I can see into her as if into a mirror; and I can see now that she loves you ...' (iv, p. 202). [Thus a mirror is mentioned when deception is taking place—Murzavetskaya is pretending that she is acting on her own initiative and Berkutov is pretending to be in love with Kupavina.]

Rich Brides

ACT TWO: A pier-glass is described as hanging on the wall in Belesova's house. [She is not as she seems—she is described as Gnevyshov's ward, but in reality is his mistress.]

ACT TWO, SCENE 2: Belesova learns of Gnevyshov's plans to return to his wife, and to marry her, his mistress, to the idealistic young civil servant, Tsyplunov. She agrees to comply with his plans to deceive Tsyplunov into marriage and then looks in a mirror, complaining that Gnevyshov has aged her. [Thus the mirror is linked with deception and the superficial nature of appearances.]

Truth is Fine, but Luck is Better

ACT THREE, SCENE 3: Feliksata notes: 'They are hurting Platon for no good reason, that's what! He took care and wrote the books so well that when you looked at them it was as clear as looking into a mirror who was cheating and how it was done' (iv, p. 296). [Thus a mirror is again linked with deception.]

The Unfree

ACT THREE, SCENE 1: Miron uses a mirror when tying a handkerchief around his head and pretending he has toothache. [The mirror is linked to deception. Miron is also the character most removed from reality. He lives in drunken oblivion and has delusions of grandeur.]

Talents and Admirers

ACT THREE, SCENE 2: Domna looks in a mirror when trying on a scarf Velikatov has bought her, and imagines herself as mistress of his grand estate. [Thus the mirror acts as a link with her fantasy world.]

The Handsome Man

ACT THREE, PART 1: A mirror is described as hanging on the wall in Susanna's hotel room. [She is a character blind to reality, concerned with superficial appearances.]

ACT 3, PART 1, SCENE 2: Susanna, when describing her latest love, breaks off and checks her own appearance in the mirror [thus emphasising her concern with appearances at the expense of reality].

ACT THREE, PART 2, SCENE 3: Oleshunin checks his appearance before meeting Zoya, who has falsely declared her love for him. [He too is a character deeply concerned with how he appears in the eyes of others. He is also self-deceiving and egotistical—he focuses on himself at the expense of reality. At this point in the play, he believes in Zoya's false love for him.]

Not of this World

ACT ONE, SCENE 9: The 'other-worldly' Kseniya twice looks in a mirror, the first time after she has sought reassurance from Elokhov that Vitaly loves her; the second, immediately after Elokhov has told her of Vitaly's plans to buy an estate in the country. [Thus the mirror is linked to her ideal, fantasy world.]

APPENDIX H

Table of Elements

Below is a list of the plays showing the principal elements that appear in each. The elements are numbered as follows:

1.	Realism/Idealism	8.	Blurred boundaries
2.	Deception	9.	Links to Literature
3.	Appearances	10.	Links to Theatre
4.	Blindness to Reality	11.	Mirrors
5.	Dreams	12.	Pictures
6.	Fantasy role-play	13.	Supernatural
7.	Drunkenness		

****

A Family Picture 2, 3, 4, 9, 10, 12
It's All in the Family 1, 2, 3, 4, 5, 7, 9, 11, 12
A Young Man's Morning 2, 3, 4, 9, 10, 11, 12
An Unexpected Event 1, 2, 5, 9, 10, 11
The Poor Bride 1, 2, 3, 4, 5, 6, 7, 8, 9, 10, 11, 13
Don't Get Above Yourself 1, 2, 3, 4, 7, 11, 12, 13
Poverty is No Vice 2, 3, 4, 5, 7, 10, 11
You Can't Live as you Please 2, 4, 5, 7, 8, 13
A Hangover from Someone Else's Feast 1, 2, 4, 9, 10, 13
A Lucrative Post 1, 2, 3, 4, 5, 7, 9, 10, 11, 12, 13
A Holiday Dream before Dinner 3, 4, 5, 8, 11
Incompatibility of Character 1, 2, 3, 4, 6, 8, 9, 10, 11
The Ward 1, 2, 3, 4, 5, 7
The Storm 1, 2, 3, 5, 7, 8, 11, 12
An Old Friend is Better than Two New Ones 2, 3, 5, 7, 10, 12
Don't Poke your Nose into Others' Squabbles 2, 3, 4, 5, 11, 13
You'll Find What You Seek 1, 2, 3, 4, 5, 6, 8, 12, 13
We All Have our Cross to Bear 1, 2, 3, 4, 5, 6, 9, 11
Difficult Days 2, 3, 4, 7, 9, 10, 13
Jokers 1, 2, 3, 4, 7, 12
At a Lively Spot 1, 2, 4, 10, 11, 12, 13
The Abyss 1, 2, 4, 8, 9, 10, 12

Even Wise Men Err 2, 3, 4, 5, 6, 9, 10, 11, 13

An Ardent Heart 1, 2, 3, 4, 5, 6, 7, 8, 9, 10, 11, 13

Easy Money 1, 2, 3, 4, 6, 8, 9, 10, 11, 12

The Forest 1, 2, 3, 4, 5, 7, 8, 9, 10, 12

All Good Things Come to an End 2, 3, 4, 6, 7, 9, 11

A Change in Fortune 2, 3, 4, 6, 8, 9

Hard-earned Bread 1, 2, 3, 4, 10, 11, 12

Late Love 2, 3, 4, 9, 11, 12, 13

Wolves and Sheep 2, 3, 4, 6, 7, 8, 9, 10, 11

Rich Brides 1, 2, 3, 4, 9, 11

Truth is Fine, but Luck is Better 1, 2, 3, 7, 9, 11, 13

A Last Sacrifice 1, 2, 3, 4, 8, 9, 10, 12, 13

Without a Dowry 1, 2, 3, 4, 5, 6, 7, 8, 9, 10, 12

The Heart is not Stone 1, 2, 3, 4, 10

The Unfree 1, 2, 4, 5, 6, 7, 8, 9, 10, 11, 13

Talents and Admirers 1, 2, 4, 5, 10, 11

The Handsome Man 1, 2, 3, 4, 6, 9, 10, 11

Guilty Without Guilt 1, 2, 4, 5, 7, 10, 12

Not of This World 1, 2, 5, 8, 9, 10, 11, 13

BIBLIOGRAPHY

While the list of bibliographic materials below does not claim to be fully comprehensive, that of materials in English is as near comprehensive as possible. Ostrovsky's enduring popularity in Russia has meant that there is an abundance of critical works, articles and reviews of his drama in Russian, and an attempt at a complete catalogue is beyond the scope of this publication. The bibliography lists the writings of those Soviet and Russian writers who have established themselves as the principal critics of Ostrovsky's drama, as well as those works which have particular relevance to the themes discussed in this study. These works are listed below, together with a selection of relatively minor works which aims to demonstrate typical areas of discussion in relation to Ostrovsky's writing. Also included is a selection of the principal works on Ostrovsky in other Western European languages.

M. = Moscow, L. = Leningrad

Works by Ostrovsky

The Storm, ed. Norman Henley, Letchworth, 1963

The Storm, ed. A.V.Knowles, Oxford (Blackwell Russian Texts), 1988

The Storm, The Forest, Without a Dowry, M. (Khudozhestvennaya literatura), 1964

Izbrannye sochineniya, Samara, 1996

O literature i teatre, ed. M.P.Lobanov, M., 1986

P´esy, M. (Olimp: PPP), 1993

Polnoe sobranie sochinenii, ed. M.I.Pisarev, 12 vols, St. Petersburg, 1904-1905

Polnoe sobranie sochinenii [*PSS*], ed. G.I.Vladykin, I.V.Il´inskii, V.Ya.Lakshin, V.I.Malikov, P.A.Markov, A.D.Salynskii, N.L.Stepanov and E.G.Kholodov, 12 vols, M., 1973-1980

Polnoe sobranie sochinenii, ed. I.Shiryaev, 16 vols, M., 1949-53

Prazdnichnyi son - do obeda; Svoi sobaki gryzutsya, chuzhaya ne pristavai!; Za chem poidesh´, to i naidesh´, M., 1950

Sobranie sochinenii, ed. F.I.Salaev, 10 vols, M., 1874-1890

Stikhotvornye dramy, ed. L.M.Lotman, L., 1961

Teatr i zhizn´: izbrannye p´esy, ed. A.I.Zhuravleva, M., 1995

Vsya zhizn´ – teatru, ed. N.S.Grodskaya, M., 1989

Ostrovsky's Plays in English Translation

At the Jolly Spot (Na boikom meste), tr. Jane Paxton Campbell and George R.Noyes, *Poet Lore*, 36 (1925), 1-44

Bondwomen (Nevol´nitsy), tr. Schöne Charlotte Kurlandzik and George R.Noyes, *Poet Lore*, 36 (1925), 475-541

Career Woman. Artistes and Admirers (Talanty i poklonniki), tr. Elisabeth Hanson, New York, 1976

A Cat Has Not Always Carnival (Ne vse kotu maslenitsa), tr. J.P.Campbell and G.R.Noyes, *Poet Lore*, 40 (1929), 317-72

The Diary of A Scoundrel (Na vsyakogo mudretsa dovol´no prostoty), tr. and adapted by Rodney Ackland, London, 1948. Also in *The Modern Theatre* II, ed. Eric Bentley, Garden City, 1955, pp. 37-144. Also published as *Too Clever by Half* (Applause Theatre Book Publishers, 1988)

A Domestic Picture (Semeinaya kartina), tr. E.L.Voinich in *The Humour of Russia, London, 1895*

Easy Money and Two Other Plays, tr. David Magarshack, London, 1944. [Easy Money; Even A Wise Man Stumbles; Wolves and Sheep.] (*Beshenye den´gi; Na vsyakogo mudretsa dovol´no prostoty; Volki i ovtsy.*) *Easy Money* also appears in *From the Modern Repertoire, Series II*, ed. Eric Bentley, Bloomington, 1957

Enough Stupidity in Every Wise Man (Na vsyakogo mudretsa dovol´no prostoty), tr. Polya Kasherman in *The Moscow Arts Theatre Series of Russian Plays*, second series, ed. O.M.Sayler, New York, 1923

Fairy Gold (Beshenye den´gi), tr. Camille Chapin Daniles and G.R.Noyes, *Poet Lore*, 40 (1929), 1-80

Five Plays of Alexander Ostrovsky, tr. and ed. Eugene K.Bristow, New York, 1969 [It's a Family Affair – We'll Settle it Ourselves; The Poor Bride; The Storm; The Scoundrel; The Forest.] (*Svoi lyudi – sochtemsya; Bednaya nevesta; Groza; Na vsyakogo mudretsa dovol´no prostoty; Les.*)

The Forest (Les), tr. Clara Vostrovsky Winslow and G.R.Noyes, New York, 1926

The Forest, tr. Serge Bertennson, New York, 1940 [Typewritten copy in New York Public Library]

Four Plays by Alexander Ostrovsky, tr. Stephen Mulrine, London, 1997 [The Storm; Too Clever by Half; Crazy Money; Innocent as Charged.] (*Groza; Na vsyakogo mudretsa dovol'no prostoty; Beshenye den'gi; Bez viny vinovatye.*)

Incompatibility of Temper (Ne soshlis' kharakerami!), tr. E.L.Voinich in *The Humour of Russia*, London, 1895

The King of Comedy, tr. J.McPetrie, London, 1937 [Late Love; A Sprightly Spot.] (*Pozdnyaya lyubov'; Na boikom meste.*)

Larisa (Bespridannitsa), tr. Michael Green and Jerome Katsell in *The Unknown Russian Theater*, Ann Arbor, 1991

A Last Sacrifice (Poslednyaya zhertva), tr. Eugenia Korvin-Krankovsky and G.R.Noyes, *Poet Lore*, 39 (1928), 317-410

Plays, tr. and ed. G.R.Noyes, New York, 1917 [A Protégé of the Mistress; Poverty Is No Crime; Sin and Sorrow Are Common to All; It's A Family Affair – We'll Settle it Ourselves.] (*Vospitannitsa; Bednost' ne porok; Grekh da beda na kogo ne zhivet; Svoi lyudi – sochtemsya.*)

Plays, tr. Margaret Wettlin, M., 1974 [Poverty is No Crime; The Storm; Even the Wise Can Err; More Sinned Against than Sinning.] (*Bednost' ne porok; Groza; Na vsyakogo mudretsa dovol'no prostoty; Bez viny vinovatye.*)

Poor Bride (Bednaya nevesta), tr. John Laurence Seymour and G.R.Noyes in *Masterpieces of Russian Drama I*, ed. G.R.Noyes, New York, 1933

Seek and You Shall Find (Za chem poidesh', to i naidesh'), tr. Edythe C.Haber, *Slavic and East European Arts*, 2 (1983), 95-118

The Storm (Groza), tr. Constance Garnett, London, 1899

The Storm, tr. George F.Holland and Malcolm Morley, London, 1930

The Storm, tr. David Magarshack in *The Storm and Other Russian Plays*, New York, 1960, 85-153. Also published as *The Storm*, tr. David Magarshack, Ann Arbor, 1988

The Storm, tr. F.D.Reeve in *Nineteenth-Century Russian Plays*, ed. F.D.Reeve, New York, 1973, 315-74

Thunder (Groza), tr. Joshua Cooper in *Four Russian Plays,* London, 1972

The Thunderstorm (Groza), tr. Andrew MacAndrew in *A Treasury of the Theatre I*, New York, 1967, 988-1012

The Thunderstorm, tr. Florence Whyte and G.R.Noyes, New York, 1927. Also published in *World Drama II*, ed. Barratt H.Clark, New York, 1956, 608-41

We Won't Brook Interference (Ne v svoi sani ne sadis´), tr. J.L.Seymour and G.R.Noyes, San Francisco, 1938

Without A Dowry and Other Plays, tr. Norman Henley, Ann Arbor, 1997 [Without A Dowry; A Profitable Position; Ardent Heart; Talents and Admirers.] (*Bespridannitsa; Dokhodnoe mesto; Goryachee serdtse; Talanty i poklonniki*.)

Wolves and Sheep (Volki i ovtsy), tr. Inez Sachs Colby and G.R.Noyes, *Poet Lore*, 37 (1926), 159-253

You Can't Live Just As You Please (Ne tak zhivi, kak khochetsya), tr. Philip Winningstad, G.R.Noyes and John Heard, *Poet Lore*, 49 (1943), 203-40

Earliest Translations of Ostrovsky's Plays into Other Western European Languages

L'Orage. Drame en cinq actes et en prose. Par A.N.Ostrovski. Traduit par A.Legrelle, Paris, 1885 [*Groza*]

Chefs-d'oeuvre dramatiques de Ostrovsky. Traduits du russe avec l'approbation de l'auteur et précédés d'une étude sur la vie, les oeuvres de A.N.Ostrovsky par E.Durand-Gréville, Paris, 1889 [*Ne v svoi sani ne sadis´; Snegurochka*]

Alexandre Ostrovsky: Das Gewitter. Drama in fünf Aufzügen, tr. Alexei Markov and Richard Zeyss, Berlin, 1893 [*Groza*]

A.N.Ostrovsky: Vassilissa Melentieva. Dramma in cinque atti e sette quadri, tr. Aldo Oviglio, Milan, 1894

A.N.Ostrovsky. La Gropada, tr. Narcis Oller, Barcelona, 1911 [*Groza*]

Ostrovsky Criticism in English

Beasley, I., 'The Dramatic Art of Ostrovsky', *Slavonic and East European Review*, 6 (1927), 603-17

Beasley, I., 'The Dramatic Art of Ostrovsky' (unpublished doctoral thesis), University of London, 1931

Bristow, Eugene K., 'Preface', 'Introduction' and 'Notes', in *Five Plays of Alexander Ostrovsky*, New York, 1969

Cox, Lucy, 'Form and Meaning in the Plays of Alexander Ostrovsky' (unpublished doctoral thesis), University of Pennsylvania, 1975

Ehre, Milton, 'The Forest', in *Reference Guide to Russian Literature*, ed. Neil Cornwell, assoc. ed. Nicole Christian, London, 1998, 605-6

Esam, I., 'Folkloric Elements as Communication Devices. Ostrovsky's Plays', *New Zealand Slavonic Journal*, 2 (1968), 67-88

Esam, I., 'An Analysis of Ostrovsky's *Ne ot mira sego* and the Play's Significance in Relation to the Author's Other Works', *New Zealand Slavonic Journal*, 4 (1969), 68-91

Esam, I., 'The Style of *Svoi lyudi – sochtemsya*', *New Zealand Slavonic Journal*, 10 (1972), 79-105

Esam, I., 'A Study of the Imagery Associated with Beliefs, Legends and Customs in *Bednost´ ne porok*', *New Zealand Slavonic Journal*, 11 (1973), 102-22

Grylack, B.R., 'The Function of Proverbs in the Dramatic Works of Alexander Ostrovsky' (unpublished doctoral thesis), New York University, 1975

Hanson, L., 'Introduction', in *Career Woman. Artistes and Admirers*, vii-xxxvi

Henley, Norman, see end materials in his translation of *Groza*, Letchworth, 1963

Henley, Norman, 'Ostrovskij's Play-Actors, Puppets, and Rebels', *Slavic and East European Journal*, 14 (1970), 317-25

Henley, Norman, Review of Ostrovsky's *Artists and Admirers*, *Slavic and East European Journal*, 15 (1971), 382-5

Hochman, S., ed., *The McGraw-Hill Encyclopedia of World Drama* IV, New York, 1984 [Discussion of Ostrovsky: pp. 53-66]

Holland, George F., 'The Drama of Ostrovsky', *The Curtain*, 9 (1930), 17-18

Hoover, Marjorie L., *Alexander Ostrovsky*, Boston, 1981

Kaspin, Albert, 'Ostrovsky and the *Raznochinets* in his Plays' (unpublished doctoral thesis), University of California, 1957

Kaspin, Albert, 'Dostoevsky's Masloboyev and Ostrovsky's Dosuzhev: A Parallel', *Slavonic and East European Review*, 39 (1961), 222-7

Kaspin, Albert, 'A Re-Examination of Ostrovsky's Character Lyubim Tortsov', in *Studies in Russian Literature in Honor of W.Lednicki*, ed. Z.Folejewski, The Hague, 1962, 185-91

Kaspin, Albert, 'A Superfluous Man and an Underground Man in Ostrovsky's *The Poor Bride*', *Slavic and East European Journal*, 6 (1962), 312-21

Kaspin, Albert, 'Character and Conflict in Ostrovskij's *Talents and Admirers*', *Slavic and East European Journal*, 8 (1964), 26-36

Kersten, Peter A., 'The Russian Theater in the Plays of A.N.Ostrovsky' (unpublished master's thesis), University of Wisconsin, 1962

Knowles, A.V., 'Introduction', in *Groza*, Oxford (Blackwell Russian Texts), 1988, x-xxi

Knowles, A.V., 'Aleksandr Nikolaevich Ostrovskii 1823-1886: Dramatist', in *Reference Guide to Russian Literature*, ed. Neil Cornwell, assoc. ed. Nicole Christian, London, 1998, 602-4

Kropotkin, P., *Ideals and Realities in Russian Literature*, London, 1905 [Discussion of Ostrovsky: pp. 202-14]

Leach, Robert, 'The Storm', in *Reference Guide to Russian Literature*, ed. Neil Cornwell, assoc. ed. Nicole Christian, London, 1998, 604-5

Lord, Robert, *Russian and Soviet Literature: An Introduction*, London, 1972 [Discussion of Ostrovsky: pp. 167, 170-72]

Magarshack, David, 'Introduction', in *Easy Money and Two Other Plays*, London, 1944, 6-11

Magarshack, David, 'Ostrovsky – the author', *Theatre Newsletter*, 2, 49 (12 June 1948), 5-8

Magarshack, David, 'Ostrovsky produces', *Theatre Newsletter*, 2, 50 (26 June 1948), 9

Magarshack, David, 'He Created Russia's National Theatre', *Anglo-Soviet Journal*, 9 (1948), 6-10

Magarshack, David, 'Alexander Ostrovsky: The Founder of the Russian Theatrical Tradition', in *The Storm*, Ann Arbor, 1988, 5-13

Manheim, Martha, 'Ostrovsky and Vaudeville' (unpublished doctoral thesis), Columbia University, 1978

Manning, Clarence, 'Ostrovsky and the "Kingdom of Darkness"', *Sewanee Review*, 38 (1930), 30-41

Matthewson, R.W., *The Positive Hero in Russian Literature*, Stanford, 1975 [Discusses *The Storm*: pp. 57-62]

Matual, David, 'Ostrovskij in the Background of Tolstoj's *Vlast´ t´my*', *Russian Language Journal*, 121-2 (1981), 125-31

Mirsky, D.S., *A History of Russian Literature*, London, 1949 [Discussion of Ostrovsky: pp. 234-9]

Patrick, George, 'A.N.Ostrovski: Slavophile or Westerner', in *Slavic Studies*, ed. Alexander Kaun and Ernest J.Simmons, Ithaca, 1943, 117-31

Peace, R.A., 'A.N.Ostrovsky's *The Thunderstorm*: The Dramatization of Conceptual Ambivalence', *Modern Language Review*, 84 (1989), 99-110

Programme for The Rosemary Branch Theatre production of *The Storm*, May 1997

Ralston, William, 'Art VI. *Sochineniya A.N.Ostrovskogo. [The Works of A.N.Ostrovsky.]* 4 Vols. *St Petersburg: 1859-67'*, *The Edinburgh Review*, 261 (July 1868), 158-90

Rudnitsky, Konstantin, *Meyerhold the Director*, tr. G.Petrov, Ann Arbor, 1981 [Meyerhold's productions of Ostrovsky's plays: pp. 34-5, 217-24, 323-6, 329-31, 342-3, 340-52.]

Sealey Rahman, Kate, 'Ostrovsky through the Looking Glass: The Significance of Mirrors in the Plays of A.N.Ostrovsky', *Irish Slavonic Studies*, 18 (1997), 111-27

Sealey Rahman, Kate, 'Aleksandr Ostrovsky – Dramatist and Director', in *The Cambridge History of Russian Theatre*, Cambridge [forthcoming]

Setchkarev, V., 'From the Golden to the Silver Age (1820-1917)', in *Companion to Russian Studies, II: An Introduction to Russian Language and Literature*, ed. R.Auty and D.Obolensky, Cambridge, 1977, 135-85 [Discussion of Ostrovsky: pp. 152-3]

Sleptsov, Vasily, 'On Alexander Ostrovsky', in *The Complection of Russian Literature*, ed. Andrew Field, New York, 1971, 152-5

Slonim, Marc, *Russian Theater: From the Empire to the Soviets*, London, 1963 [Discussion of Ostrovsky: pp. 73-80]

Terras, Victor, ed., *Handbook of Russian Literature*, New Haven, 1985 [Discussion of Ostrovsky: pp. 324-6]

Terras, Victor, *History of Russian Literature*, New Haven, 1991 [Discussion of Ostrovsky: pp. 371-5]

Theatre Newsletter, 1, 5 (21 September 1946), 2 [Review of a production of *Diary of a Scoundrel*, Questor's Theatre, Ealing, London]

Theatre Record, 21 and 22 (1992), pp. 1218-22, 1316 [Reviews of an RSC production of *Artistes and Admirers*, October 1992, The Pit, The Barbican, London]

Valency, Maurice, *The Breaking String*, London, 1966 [Discussion of Ostrovsky: pp. 32-40]

van Baak, J.J., 'The Function of the Social Setting in "Groza" by A.N.Ostrovskij', in *Zugänge zu Ostrovskij/Approaches to Ostrovsky*, ed. A.G.F.van Holk, Publications of the Slavic Institute of the University of Groningen, 1, Groningen, 1979, 117-46

van Holk, A.G.F., 'Thematic Analysis of Ostrovsky's *Poverty is No Crime*', *Essays in Poetics* 3, 2 (1978), 41-76

van Holk, A.G.F., ed., *Approaches to Ostrovsky*, Groningen, 1979

van Holk, A.G.F., 'Semiotic Structures in Ostrovskij's plays', in *Approaches to Ostrovsky*, Groningen, 1979, 147-235

van Holk, A.G.F., 'The Syntax of the Slovo-er: On the Thematic Composition of A.N.Ostrovskij's *An Advantageous Job*', *Russian Linguistics* 8, 3 (1984), 215-50

van Holk, A.G.F., 'The Key Scene in Ostrovskij's *The Thunderstorm*: On the Analysis of Modal Profiles', *International Journal of Slavic Linguistics and Poetics* , 31-2 (1985), 481-93

Varneke, B.V., *History of the Russian Theatre: Seventeenth through Nineteenth Century*, tr. B.Brascol, New York, 1951 [Discussion of Ostrovsky: pp. 319-50]

Wan, Ning, 'Female Characters in A.Ostrovsky's The Storm and Cao Yu's The Thunderstorm' (unpublished doctoral thesis), University of Pittsburgh, 1985

Wettlin, Margaret, 'Alexander Ostrovsky and the Russian Theatre Before Stanislavsky', in her *Plays*, M., 1974, 7-79

Whitmore Williams, Harold, *Russia of the Russians*, London, 1920 [Discussion of Ostrovsky: pp. 272-3]

Whittaker, Robert, 'The Ostrovskij-Grigor´ev Circle Alias the "Young Editors" of the *Moskvitianin*', *Canadian-American Slavic Studies*, 24 (1990), 385-412

Zohrab, Irene (née Esam), 'Problems of Style in the Plays of Ostrovsky', *Melbourne Slavonic Studies*, 12 (1977), 35-46

Zohrab, Irene (née Esam), 'F.M.Dostoevsky and A.N.Ostrovsky', *Melbourne Slavonic Studies*, 14 (1980), 56-78

Zohrab, Irene (née Esam), 'Problems of Translation. The Works of A.N.Ostrovsky in English', *Melbourne Slavonic Studies*, 16 (1982), 43-88

Zohrab, Irene (née Esam), 'Without A Dowry', in *Reference Guide to Russian Literature*, ed. Neil Cornwell, assoc. ed. Nicole Christian, London, 1998, 606-7

Ostrovsky Criticism in Russian

Aikhenval´d, Yu., *Siluety russkikh pisatelei*, M., 1909 [Discussion of Ostrovsky: pp. 168-72]

Alpers, B.V., '*Serdtse ne kamen´* i pozdnii Ostrovskii', in *Teatral´nye ocherki*, 2 vols, M., 1977, I, 405-546

Anastas´ev, A.N., *Groza Ostrovskogo*, M., 1975

Brodskii, N.L., ed., *A.N.Ostrovskii i F.A.Burdin: neizdannye pis´ma*, M.-Petrograd, 1923

Chernykh, L.V., 'A.N.Ostrovskii', in *Russkaya literatura i fol´klor, vtoraya polovina XIX veka*, ed. A.A.Gorelov, L., 1982, 369-417

Danilov, S.S., *Ocherki po istorii russkogo dramaticheskogo teatra*, M., 1958 [Discussion of Ostrovsky: pp. 315-63]

Davydova, Marina, 'Za zerkal´noi dver´yu: *Groza* v Moskovskom TYUZe, postanovka Genrietty Yakovskoi', *Nezavisimaya gazeta*, no. 048 (1373), 18 March 1997

Derzhavin, K.N., *Aleksandr Nikolaevich Ostrovskii 1823-1886*, L.-M., 1950

Derzhavin, K.N., 'A.N.Ostrovskii', in *Russkie dramaturgi XVIII - XIX vv.*, ed. B.Bursova, 3 vols, L.-M., 1962, III, 75-163

Dmitriev, Yu.A., *Akademicheskii Malyi teatr 1917-1941*, M., 1984 [Contains details of productions of Ostrovsky plays at the Maly]

Dobrolyubov, N.A., 'Temnoe tsarstvo' and 'Luch sveta v temnom tsarstve', in *Russkie klassiki*, ed. Yu.Oksman, M., 1970, 70-188

Dolgov, N.N., *A.N.Ostrovskii: zhizn´ i tvorchestvo*, M.-Petrograd, 1923

Dostoevskii, F.M., 'A.N.Ostrovskii', *Grazhdanin*, 13 (26 March 1873)

Dubinskaya, A.I., *A.N.Ostrovskii: ocherk zhizni i tvorchestva*, M., 1951

Durylin, S.N., *Mastera sovetskogo teatra v p´esakh A.N.Ostrovskogo*, M., 1939

Efros, N.E., *A.N.Ostrovskii*, Petrograd, 1922

Filippov, V.A., *Dnevniki i pis´ma, teatr Ostrovskogo*, M.-L., 1937

Filippov, V.A., 'Yazyk personazhei Ostrovskogo', in *A.N.Ostrovskii - dramaturg*, ed. V.A.Filippov, M., 1946, 122-31

Filippov, V.A., *Velikii russkii dramaturg A.N.Ostrovskii*, M., 1948

Filippov, V.A., ed., *Slovar´ k p´esam A.N.Ostrovskogo*, M., 1993

Fokht, U.R., ed., *Razvitie realizma v russkoi literature*, 3 vols, M., 1973, II [Discussion of Ostrovsky: pp. 314-17]

Fomin, A.A., 'Polozhenie russkoi zhenshchiny v sem´e i obshchestve po proizvedeniyam A.N.Ostrovskogo', *Russkaya mysl´*, 1 (1899), 120-34; 2, 72-92; 4, 27-57

Fomin, A.A., 'Svyaz´ tvorchestva Ostrovskogo s predshestvovavshei dramaticheskoi literaturoi', in *Tvorchestvo A.N.Ostrovskogo*, ed. S.K.Shambinago, M.-Petrograd, 1923, 1-25

Gerasimov, Yu.K., ed., *A.N.Ostrovskii i literaturno-teatral´noe dvizhenie XIX-XX vekov*, L., 1974

Gitel´man, L.I., 'Iz opyta osvoeniya dramaturgii Ostrovskogo zarubezhnym teatrom', in *A.N.Ostrovskii i literaturno-teatral´noe dvizhenie XIX-XX vekov*, L., 1974, 257-78

Golovina, V.Z., 'Moe znakomstvo s A.N.Ostrovskim', Istoricheskii vestnik, 125 (1911), 125

Golubentsev, N.A., *A.N.Ostrovskii v portretakh i illyustratsiyakh*, M., 1949

Grigorenko, V.V., ed., *A.N.Ostrovskii v vospominaniyakh sovremennikov*, M., 1966

Grigor´ev, A.A., 'Posle "Grozy" Ostrovskogo: pis´ma k Ivanu Sergeevichu Turgenevu', *Russkii mir*, 5, 6, 9, 11 (1860)

Kashin, N.P., 'A.N.Ostrovskii i starinnaya drama', *Ezhegodnik Imperatorskikh teatrov*, 4, St. Petersburg (1909), 16-56

Kashin, N.P., *Etyudy ob A.N.Ostrovskom*, 2 vols, M., 1912

Kashin, N.P., 'A.N.Ostrovskii v frantsuzskoi literature', *Zhurnal ministerstva narodnogo prosveshcheniya*, 10, Petrograd (1915), 319-49; 11, 37-61

Kashin, N.P., 'Simvolika Ostrovskogo', *Zhizn´*, 3 (1922), 5-26

Kashin, N.P., 'Otnoshenie k Ostrovskomu zapadnykh stseny i nauchnoi literatury', in *Tvorchestvo A.N.Ostrovskogo*, ed. S.K.Shambinago, M.-Petrograd, 1923, 25-58

Kashin, N.P., 'Smena klassov v russkom obshchestve po proizvedeniyam A.N.Ostrovskogo. K stoletiyu so dnya rozhdeniya (1823-1923)', *Pechat´ i revolyutsiya*, 3, M. (1923), 1-13

Kashin, N.P., 'Ostrovskii i Mol´er', *Slavia*, 5, Prague (1926-7), 107-35

Kashin, N.P., 'O razrabotke arkhiva A.N.Ostrovskogo', *Literaturnoe nasledstvo*, 7-8, M. (1933), 407-17

Kashin, N.P., ed., *A.N.Ostrovskii. Sochineniya*, M., 1937

Kashin, N.P., 'O yazyke A.N.Ostrovskogo. Nablyudeniya i zametki', in *A.N.Ostrovskii - dramaturg*, ed. V.A.Filippov, M., 1946, 60-78

Kholodov, E.G., *Masterstvo Ostrovskogo*, M., 1967

Kholodov, E.G., *Ocherk zhizni i tvorchestva*, Yaroslavl´, 1968

Kholodov, E.G., 'Katerina Kabanova (opyt kharakteristiki geroini dramy A.N.Ostrovskogo "Groza")', in *Russkaya klassicheskaya literatura: razbory i analizy*, ed. D.Ustyuzhanin, M., 1969, 244-69

Kholodov, E.G., 'A.N.Ostrovskii v 1855-1865 godakh', *PSS* ii, 658-90

Kholodov, E.G., 'A.N.Ostrovskii v 1873-1877 godakh', *PSS* iv, 460-93

Kholodov, E.G., *Dramaturg na vse vremena*, M., 1975

Kholodov, E.G., *Yazyk dramy: ekskurs v tvorcheskuyu laboratoriyu A.N.Ostrovskogo*, M., 1978

Kogan, L.R., *Letopis´ zhizni i tvorchestva A.N.Ostrovskogo*, M., 1953

Kolosova, E.M., ed., *A.N.Ostrovskii i russkie kompozitory: pis´ma*, M., 1937

Kostelyan, B.O., *Bespridannitsa A.N.Ostrovskogo*, L., 1982

Kropachaev, N.A., *A.N.Ostrovskii na sluzhbe pri imperatorskikh teatrakh: vospominaniya ego sekretarya*, M., 1901

Kuleshov, V.I., *Istoriya russkoi kritiki XVIII - XIX vekov*, M., 1972 [Discussion of Ostrovsky: pp. 392-4]

Lakshin, V.Ya., 'Tri p´esy A.N.Ostrovskogo', in *Groza, Les, Bespridannitsa A.N.Ostrovskogo*, M., 1964, 5-18

Lakshin, V.Ya., 'Mudretsy Ostrovskogo – v istorii i na stsene', *Novyi mir*, 12 (1969), 208-44

Lakshin, V.Ya., 'Ostrovskii (1843-1854)', in *PSS* i, 462-93

Lakshin, V.Ya., *A.N.Ostrovskii*, M., 1976

Lakshin, V.Ya., *Teatr Ostrovskogo*, M., 1986

Lakshin, V.Ya., 'Mudrost´ Ostrovskogo', in *P´esy A.N.Ostrovskogo*, M., 1993, 5-12

Lebedev, Yu.V., *Dramaturg pered litsom kritiki: vokrug A.N.Ostrovskogo i po povodu ego. Idei i temy russkoi kritiki*, M., 1974

Levin, Yu.D. and A.V.Fedorov, eds., *Russkie pisateli o perevode XVIII-XX vv.*, L., 1960 [Extracts of Ostrovsky's comments on translation: 348-53]

Linin, A.N., *Literatura po A.N.Ostrovskomu*, Vladikavkaz, 1924

Linin, A.N., *K.voprosu o vliyanii Gogolya na Ostrovskogo*, Rostov-on-Don, 1935

Lobanov, M.P., *Ostrovskii*, M., 1989

Lomov, A.G., *Frazeologiya v tvorcheskoi laboratorii A.N.Ostrovskogo*, Tashkent, 1987

Lotman, L.M., *A.N.Ostrovskii i russkaya dramaturgiya ego vremeni*, L., 1961

Lotman, L.M., 'Dramaturgiya A.N.Ostrovskogo', in *Istoriya russkoi dramaturgii vtoroi poloviny XIX - nachala XX vekov do 1917 g.*, M., 1987, 38-155

244

Lunacharskii, A.V., 'Ob Aleksandre Nikolaeviche Ostrovskom i po povodu ego', *Izvestiya VTsIK*, 78 and 79 (1923)

Mendel´son, N.M., *Aleksandr Nikolaevich Ostrovskii v vospominaniyakh sovremennikov i ego pis´makh*, M., 1923

Meshcheryakov, N.L., *Russkie kritiki ob Ostrovskom*, M., 1923

Muratova, K.D., *Bibliografiya literatury ob A.N.Ostrovskom (1847-1917)*, L., 1974

Nelidov, F.F., 'A.N.Ostrovskii v kruzhke "Molodogo Moskvityanina"', *Russkaya mysl´*, 3, M., 1901, 1-33

Nemtsev, V.I., 'Zhenikhi *Bespridannitsy*: opyt sovremennogo prochteniya p´esy Aleksandra Ostrovskogo', *Nezavisimaya gazeta*, no. 066 (1319), 11 April 1997

Pavlova, T. and E.G.Kholodov, eds., *A.N.Ostrovskii na sovetskoi stsene: stat´i o spektaklyakh moskovskikh teatrov raznykh let*, M., 1974

Pirogov, G.P., *A.N.Ostrovskii, seminarii*, L., 1962

Pisarev, D.I., 'Motivy russkoi dramy', *Russkoe slovo*, 3, 1864

Pospelov, G.N., 'Dramaturgiya A.N.Ostrovskogo', in *Istoriya russkoi literatury 19 veka*, M., 1962, 515-98

Prokhorov, E.I., 'Ostrovskii i Gogol´', *Literaturnoe nasledstvo*, 88, 1 (1974), 439-48

Prygunov, M.D., *Neizdannye pis´ma iz arkhiva A.N.Ostrovskogo*, M.-L., 1932

Revyakin, A.I., *A.N.Ostrovskii: zhizn´ i tvorchestvo*, M., 1949

Revyakin, A.I., *A.N.Ostrovskii v Shchelykove*, Kostroma, 1957

Revyakin, A.I., *Moskva v zhizni i tvorchestve A.N.Ostrovskogo*, M., 1962

Revyakin, A.I., *A.N.Ostrovskii v vospominaniyakh sovremennikov*, M., 1966

Revyakin, A.I., *Iskusstvo dramaturgii A.N.Ostrovskogo*, 2nd edn. , M., 1974

Revyakin, A.I., 'Itogi i zadachi izucheniya dramaturgii Ostrovskogo', in *Nasledie A.N.Ostrovskogo i sovetskaya kul´tura*, ed. G.I.Vladykin, 1974, 5-41

Salynskii, A.D., 'A.N.Ostrovskii v nashi dni', in *PSS* i, 8-22

Shambinago, S.K., *Tvorchestvo A.N.Ostrovskogo*, M.-Petrograd, 1923

Shtein, A.L., ed., *A.N.Ostrovskii: Sbornik statei i materialov*, M., 1962
Shtein, A.L., *Tri shedevra A.Ostrovskogo: Groza, Les, Bespridannitsa*, M., 1967
Shtein, A.L., *Master russkoi dramy*, M., 1973
Shtein, A.L., *Uroki Ostrovskogo*, M., 1984
Sinyukhaev, G., 'Ostrovskii i narodnaya pesnya', *Otdelenie russkogo yazyka i slovesnosti. Izvestiya*, 28, Petrograd, 1923, 9-70
Skabichevskii, A.M., 'Zhenshchiny v p´esakh A.N.Ostrovskogo', *Severnyi vestnik*, 8, St. Petersburg, 1887, 151-90
Stepanov, A.N., ed., *Biblioteka A.N.Ostrovskogo*, L., 1963
Sukhikh, I.N., *Drama A.N.Ostrovskogo 'Groza' v russkoi kritike*, L., 1990
Uspenskii, L. and V., 'Ostrovskii-yazykotvorets', in *A.N.Ostrovskii: Sbornik statei i materialov*, ed. A.L.Shtein, M., 1962, 184-265
Varneke, B.V., 'Tekhnika Ostrovskogo', *Izvestiya po russkomu yazyku i slovesnosti*, 1, L., 1928, 134-40
Vladykin, G.I., 'A.N.Ostrovskii', in *Sobranie sochinenii A.N.Ostrovskogo*, 10 vols, M., 1959, I, v-lxiv
Vladykin, G.I., ed., *A.N.Ostrovskii v russkoi kritike*, M., 1966
Vladykin, G.I., ed., *Nasledie A.N.Ostrovskogo i sovetskaya kul'tura*, M., 1974
Zhuravleva, A.I., *Ostrovskii-komediograf*, M., 1981
Zhuravleva, A.I., *Aleksandr Nikolaevich Ostrovskii*, M., 1997

Ostrovsky Criticism in Other Languages

Kasin, N., 'Ostrovskij und Gozzi', *Zeitschrift für slavische Philologie*, 7, Leipzig, 1930, 94-109
Patouillet, J., *Ostrovski et son théâtre de moeurs russes*, Paris, 1912
Patouillet, J., 'Le Centenaire du Molière russe: Alexandre Ostrovski (1823-1886)', *La vie des peuples*, 10, Paris, 1923, 84-105
Patouillet, J., 'Les idées de A.N.Ostrovskij sur l'art dramatique', *Revue des Études Slaves*, 9, Paris, 1929, 48-70
Steltner, Ulrich, *Die künstlerischen Funktionen der Sprache in den Dramen von A.N.Ostrovskij*, Giessen, 1978
van Holk, A.G.F., *Zugänge zu Ostrovskij/ herausgegeben von A.G.F.van Holk*, Bremen, 1979

246

Other Relevant Materials

Abrams, M.H., *The Mirror and the Lamp: Romantic theory and the critical tradition*, New York, 1953

Anderson, R., 'Notes from the Underground: The Arrest of Personal Development', *Canadian-American Slavic Studies*, 24 (1990), 413-30

Anikst, A., *Teoriya dramy v Rossii ot Pushkina do Chekhova*, M., 1972

Aronson, Elliot, *The Social Animal*, 5th edn., New York, 1988

Barratt, Andrew and A.D.P.Briggs, *A Wicked Irony: The Rhetoric of Lermontov's A Hero of Our Time*, Bristol, 1989

Berne, Eric, *Games People Play: The Psychology of Human Relationships*, London, 1968

Boyle, A.S., *Seneca's Phaedra: Introduction, Text, Translation and Notes*, Liverpool, 1987

Chernyshevskii, N.G., 'Zametki o zhurnalakh', *Sovremennik*, 4, 1857

Consigny, Scott, 'The Paradox of Textuality: Writing as Entrapment and Deliverance in *Notes from Underground*', *Canadian-American Slavic Studies*, 12 (1978), 341-52

Dobrolyubov, N.A., *Selected Philosophical Essays*, tr. J.Finsburg, M., 1948

Dostoevskii, F.M., *Dvoinik*, in his *Polnoe sobranie sochinenii*, 30 vols, L., 1972, I, 109-230

Dowler, Wayne, *An Unnecessary Man: The Life of Apollon Grigor'ev*, Toronto, 1995

Eagle, Herbert, 'Lermontov's "Play" with Romantic Genre Expectations in *A Hero of Our Time*', *Russian Literature Triquarterly*, 10 (1974), 299-315

Encylopaedia Britannica, The, 27, 15th edn., Chicago, 1997

Gilroy, Marie, *Lermontov's Ironic Vision*, Birmingham, 1989

Gippius, Vasily, '*The Inspector General*: Structure and Problems', in *Gogol from the Twentieth Century: Eleven Essays*, ed. Robert A.Maguire, Princeton, 1974, 216-65

Gogol, Nikolai, *Diary of a Madman and Other Stories*, tr. and intro. by Ronald Wilks, London, 1972

Gogol, Nikolai: *The Complete Tales of Nikolai Gogol*, ed. Leonard J.Kent, 2 vols, Chicago, 1985

Gogol, Nikolai, *Plays and Petersburg Tales*, tr. Christopher English, Oxford, 1995

Holquist, J.M., 'Plot and Counter-Plot in *Notes from Underground*', *Canadian-American Slavic Studies*, 6 (1972), 225-38

Johnson, Frank A., 'Some Problems of Reification in Existential Psychiatry: Conceptual and Practical Considerations', in *Theories of Alienation: Critical Perspectives in Philosophy and Social Sciences*, ed. R.Felix Geyer and David R.Schwitzer, Leiden, 1976, 77-102

Kul'tura, no. 16 (7127), 29 April - 13 May 1998

Lyon Clark, Beverly, *Reflections of Fantasy: The Mirror-Worlds of Carroll, Nabokov and Pynchon*, New York, 1986

Maguire, Robert A., ed., *Gogol from the Twentieth Century: Eleven Essays*, Princeton, 1974

Merezhkovsky, Dmitry, 'Gogol and the Devil', in *Gogol from the Twentieth Century*, Princeton, 1974, 57-102

Mersereau, J., *Mikhail Lermontov*, Carbondale, 1962

Reid, Robert, *Lermontov's 'A Hero of Our Time'*, London, 1997

Remizov, A.M., *Ogon' veshchei: sny i predson'e*, Paris, 1954

Revyakin, A.I., *Istoriya literatury XIX veka*, II, M., 1963

Senelick, Laurence, tr. and ed., *Russian Dramatic Theory from Pushkin to the Symbolists: An Anthology*, Austin, 1981

Stilman, Leon, 'The "All-seeing" Eye in Gogol', in *Gogol from the Twentieth Century*, Princeton, 1974, 376-89

Terras, Victor, *Belinskij and Russian Literary Criticism: The Heritage of Organic Aesthetics*, Wisconsin, 1974

Turner, C.J.G., *Pechorin: An Essay on Lermontov's 'A Hero of our Time'*, Birmingham, 1978

Varneke, B.V., *Istoriya russkogo teatra XVII-XIX vekov*, M.-L., 1939

Weber, H.B., 'Belinsky and the Aesthetics of Utopian Socialism', *Slavic and East European Journal*, 15 (1971), 293-302

Woodin Rowe, William, *Through Gogol's Looking Glass: Reverse Vision, False Focus and Precarious Logic*, New York, 1976

Ziolkowski, Theodore, *Disenchanted Images: A Literary Iconology*, Princeton, 1977

INDEX